# THE PORNOGRAPHER'S DAUGHTER

# THE PORNOGRAPHER'S DAUGHTER

*A Memoir of Childhood, My Dad, and* Deep Throat

## KRISTIN BATTISTA-FRAZEE

Skyhorse Publishing

Skyhorse Publishing books may be purchased in bulk at special discounts for sales promotion, corporate gifts, fund-raising, or educational purposes. Special editions can also be created to specifications. For details, contact the Special Sales Department, Skyhorse Publishing, 307 West 36th Street, 11th Floor, New York, NY 10018 or info@skyhorsepublishing.com.

Skyhorse® and Skyhorse Publishing® are registered trademarks of Skyhorse Publishing, Inc.®, a Delaware corporation.

Visit our website at www.skyhorsepublishing.com.

10 9 8 7 6 5 4 3 2 1

Library of Congress Cataloging-in-Publication Data is available on file.

Cover design by Brian Peterson
Cover photo credit: Thinkstock

Print ISBN: 978-1-62914-434-4
Ebook ISBN: 978-1-63220-091-4

Printed in the United States

# Contents

# *Acknowledgments*

This book would not be without the kindness of strangers, the help of my friends, and the support of my family. First, and most importantly, a debt of gratitude goes to my parents, Anthony Battista and Frances Battista, for having lived and survived a life that gave me something incredible to write about. They honestly shared their story with me and provided their unwavering love and support. Simply, without them this book would not have been possible.

To my husband, Brian Frazee, and my daughter, Grace Frazee, for their love and forgiveness for the hundreds of hours they let me steal away from their lives to write. I love you both and I don't think there are enough words to say thank you. I hope this endeavor makes you both proud. To Grace, thanks for thinking it's cool Mom wrote a book but remember, this a story about your family heritage—learn all you can from it.

Thanks to everyone at Skyhorse Publishing and my editor, Holly Rubino. Holly, your funny and light-hearted approach to our work made every second of the editing process enjoyable. Thank you for taking on this project and for just being you.

To Craig Kayser, my literary agent, thank you for lighting my path to becoming a storyteller and writer. You always told me the truth, even when I didn't want to hear it, which improved our work. I'm grateful for your insight, intelligence, and devotion to this project.

Jeremy Hawkins, The Distillery Editing Services, thanks for lending your skills to fine-tune this book. I learned so much from you, and I'm grateful for your efforts to make the words on these pages sing. Your book, *The Last Days of Video*, is going to be excellent and I can't wait to buy it.

To my writing group: Six Great Books, Molly Mahoney Matthews, Janet Hall Warner, Kelly Hand, Donna Drew Sawyer, and David Bonck, you all provided the best guidance, sounding board, and collective wisdom to help me keep this project going. You erased any self-doubt that crept in from time to time and you are each gifted writers. I am so fortunate to have you in my life.

I'm indebted to the Writer's Center in Bethesda, Maryland, for the wonderful teachers and other aspiring writers I met there. Rick Walter, thank you for being the first to tell me this story had the qualities of becoming a book and that I could accomplish this task. Your early encouragement and mentoring set me on the right path to making this book a reality. Barbara Esstman, thank you for impressing upon me the importance of improving my writing craft. You were so right.

I've been fortunate to have Steve Barnett and David Koechner as champions in our effort to create this story into something great for television. I could not have found better guardians for this project. Both of you have both artfully conceived the rich potential of this story and have true vision. To Steve Barnett, your enduring excitement and dedication has made all the difference in the world and for this I am forever grateful.

To my family for their love and excitement about this book; Jerry Parrotto, Sandra Parrotto, Connie Parrotto Hudson, Chris Battista, Stephen Battista, Alexis Battista, Rose Martini, and Angie Battista. Also to my in-laws Carol, George, and Leanne. Your words of encouragement always inspired me.

To my aunt, Dolores Parrotto Giesman, thank you for being the first true writer in the family and for the many hours you spent editing my graduate school papers. You helped me become a writer by your example and your insistence on excellence was never forgotten.

To my grandmother, Maria Parrotto, thank you for being so unforgettable and ballsy, and although you will never read this, I hope you know how much you inspired the women in our family. In these pages, you'll inspire women everywhere to be as loyal, brash, outspoken, and loving as you are. Without you, this story wouldn't have been nearly as interesting. You're truly unforgettable.

Many thanks to Tara Fort, Eric Danville, Chris Conrad, Danny Miller, Theresa Flynt, Belisa Vranich, Kelley Wyatt Mautz, Brian Scott Gross, Jeannie Campbell, Gabe Doppelt, and the many friends and work colleagues who stood in my corner and taught me so many things that will lend to the success of this book.

# *Prologue*

"**S**mut!"

That's my Grandma Maria talking. We're in her kitchen in South Philly. I'm about fourteen and I'm sitting on a pink barstool at a gray-speckled Formica countertop. I'm eating something amazing like broccoli and spaghetti or hot buttered Italian rolls from Cacia's Bakery. But I'm also listening carefully because I know exactly what she's talking about, and it's a story I've been waiting to hear for a long, long time.

"He was involved in that smut!" she said, shaking her hands wildly to punctuate the end of her sentence.

This was something I imagined a churchgoer might say in righteous indignation, flurries of spit flying from twisted lips, a rosary twitching in her hand. But that wasn't really my Grandma Maria, my mom's mom. The only time she entered a church was for weddings or funerals, and she would roll her eyes as my grandfather diligently went off to church every Sunday morning. Maria was a free-thinking, hell-on-wheels type who, once safely outside of church, would cast aside a Bible quicker than a dead rat. She always said "religion was for the weak minded."

So it was strange to hear her so passionately wield the word *smut* against my father.

Now the family's dirty secret was becoming more real to me. It was something always whispered about, and let's just say I'd always sensed what went on with my dad. But I didn't really know any of the nasty details. I knew my father, Anthony Battista, had been arrested ten years before, in the mid-1970s, for distributing a movie about sex, and I knew that many legal troubles had followed. But why someone would be in trouble about a movie was still a mystery to me. I just didn't know how to ask about this. Or maybe I didn't want to know. I was a kid and sex was just a beautiful rumor for me. Sex had more to do with the most popular girl in school, Diane, "liking" the coolest guy, Chris, or whatever their names were. I was a teenager, at an age when the meaning of sex was just beginning to change. It would no longer be about holding hands in the hallway.

What Grandma Maria told me about my father didn't ruin what sex meant for me; it just added a complicated dimension. My gutsy grandma was the first person who would challenge me to face the truth about my dad's involvement in pornography. I suppose telling me this was her way of protecting me in what she saw as my long haul through a life of stigma. The way she saw it, many people, rightly or wrongly, believed that being associated with pornography was shameful. This was also a form of commiseration.

I sat on the pink barstool, watching Grandma Maria move from stove to sink, stirring a big pot of gravy and frying meatballs. It sure sounded like my dad had done something bad. But so what? I knew everything would turn out okay. On the other hand, I realized that my father's involvement in pornography was the most notorious thing that had happened in our family.

I just listened to her and marveled that our family sounded more interesting than any TV show like *Dynasty, Dallas*, or *Falcon Crest*. Talking while cooking, Grandma Maria experienced this family event like it had happened yesterday. She flashed between anger, tears, and reflection at different points in her storytelling. She said, "But I love your father, he always did right by you," and then in the next breath she would accuse him of being a bastard and doing horrible things to her daughter. Obviously she was conflicted about her son-in-law's complicated career. And so was I.

"How did he get involved with that movie?" I asked her.

"Well, Mommy," she said ("Mommy" was her funny nickname for all her grandkids), "you know your Uncle Tony got him involved. I never trusted Uncle Tony all that much."

"Uncle Tony" was Anthony Arnone, and he was not really my uncle but rather my father's close friend from college. When I was growing up, anyone close to my family became "Uncle This" or "Aunt That" and this naming happened as if the DNA of the person became bonded to my family's DNA out of thin air. These honorary titles always indicated if you were in or out of the family's good graces. People who fell out of favor were suddenly called by their first names again, or worse, just "son of a bitch."

So as Grandma Maria told me this story, it was really hard for me to fathom why my father would want to work in the porn business. Someone doesn't just stumble into the porn industry, does he? It wasn't like a guy standing on a street corner had flashed my father the inside of his trench coat and said, "You wanna work in porn?" rather than "You wanna buy a watch?" Clearly, this was not a common career path or something you studied in college.

"I guess it was about August of 1973," Grandma Maria explained. "Right before your third birthday, your father got a call from Uncle Tony to see if he wanted to distribute that dirty movie in the Philadelphia area. They'd already opened their smutty theater, The Premier, in Orlando. Of course I didn't know anything when it was happening. Cloak and dagger, you know. Only found out after the fact."

Apparently my mother had kept Grandma Maria on a need-to-know basis, and I sensed that, for Grandma Maria, keeping secrets was as serious a crime as kidnapping or murder or, for that matter, dealing in porn.

"He had a good job as a stockbroker, Mommy, so I don't understand why he did such a stupid thing. Your mother . . ." Her voice quivered and she placed her hands to her forehead. Then she ran the hot water and started to clean the pots and pans. Grandma Maria regained her composure as the bubbles of the soapy water rose. I realized cleaning must have had a calming effect for her.

I grabbed a dishtowel and dried the pans as she handed them to me. "Your mother suffered so much," she went on. "When I got the call from your mother that your father was arrested, I just didn't know what to think."

I doubt anyone had known what to think. Sort of like when you discover your neighbor is a drug dealer or the seemingly happiest couple on Earth suddenly gets divorced because of the husband's affair with a babysitter. It makes people feel uncomfortable, even violated, when they discover that such shocking secrets have been kept from them. It's a betrayal of trust.

Before his arrest, my father had been a top salesman at W. E. Hutton, a huge investment company in Philadelphia. The money was good and everyone thought of him as very successful. He'd even scored a free trip to Hawaii for selling mutual fund products. I have often envisioned my parents on that trip, sitting under palm trees in lounge chairs with tropical drinks in hand and crystal clear water lapping at their feet. Having already tasted paradise, why would my father sell porn?

The possibilities as to why are endless. Maybe such a person simply loves naked women, like a lot. Or the person is a closet pervert and working in porn is the perfect opportunity to make his shameful hobby into a career. It's also a great job for a voyeur, someone who has tired of peeking through bedroom windows and now wants the chance to admire willing exhibitionists. Or could it have been a love of avant-garde films?

No. None of these reasons made sense. My father wasn't a pervert. He wasn't into obscure films. He had an economics degree, which wasn't controversial at all. He even voted for Nixon!

The only logical choice, as I saw it then, and as I see it now, was the money. *Deep Throat* had an enticing, high-profit allure. My father must have thought, *This is hot, so people all over the country are going to pay to see it.* And if you've got an in on distribution and its big margin, well then you'd be a fool to pass it up. My father's job at W. E. Hutton and the high-powered business culture and the trips to Hawaii must not have been enough to keep him from picking this nice ripe apple dangling from the tree.

By the time Grandma Maria and I were finished talking that day, it was late and the kitchen that had been a huge mess earlier in the evening was now spotlessly clean. You could eat off the floor in my grandmother's kitchen.

"So did you ever forgive him, Grandma?" I asked.

"Of course, Mommy. He gave me you, the best granddaughter in the world," Grandma Maria said in a lighthearted way designed to keep my image of my father intact.

It was time to go. I left that day with more questions than answers. But at least I knew a little bit more. I wondered if what my father did was wrong. It was hard for me to imagine he would break the law or hurt anyone. He was always a kind and generous person and a loving father. As a husband, he seemed to struggle and there was always strain in my parents' relationship that I didn't fully understand. Over the next several years, as I matured into an adult, I would learn much more, which I detail on the following pages. Between my memories as a child during the time my dad distributed *Deep Throat* and hearing stories from my Grandma Maria and other family members, I realized that my father was like a jigsaw puzzle with a million little pieces, and I was always trying to see the full picture.

# 1

## *Stockbroker to Pornbroker*

"Grosses this week at the Premier are up, and *Deep Throat* is still bringing in the crowds," said Tony Arnone, my father's business partner and old college friend.

Dad held the phone closer to his ear lest one of the other salesmen working at the twenty identical desks lined up in the cavernous trading room at W. E. Hutton would hear the man my family called "Uncle Tony" on the other end of the line.

"Look, I don't want to keep you," Tony continued, "but a business opportunity has come up. You remember me mentioning Lou Perry?"

Dad whispered into the phone. "Your *Deep Throat* contact?"

"The producers are moving the movie nationwide, and pronto," said Tony. "They need distributors in the Northeast. I think you'd be perfect. All you'd have to do is call up some theaters and pitch them the movie. You get 5 percent of the distributor's cut of the gross from whatever theaters you sign."

My father peered left and right at the large office space. What would his co-workers think if they knew he was having this conversation while on the clock at W. E. Hutton? "Doesn't sound too hard," he said after a moment. "Thanks for the offer. I'll think about it."

"Man, don't think too much. These people are ready to go."

My father knew making a few phone calls and booking sales was basically what he did as a broker, so in that regard, he was incredibly well suited for this opportunity. And he knew *Deep Throat* would basically sell itself. The film had premiered in Times Square at the World Theater in June 1972 and had been showing in theaters for more than a year. By then, August 1973, it was still hugely popular. In fact, its popularity accelerated. In January of that year, the *New York Times Magazine* had published an article titled "Porno Chic" that described *Deep Throat* as a cultural phenomenon, and the article's author, Ralph Blumenthal, had even hypothesized that, based on *Deep Throat*'s huge crossover success, hardcore pornography would one day merge with traditional movies.

The reasons for the movie's success are myriad. For one, the film defied convention in that it incorporated a complete plot (albeit a flimsy one). It also boasted a keen sense of humor. The notion of a woman having a clitoris in the back of her throat—perhaps the weirdest and most notorious aspect of *Deep Throat*—was not seen by most as obscene, but rather hilarious. The film was a household name, even before its bizarre and rather arbitrary connection to the Watergate scandal, with which the term "Deep Throat" is now more popularly associated.

My father had seen the movie shortly after its premiere when he and a group of co-workers had gone to a local theater on their lunch hour to check it out. He appreciated the movie's unconventional, offbeat storyline, and he was strangely curious about Linda Lovelace's unique skill set, which left the average viewer dumbfounded about the gag reflex (or, in this case, the lack thereof). The director, Gerard Damiano—himself transformed from Queens hairstylist to porn director—knew he had found a gem when he discovered Linda Lovelace. It seemed part luck and part genius that Damiano was able to pull this movie together in such a short amount time and with very little money.

After they left the theater, a co-worker said to my father, "If my wife could do what Linda Lovelace can do, I might be worried."

My father laughed. "I just found the plot so weird," he said. "My wife would probably find it funny. That wacky doctor character, Harry Reems, actually seemed to have some acting talent."

As my father tells it now, he returned to work that afternoon having no idea that someday he would be involved with the film. But fast-forward a year and everything had changed—*Deep Throat* was an all-out sensation. My dad knew that if he didn't cash in, someone else surely would.

But there was much more to *Deep Throat* than just a very good business opportunity for my father. This movie was redefining our culture in a controversial way. In April 1973, *Deep Throat* was banned in New York City as part of Mayor Lindsey's vow to clean up Times Square. Judge Joel Tyler, in a Manhattan Criminal Court, ruled that the film was indecent and closed down the showing at the World Theater. The headline on the marquee of the World Theater—"Throat Cut, World Mourns"—seemed to signal the end of *Deep Throat*. But, in fact, it was just the beginning of the phenomenon. The trial leading up to its ban made the film wildly popular in other parts of the country, which helped fuel rumors that the early court proceedings had actually been staged to create buzz.

At about the same time, in June 1973, the Supreme Court decision in Miller versus California granted greater power to states in setting their own "community standards" and established the "Miller Test" for communities to decide for themselves if material was obscene. Marvin Miller, the owner of a small mail-order business, was convicted of sending sexually oriented ads through the mail. Before this decision, communities had had to apply a national standard to enforce obscenity laws. But Miller versus California clarified that obscenity was no longer solely protected by the First Amendment, which was the beginning of local governments prosecuting obscenity cases around the country, making it illegal in some places (but not all places) to show *Deep Throat* and other films. Miller versus California made it possible to hold the federal obscenity trials in Bible Belt states and conservatives went into a feeding frenzy to enforce what they saw as the high moral standards of their communities.

*Deep Throat* also reshaped the sexual landscape for both men and women and carried the torch for sexual pioneers Alfred Kinsey, Williams Johnson, and Virginia Masters and the free love time of the 1960s. Sex was something to be embraced and enjoyed, not hidden. The birth control pill was now taken by many women and sex was free of consequence as well, unleashing a time of experimentation.

The film became a part of the mainstream during a time in our country when people had a growing distrust of its government. My father's generation had experienced so much turmoil in the 1960s—the Civil Rights movement, the assassinations of John F. Kennedy, Robert Kennedy, and Dr. Martin Luther King, not to mention the agony of the Vietnam War. Then, on the brink of the 1970s, came the Nixon Watergate scandal. The country was ripe for social change. By the end of its multi-year run, the film had grossed hundreds of millions of dollars from a $25,000 initial investment.

My father told me he did not give much thought to the obscenity controversy the movie was stirring across the country or that distributing it might be a risky venture. He believed, perhaps naively, that because Philadelphia was not a small town or located in the Deep South, he was not risking any legal repercussions.

And anyway, this would only be a part-time gig.

On his way home after work from bustling downtown Philadelphia to suburban Upper Darby, my father would often pick up flowers for my mother. (My mother loved any flower except for carnations; she always called carnations "funeral flowers" and said that they reminded her of an open casket wake, which was the typical way Italians honored the dead.) When he entered the door of our modest row house on Spruce Avenue, he would announce, "I'm home!" and call out to my mother, "Smells good, Frannie. What are you cooking?" Usually I would be watching *The Electric Company* or *Sesame Street* in the living room, and I'd jump up to greet him. "How's my little girl today?" he would ask as he lifted me from the floor and gave me a big hug. It was always so exciting to feel weightless for a half a second. As he made his way to the kitchen—with me watching curiously from behind—he would peer around the doorway to see my mother, with her tall slender frame and jet-black hair pulled into a tight ponytail, busy at the counter or stirring a pot on the stove. My father would stand behind her with the flowers until she turned around. "Oh Anthony, they're beautiful!" I remember her saying many times, tilting her head slightly to kiss him on the cheek.

On the day my father received the offer from Tony Arnone to distribute *Deep Throat*, he told my mother at dinner matter-of-factly about his decision. "I'm going to take Tony up on it," he said. Then he added, "I think I could make us great extra money."

My mother told me later that she doesn't remember giving it much thought. She could sense that his gut instincts told him this was a good move and she knew he never ignored his gut instincts. And anyway, she'd been fine with him investing in the Premier Theater. This didn't seem like a much bigger deal.

In the end, she trusted him.

"If you think it'll be worthwhile," she said confidently, looking at the white dahlias he'd brought her that evening.

And that was that.

❧

A couple of weeks after talking to Tony Arnone, my father began distributing *Deep Throat* in earnest. "All of a sudden I was getting lots of phone calls at my office," my father told me when we talked many years later about his distributing days. "A cottage industry had sprung up overnight."

"How did you get any W. E. Hutton work done?" I asked him. If his phone was ringing off the hook as he described, I imagined that his co-workers at W. E. Hutton must have thought he was selling a helluva lot of stocks. Distributing *Deep Throat* gave a whole new meaning to the term *moonlighting*; this wasn't like waiting tables or stocking shelves at a retail store late at night. This tapped into an insatiable demand for racy content and created an outlet for people to express their sexuality. Sex was no longer something to be hidden. My father's new venture was also part entrepreneurial American dream, part pure craziness.

"I worked long hours," my father answered simply. Then he confessed, "But there were some days that *Deep Throat* business was all I did."

He landed a few small bookings across town, but for his first major booking, he selected the venue strategically: the Midtown Theater, a massive nine-hundred seat, velvet-draped classic movie theater located on Chestnut Street in downtown Philadelphia. Not only was the Midtown in a plum location, it was also part of the huge Budco theater chain and it was the epitome of the 1970s movie-going experience in Philadelphia. If he could land the Midtown, he knew he'd have a leg up in developing a huge clientele in the Philadelphia area.

And, coincidentally, the Midtown is where my father had taken my mom on their first date.

Mitch Goldman, the Budco booking agent, contacted my father and over the next few weeks they discussed the possibility of booking the Midtown. Goldman wanted the movie. Badly. But there was one huge problem . . . they had to convince Claude Schlanger, the conservative owner of the Midtown, to take the film.

"Anthony, man, I want this movie," Goldman said to my father in his fast-talking New York accent. "But I'm telling you, convincing Schlanger will be like convincing Jesus to sin. He's a strict German Catholic, for Christ's sake."

"You sure? With a name like Schlanger?" my dad said laughing. "This movie is perfect for him."

"No, he's an uptight Kraut, I'm telling you," Mitch said.

"Okay, I get you. You want me to call him? Just tell me what to do."

According to my father, hearing this was an epiphany for Goldman. "Anthony, you know, that's a great idea. He'll love you. You're both Villanova grads. You could chat him up about basketball. And you're Catholic, right?"

"Well . . ."

"Why would he want to take advice from an obnoxious Jew like me?" Goldman asked, snorting laughter through his nose. "Our races don't exactly have a good history, if you know what I mean."

"I'd hardly say I was Catholic, Mitch. My mother does the praying in our family. But if you think it would help, I'll call him."

My father banked on charming Schlanger with the latest Wildcat basketball scores and reminiscing about the old days on campus. But after repeated attempts, Schlanger remained adamant: he did not want to be involved in pornography. (It didn't help that *Deep Throat* had already showed a year earlier at Theater 1812, also on Chestnut Street, and that it had come and gone without much fanfare.) No matter what my father said and no matter how much evidence he provided of *Deep Throat*'s recent success across the country, Schlanger would not sign on.

Eventually Goldman took over again and he became relentless. He called Schlanger daily and said things like, "You're a smart guy, Claude. Can you honestly walk away from all this money? Other theaters around the country are making tens of thousands!"

Finally, about a month later, Schlanger surrendered; he had a sudden Hollywood movie cancellation and needed to fill a hole in his schedule. He decided to give *Deep Throat* one week.

Goldman and my father were thrilled. But there were still two more hurdles to clear. First, Goldman and my father wanted to charge $5 per ticket, but Schlanger argued that this was an outrageous price; the average cost of a movie ticket in those days was $1.50. My father was adamant that the public would be willing to pay. He persisted. Finally, after much haggling, Schlanger compromised on $4 per ticket.

The second problem was much more daunting.

The Peraino family—the notorious mob-connected owners of *Deep Throat*—announced they did not want to book with the Midtown because Schlanger would only agree to pay by check. The Perainos preferred cash collected at the end of every night by a "checker." My father felt uneasy, of course, that the Perainos only wanted to deal in cash. But they owned the film, so however they conducted business was their prerogative.

In the short time my father had been distributing, he had discovered that dealing with the Perainos was tumultuous and never predictable. But anyone who entered the porn business in those days—especially if they wanted to show *Deep Throat*—had to deal with the Perainos, for better or worse. Lou Peraino (a.k.a. Lou Perry) was the producer of *Deep Throat*. Lou's father, Anthony Peraino (a.k.a. the "old man") was the head of the family and had given Lou the initial investment money to produce the film. And Lou's uncle, Joe "The Whale" Peraino (nicknamed for his three-hundred-pound girth), acted as general manager for the *Deep Throat* distributing business. They were a motley crew, and together they cast an intimidating shadow.

My father has described the Perainos to me as "the gang that couldn't shoot straight," after the Jimmy Breslin novel of the same name about mob boss Joey Gallo and the famous screw-ups of his Brooklyn crew. They were unpredictable and arbitrary in the way they made decisions. Above all, they seemed to have secrets, scary secrets, which left people wary and unable to gauge their intentions. There were also many rumors about their mob ties and the physical retaliation people might face if they went against the family. My father never admitted to having any fear in dealing with the Perainos. But he did confess to purposely holding them at arm's length, like a snake charmer handling a poisonous snake. The lesson here was simple: be close enough to benefit from the business at hand, but not so close as to become enmeshed in something dangerous. And be careful not to get bitten.

While the Midtown deal was in negotiations, the Perainos' fledging distribution network was coming together at a rapid, but disorganized, pace. Tony Arnone had established strong ties with the Perainos in the early 1970s while expanding his adult theater business all over south Florida. During that time, he had secured the Perainos' permission to create a national distribution network for *Deep Throat*. Thus Tony was my father's go-to contact for distributing... until, that is, he was abruptly removed from the job following a quick succession of events.

In the fall of 1973, Anthony Peraino expressed interest in partnering with Tony Arnone and my father at the Premier Theater in Orlando. Essentially, the Perainos wanted a foothold in the brick-and-mortar porn business in Florida.

But my father and Tony both knew this was an offer they *had* to refuse. Aligning too closely with the Perainos would be a bad idea. They thought it was possible they would lose the business due to mismanagement or they could be pushed out altogether.

"I think we need to separate from the Perainos," Tony said.

My father agreed, nodding. "They seem to be involved in some bad stuff," he said.

"Okay, let's just tell them we're interested in a localized, small business. I'll say I know that they're going to be big time and that's just not what we're after."

"You think they'll buy that line?" Dad asked.

"God, I hope so. Hopefully they already realize we're just not like them," Tony replied.

Separating from the Perainos was key. When considering the future of their theater and the possibility of other theaters to come, my father and Tony knew any legal or personal complications with the Perainos would put them at great risk.

Tony Arnone hoped to decline the Perainos' offer in a respectful way, so as to not offend the family while still retaining his access to showing *Deep Throat*. After a tense meeting, Anthony Peraino accepted his and my father's decision by graciously saying, "Let's part now while we can part as friends."

But declining the Perainos' offer came with consequences; immediately after their refusal, Tony lost his partnership to distribute *Deep Throat* nationally and became just another theater owner showing the film.

The question now was: since my father was still a regional distributor, who would his *Deep Throat* contact be?

The answer was a man named Bobby DeSalvo, a unique character in the twisted story of *Deep Throat*. Bobby had come out of nowhere. Just a few months prior to the Midtown deal, he had been introduced to the Perainos after Tony caught him showing an unauthorized copy of *Deep Throat* in Lake Worth, Florida. Tony had informed Lou Peraino about the showing because he knew it was a huge problem for anyone to cut into the Perainos' business.

Lou then paid Bobby an in-person visit. But instead of threatening Bobby as everyone had expected, Lou was so charmed by Bobby that he handed over the rights to show *Deep Throat*. Lou even made Bobby a partner in their national distributing scheme. Lou liked Bobby because he had had the guts to defy them by showing the bootleg copy of *Deep Throat*. He viewed Bobby as one of them—an Italian street guy with ambition.

Fortunately for my father, Bobby was very likeable. If my father could no longer have Tony Arnone as his liaison, he was at least happy to have Bobby to deal with the Perainos directly instead of having to do so himself.

So it was Bobby, the Perainos' trusted advisor, who stepped in to save the Midtown theater deal and who convinced the Perainos that the Midtown would make a ton of money by helping them break into the Philly market. And it was Bobby who instructed my father to book the theater and to take payment by check for that week.

⋘⋙

On January 10, 1974, *Deep Throat* opened at the Midtown. The first show would be at noon. When my father awoke that morning, a hard wind was blowing in from the north and the windchill was about 10 degrees Fahrenheit. He had waited for this day with nervous anticipation, like a child counting the days until Christmas, but now he wasn't sure if people would venture out on such a painfully cold day.

Nevertheless, this day offered my father a great hope: to be free from both the vacillations of the financial markets and the whims of his investment clients. *Deep Throat's* opening had all the feel of launching his own small enterprise. And it smelled like real money, quick money.

Before my father left the house that morning for his usual day at W. E. Hutton, my mother told him, "I feel it, Anthony. It'll be a hit."

"I hope you're right, honey," my father said nervously. Then he kissed her on the cheek and ran out the door. My mother was just as excited as he was and she called after him, "Let me know if you hear anything!"

As soon as my father reached his office at 9 a.m., Goldman called and said, "Anthony, there's a line around the corner."

"What?"

"A line around the corner of the Midtown! Hundreds of people!"

"Jesus Christ, Mitch!" my father said in a hoarse whisper so his co-workers wouldn't hear.

An hour later, Goldman called again and his voice sounded giddy. "Anthony, all nine hundred seats in the theater are full!"

My father could barely contain his excitement. He wanted to jump onto his desk and howl like a wolf. But he realized that the trading room was now bustling around him, so he sat still and responded politely, as if talking to one of his clients:

"Thank you very much for letting me know, Mr. Goldman. I'll be sure to get back to you later about making further buys."

Dad realized he had hit the jackpot. He immediately called my mother and told her in a whisper what was happening.

"Oh, my goodness!" my mother said "I told you it would be a big hit. This is great, honey."

At lunchtime, he had to see the crowds for himself, so he walked briskly in the cold to Chestnut Street. He peered up the street, and even though he knew what he was going to see, he was still shocked to discover a line of people stretching a hundred yards down the block.

*Jesus, I can't believe all the people,* he thought. *They must be freezing their asses off!*

My father came home that night over the moon about his apparent success. As my mother remembers it, he looked wild-eyed and disheveled, like someone had ransacked his suit into a wrinkled mess. Even though it was freezing out, he was sweaty around the temples from running home from the EL stop.

"Frannie, I can't believe it! The crowd outside the theater was unbelievable. I wish you could see it," said my father, grabbing her around the shoulders and planting a big kiss on her lips.

"That's just . . . just great news," she cooed, truly happy that everything seemed to be working out.

"Do you mind if I run downtown after dinner?" he asked. "I want to see how the crowds are tonight."

She smiled. "Come on. Let's eat real quick so you can go."

My father ate quickly, then set off on his impromptu field trip. During the drive, he recalled the numerous calls from Goldman updating him about the massive crowds outside the theater. It was *Deep Throat*'s grand return to Philadelphia, all made possible by my father.

That week, *Deep Throat* grossed $73,000 at the Midtown, breaking the house record previously held by *The Sound of Music*, which had grossed $40,000 in the same amount of time. Claude Schlanger was ecstatic and, conveniently forgetting his earlier protests, said to my father, "I knew that was what people wanted to see."

*Deep Throat* played at the Midtown for nine weeks and it grossed a weekly average of $50,000. Goldman soon moved it to other Budco theaters like the Goldman Theater on Fifteenth and Chestnut Street, where it was equally successful. The film played in all the Budco theaters in Plymouth, White Marsh, Exton, and Wilmington, Delaware, just to name a few.

And this was just the beginning. Before my father knew what was happening, he had become the primary Northeastern contact point for theater owners to gain access to *Deep Throat*. He didn't even have to pick up the phone, as he'd expected. Instead, the theater owners called him. And when they called, which they all inevitably did, my father had the perfect sales pitch: not only was the Midtown making a mint, but when *Deep Throat* had played at my father's theater in Orlando, Dad and Tony had earned back their initial investment of $25,000 in just one weekend. How could any businessperson argue with numbers like that?

No one could. Everyone wanted a piece of this instant success and my father was in a perfect position to provide it.

*Deep Throat* was generating about $70,000 a week in each of the theaters where Dad had placed it. In 1973, he earned an additional $25,000 to $30,000 from distributing and, one by one, he landed all the large movie houses in Philadelphia. Considering that his annual salary at W. E. Hutton was $40,000 on a draw versus commission basis, this was excellent pay for a lot less work.

Not bad for a part-time job.

⁓⁓

After the Midtown booking, my father was so busy that he enlisted the help of his uncle, Ercole Dicolla.

Uncle Coke, as he was known in our family, was a tough World War II veteran who had proudly served in the navy as a gunner on a destroyer in the Pacific. "To fight those Japs," as he would say. Uncle Coke had never written home during the war and his sister, Grandma Emma, made a number of trips to the Red Cross to confirm he was still alive. "If I was dead, people would find out soon enough," he joked later. He smoked unfiltered Lucky Strike cigarettes, one after the other, and I clearly remember his full head of silver hair that punctuated the top of his short, stout body.

Uncle Coke and my father were very close. Dad could tell Uncle Coke many things about the *Deep Throat* business that he couldn't share with his own father, Antonio. He knew Antonio would never understand the thrill of participating in this bustling new enterprise and would also disapprove of dabbling in porn. But Uncle Coke understood the street mentality and he could provide a unique perspective on this unusual business.

Uncle Coke was the complete opposite of the traditional elders in our family, thus he was the perfect *Deep Throat* accomplice. He was a rebel, known for developing little criminal schemes of his own. Like when he was a bus mechanic at the Southeastern Pennsylvania Transportation Authority (SEPTA) and he and his buddy Joe Fortuna (who looked like actor Joe Pesci) would drive city buses around the block at the end of their routes to steal a portion of the day's fares from the box. They gave co-workers a percentage to keep them quiet, then converted the rest of the coins into dollars.

Although the SEPTA scam was clearly a crime, Uncle Coke gave the money to the local Catholic Church for children who needed shoes, clothes, and books for school. He said he always gave the money to the nuns, since he was sure that if a priest got hold of the cash, it would never end up with the children who needed it. Uncle Coke also coached a boys baseball team and every year they had new uniforms and equipment. As my father said, "Uncle Coke had larceny in his heart." But Uncle Coke didn't use the money to buy a bigger house or more possessions; he lived modestly and happily in the basement level of a row home with his wife, Aunt Lil. Since the basement was a walk-out, this made it easier for Aunt Lil to get outside. She weighed almost four hundred pounds and walking the stairs was almost impossible given her large size.

All of this adds up to the fact that Uncle Coke was a willing and able business partner in my father's *Deep Throat* endeavors. He was the in-person contact for the Johnston Theater for Dad and he became a checker and a sweeper in the *Deep Throat* distributing system. A checker and sweeper was managed by a regional distributor and they were the engine that made the distribution system run. Uncle Coke would also travel to New York City by bus or train to pick up the film at a designated location to bring it back to Philadelphia. The film was transported in large metal containers and weighed about thirty to forty pounds, and he would put this in a suitcase to conceal the contents. Uncle Coke treated the film like contraband and he never told anyone about his daytrips to New York.

Uncle Coke would deliver the film to all the theaters in Philadelphia every afternoon and at the end of each night he would collect the evening's profits. He put the cash and the film into a suitcase and brought it all to my father. Then, twice a month, my father would fly to Florida to take the money to the Perainos' office in Wilton Manors, a suburb of Fort Lauderdale. Mickey Cherubino, Lou Peraino's son-in-law, would collect and ship the money by rented truck to the Perainos' office in Brooklyn, New York.

This wildly circuitous route did not make much sense to my father at the time. But in hindsight, he would understand . . .

This all made the film, and the money, much more difficult for the FBI to track.

On one of these regular visits to Fort Lauderdale to check in with Mickey, Dad had trouble opening the door to the Perainos' office. He pushed open the door with a shove because something was blocking the doorway. He was only able to open the door halfway, creating just enough space to squeeze through.

Mickey Cherubino sat at a desk in the far corner of the room and he looked up as my father struggled in. The humming noise of the air conditioner filled the space, along with a cool blast of air Dad felt as he entered the room.

"Hey, Anthony! Welcome back to Florida," Mickey said, waving him over. Mickey was wearing a Hawaiian shirt and sandals.

My father peered around the room in amazement as he realized what had been blocking the door. Cash was piled to the ceiling, stuffed in drawers, stored in overflowing boxes. The room was filled to the brim with money.

"Hey, Mickey, is Lou or Bobby around this week?" my father inquired nervously, just making conversation.

"No, they're in Brooklyn. Won't be back until next week. So how's business been in Philly?"

"Good. The bookings are doing well and the film is still real popular. It looks like, from around here, the film is still doing pretty good everywhere else," he said, referencing the piles of cash filling the room.

"Yeah, yeah, business is good. Okay, hand over the suitcase and let me get you sorted out," said Mickey.

My father was numb to what was obviously going on around him. It was an out-of-control cash business. A part of him had to know that all of this was rife with fraud but he rationalized his involvement; as long as he didn't know where all this money was going and as long he paid taxes on all his income from the movie, he was safe. He just wanted to keep his drop-offs brief and all about business.

Fortunately for my father, it was easy to stay removed from the Perainos' day-to-day dealings, simply because they never wanted outsiders to visit their Brooklyn office. That was a special privilege that only Bobby DeSalvo enjoyed, which was fine with my father. He never wanted to set foot in the New York office for fear that he might witness something he shouldn't.

Dad left Florida that day realizing he was in an unusual circumstance and wondering how long his distributing of *Deep Throat* would last. He was working hard at his day job and just hoped he could keep doing what he was doing for as long as he could. He knew all too well from sales that there is no such thing as a free lunch and that he would just have to make the most of this opportunity while he could.

# 2

# *The Beach*

"**B**rian!" I yell from the top of the stairs. "Where's the beach bag with all the pockets?"

"I think it's in the guest room closet," my husband responds. "What about the green duffle bag?"

"It's probably in the same closet. I'll look."

We're rushing around packing for a trip to the beach after a busy day at work. I'm exhausted. Grace, my daughter, flies into the room, flops onto the bed, and says to me, "I can't wait to go to the beach, Mom. When will we get there?"

Before I can respond, Brian is in the doorway answering her question.

"We should leave by 5:00 a.m.," he says. "If we do, we'll be there about 9:00 a.m."

"God, why so early?" I say, whining through work fatigue. "Isn't this the start of vacation? It should mean more sleep."

Brian looks at me, realizing I'll have to be convinced. "We both hate traffic," he says. "The longer we wait, the more traffic and accidents we'll run into on the beltway."

I hear the word *accidents*, glance at my daughter, and begrudgingly agree. "Fine," I say. Brian's logic is just too sound and, as I get older, I'm more and more fearful of dying in a tragic accident.

"We'll be the first on the beach," he reassures me.

Grace bounces out of the room. "Yay! I can't wait to get to the beach!"

I can't wait either, despite my irritation and exhaustion. I was raised on yearly doses of beach vacations. My earliest memories are of my father, mother, and entire family converging on the Jersey Shore for extended periods every summer. Those trips, and the trips with my husband and daughter now, are the happiest memories I possess.

This evening, I wander around our house for hours, double-checking bags obsessively to make sure we have everything. The anticipation of the summer's first beach trip starts for me in early spring. As soon as the sun starts to warm away the winter, I begin rummaging for bathing suits, towels, and sunscreen. I think I'm driven to do this because it's easy to become intoxicated by the beauty of an ocean view, and I crave the feeling of the sun penetrating vitamin D into my skin. The beach has always elicited for me feelings of calm and revival.

I have trouble getting to sleep knowing I'll be coaxed into the car so early tomorrow morning. But as I lie quietly in bed next to my lightly snoring husband, I see sunsets, sunrises, calm oceans, choppy oceans, kids climbing on sand mountains, and adults toasting in celebration of just being at the beach. My mind wanders to my childhood trips to the Jersey Shore. I smile and finally drift off to sleep.

~⚬⚬~

As a child, I never slept well the night before our summer vacations to Ocean City, New Jersey. We would spend up to six weeks each summer at a rented beach house, though on the weekdays my father would commute to work in Philadelphia, leaving my mother and me to our own devices. Then, on the weekends, our clannish Italian Catholic family, from both sides, would congregate to eat huge meals together, which added another rich dimension to our summers. It was a revolving door of grandparents, aunts, uncles, and cousins. Adult family members would sit under umbrellas discussing politics and the

Phillies, while kids would tiptoe to the water's edge, then run away screaming from the waves crashing on the shoreline.

I remember the smell of the salty air and the feel of the wheels of my stroller rattling over the Ocean City boardwalk. I remember my requests for ice cream, salt-water taffy and fudge, and being indulged only occasionally with waffles and ice cream. And I remember spending hours on the same rides at the amusement pier, my favorite being the little boats that just went in circles and that had a little horn I could toot while pretending to be a boat captain.

My parents loved the beach and they prepared for our vacations just like I do today. Dad would strategically pack the car with beach chairs and umbrellas, just as my husband does now, and Mom would gather beach essentials, like the perfect pail and shovel to make sandcastles, just as I do for my daughter. At times, the hurried pace of packing gave way to stress and anxiety and on our car trips to Ocean City, I would sometimes overhear my parents' conversations as these emotions surfaced. This was one such conversation from the summer of 1973.

I was sitting at the kitchen table picking at my breakfast, a three-year-old giddy for summer vacation to begin, and watching my mother prepare our sandwiches for our trip. "Can't you take any time off and stay at the beach for a week?" my mother asked my father.

"I just have too much going on right now, Fran," my father replied. "We'll have long weekends. Isn't that enough?"

"I guess it'll have to do," said Mom. She slammed a knife on the counter and walked to the next room.

My father followed her. I jumped up and followed them both, too. "Business is good right now, Fran," said Dad. "The Premier is making good money. You should be glad I have these opportunities."

"Yeah, sure I'm glad," said Mom sarcastically, as she busied herself with the packing.

"You should be," my father fired back. He stormed out of the room.

The moment we arrived at the beach house later that day, I jumped out of the backseat of the car and onto the gravel drive, shouting, "Come on. Let's go!" My mother rose slowly from the passenger seat, still quiet from the argument earlier. She quickly grabbed some bags and hustled into the house. Dad peered over the open trunk lid, knowing their discussion wasn't over. I pulled my little suitcase into a room with two twin beds and took out my bunny, coloring books, and the frosty pink lipstick I had stolen from my mother. Then I heard arguing in the background.

"Well, you can give me the silent treatment or enjoy being at the beach," Dad said.

"It's not that I don't appreciate the beach," she said, "or that we get this beach house for six weeks, Anthony. I just want your daughter and me to get as much of your attention as work. It's always about work. And now you have this theater, so you talk more to Tony Arnone than you do to me."

"Frannie, I just want us to have a comfortable life and that means working hard now."

Peering at them now from the hallway, I saw my mother's face soften—she knew that my father was being sincere about wanting to provide for the family.

My father took advantage of his opening and said, "Let's unpack and get to the beach. It's a beautiful day!"

She nodded in agreement and walked to the back of the house to finish unpacking. I retreated to my bedroom and began smearing Mom's lipstick all over my lips and kissing the mirror. A short while later, Mom came into my room and found me covered in lipstick. With her hands on her hips, she shouted, "Anthony, I'm going to kill your daughter!"

When Dad entered the room and saw me, the three of us dissolved into silly laughter.

We were at the beach where it was impossible for us not to be happy.

⁓⌒⊙⌒⁓

Fifty miles away from Ocean City and six years before she became my mother, Frances Parrotto rushed up the stone steps of the Drexel Brook Country Club in the Philadelphia suburbs. The clicking of her high-heel pumps was the loudest noise in the hush of the early evening. She was twenty-one years old.

Frances was late meeting a group of girlfriends for drinks. She hated to be late and she was certain her friends Nancy and Carol were already inside dancing with the cutest guys. It was 1964 and this social club was a popular hangout for twenty-somethings on Friday nights.

"Hello, I'm here to meet Nancy Pagano," she said, smiling sweetly at the doorman. "I'm Frances Parrotto."

"Yes, let me check the guest list." He reviewed the list and a puzzled look crossed his face. "I'm sorry, the Paganos don't have your name on the list."

"Oh, gosh." She blushed flirtatiously. "Well, I *am* supposed to meet Nancy and . . . um . . . I'm already late and I traveled all the way from the city. Could I go find her and bring her up to the front?"

The doorman's face softened instantly. "I know Nancy and if you say you're a friend of hers, I say it's alright to go on ahead inside. Have a nice evening, Miss."

"Oh, thank you. You're just so nice," my mother gushed.

She had the bone structure and subtle grace that resembled Jackie Kennedy, so it wasn't hard to charm her way in.

And if she hadn't charmed her way in? Then she might not have met Anthony.

The club was busy. Women, dressed in their finest outfits, powdered and preened in the hopes of meeting their future husbands, and the men, tired junior executives, donned suits with loosened ties, having just left work. Anthony was among them, blowing off steam with co-workers, and he spotted Frances from across the room. He told me it was the blue dress she wore that first caught his eye. The form-fitting style accentuated her broad shoulders. She was standing against the wall and swaying to the music, an invitation to be asked to dance. He hoped his stark-white dress shirt offset his olive complexion in a good way and that the tailored jacket he was wearing hid his slightly overweight frame. He hoped that the trendy black-rimmed glasses he'd selected would detract a bit from the fact that, at the old age of twenty-three, he was already balding.

Anthony was not a good dancer but he figured that if he had any chance at all with the beautiful girl in the blue dress, then the dance floor was in his near future. Finally, he worked up the nerve to approach her. They made small talk over the loud music as they danced. She asked what he did for a living and where he was from. He said he was a jewelry insurance underwriter at Royal Global Insurance and that it was his first job out of college; he had just graduated from Villanova.

It was an unmemorable conversation, my mother told me. But when the song was over, Anthony invited her for a drink and, to his relief, she accepted. She was accustomed to having drinks bought for her. After the drink, Anthony didn't overstay his welcome and departed Frances's company by asking for her phone number. She gave it to him, later claiming to me she was indifferent about whether he would call.

He called her a few days later.

"Hi, this is Anthony. I met you a few nights ago at the Drexel Brook," he stammered slightly.

"Oh . . . hello. How are you?"

"I'm okay. You remember me?"

"Well, sure. The jewelry insurer, right?"

"Yeah, that's me. Well, I was wondering . . . I was wondering if you'd like to catch a movie at the Midtown and dinner in Chinatown this Saturday."

"Sure, that would be nice," she said, thinking she hadn't been on a date in a few weeks.

"Great. Let's say I'll pick you up at seven?"

"Yeah, that sounds fine. Oh, by the way . . . when you come to pick me up, I have to tell you, my mother has an ocelot cat."

"A what kinda cat?"

"An ocelot. She's a South American jungle cat. I just want to let you know ahead of time. Kitty looks intimidating, but she's really sweet."

"Okay, thanks for the heads up," he said.

It was a fair warning since Kitty, by instinct, would stalk around new people. You just didn't know if the big creature was going to pounce or purr. The cat was a good indicator to any future spouse about his future mother-in-law. The pet ocelot solidified Frances's mother Maria's eccentric style. The wild cat was a perfect reflection of her personality—protective of her young and a bit on the wild side. And Kitty was beautiful, with a gorgeous, thick, tawny coat with swirls of black markings that changed from stripes to spots. Her underbelly was a cream color with the same black markings. On trips to the Jersey Shore, Maria would walk Kitty on a leash at the beach late in the evenings and let her swim in the ocean. It was like the parting of the Red Sea for anyone in their path.

Of course, Anthony braved the wildlife—he wouldn't let anything get in the way of taking Frances on a date.

Still, after a few dates, Frances just wasn't that interested in Anthony. She came home from one date with him and told her mother, "He seems like a braggart. Always talking about his career like it's the most important thing. I don't want to go out with him again."

"Maybe he's nervous, Frannie, and you should give him one more chance," her mother said, realizing Frances was already twenty-one years old and had one broken engagement from her high school sweetheart, Bobby.

Frances protested, "Nah . . . I just don't like his personality. He seems so full of himself," and she drifted away from the conversation and headed off to bed.

Anthony, of course, did not feel the same way. He kept trying to contact her, but Frances avoided his phone calls.

He was puzzled since he thought the dates had gone well. He did a checklist in his mind: I took her to nice place, I was nice to her mother and that crazy ocelot, and I was a perfect gentleman. I'm also a decent-looking guy with a college degree. What gives?

Anthony sought advice from friends. He had no idea what to do. Finally a co-worker told him, "Look, a girl like this, who knows you like her, just don't call her too much. Just every once in a while to say hello and don't even ask her out so you don't look desperate."

He took the advice and played it cool. Anthony would call once every couple of months just to talk, and he never asked her out. Frances thought, *Why the hell is he calling me and not asking me out?* The intrigue and the mystery coaxed interest from this seemingly dead romance.

Then Anthony sent Frances flowers on her birthday; she thought that was the most romantic and thoughtful gesture. She was surprised he had even remembered her birthday and she was flattered he was still interested after all this time. She called to thank him for the flowers and only then did he ask her out. She accepted the invitation. It had been a year since their first date. He had been persistent in pursuing her, which was a telltale sign that he went after what he wanted and was relentless until he achieved his goal.

～◦∽◦～

Two years later, Frances went on vacation for the Fourth of July with her girlfriends to the beach in Wildwood, New Jersey, and Anthony saw this as the perfect opportunity to surprise her with a visit and to formally propose. They had been dating for a long time and he knew she would be the perfect wife. It was time.

Frances suspected Anthony's intentions were serious. But until she got a ring, she wasn't sure. Frances loved Anthony but she also liked the attention of other men. A fun flirt of hers was Bill LeBar—a Frenchman and sometime date—who also happened to be in Wildwood over that same Fourth of July weekend.

Right after work on Friday, Anthony drove to the Jersey Shore with life-changing excitement in his chest and an engagement ring in his pocket. He arrived at the rental house where Frances was staying, but no one was there. It was a beautiful day, so he assumed correctly that everyone was at the beach. Still in a suit and tie from the office, he removed his shoes and socks and rolled up the bottom of his dress pants to climb to the top of a sand dune. Once he reached the top, he shielded the sun from his eyes with his hand and scanned the beach. He saw Frances splashing near the water and flirting with Bill and he watched with jealousy as Bill playfully scooped her up in his arms and carried her toward the ocean.

Frances looked over Bill's shoulder and, to her surprise, saw Anthony.

"Put me down, Bill, that's my boyfriend."

"Who's your boyfriend? That suit?"

Bill put her down and Frances grabbed a cover-up and walked toward Anthony. She felt the heat on her cheeks from embarrassment and the sun. She hoped that Anthony knew she was not the kind of girl who would date two men seriously at once and that he would disregard what he had seen with Bill. It didn't mean anything. She was also terrified she might have blown the chance at landing herself a good husband.

When she was close enough to Anthony, she said nervously, "Well, hey you. I didn't expect to see you here."

Anthony had no expression on this face and said, "Come with me. I have something for you in the car." He thought he might as well ask. Even if she said no, at least he would give it a shot.

Frances sensed he was there to propose. But would he really do it after what he had just seen? She slid into the passenger side of the car, still wet from the escapade in the ocean with Bill.

"Frannie, it's either me or the rest of the world," Anthony said seriously. "I have something for you in the glove compartment."

She opened it and took out a tiny box that held a perfect one-carat solitaire diamond ring. She gasped and clasped her hand over her mouth in surprise.

"The ring could be bigger, but the stone is very good," said Anthony as he looked at her face for a reaction.

Frances smiled back at him. She knew he didn't care about Bill LeBar. She kissed him and was happy to be finally engaged. All of her friends were getting married and she didn't want to be the last one. She slid the ring on and held up her hand to admire the glittering stone as it caught the sunlight. Yes, she was truly happy. They celebrated that night by going to a fancy dinner at The Long Port Inn.

∽ೕ∾

My parents were married almost a year later on June 1, 1968. A few weeks before the wedding, my maternal grandparents took wedding portraits of my mother, as they had done with many new brides at their family-run photo studio.

The studio, located at the corner of Broad and Ritner streets in Philadelphia, was *the* place to go in our Italian American community for wedding, first Communion, and family portraits. The store had also been my mother's childhood home. It was a big brownstone with bedrooms on the upper floors and a kitchen and living room area behind the storefront. This was truly the first work-from-home lifestyle, before telecommuting even existed.

Grandpa Frank was the photographer and the handyman, while Grandma Maria minded the books and helped customers prepare for their photo sessions. She had a knack for calming nervous brides on their wedding day. "Now, honey," she'd say, "if you get all flustered your makeup will look terrible and your eyes will get all puffy. Do you want to look at puffy eyes in this picture for the rest of your life?" Grandma Maria also retouched photos by hand in the darkroom alongside my grandfather, using a magnifying glass and a palette of watercolor paints. My grandparents were a good team, both at running a business and at raising a family.

My mother's slim organza silk gown with delicate beading was beautiful and it was neatly matched with a pill box hat with a flowing veil. The lighting of the studio was bright and various backdrops in blue and rose were adjusted into place.

As my mother stepped into position, my grandmother gasped, "Oh Frannie, you are absolutely the prettiest bride I've seen! I knew this dress would be perfect."

It was the first time she would experience firsthand the banter between her parents as she was pushed and pulled in a million different directions to get the right shots.

"Now Frank, get the angle of Frannie from the right side. It will be so much better," Grandma Maria said.

"I was just going to do that, Mary. You don't have to tell me."

As the pictures were taken, my mother daydreamed of finally moving out of her parents' house. There was some sadness about moving away from home but also an eagerness to begin her life at age twenty-five.

Now the blending of their families would begin, taking on the good and the bad of both. The wedding brought a flurry of activity and lots of time for my parents' families to socialize and plan. Grandma Maria, who leaned toward the contemporary, clashed at times in style and taste with my father's mother, Grandma Emma, who was more beholden to Italian and Catholic tradition. To appease both of them, the ceremony was held at the neighborhood Saint Monica's Catholic Church and the reception at the Venus Lounge, a popular nightclub spot in South Philadelphia. Tony Arnone and Dad's younger brother Gabe were groomsmen. My mother's best friend Fran, sister Dolores, and sister-in-law Nancy were bridesmaids. My parents honeymooned in Miami, only to brave a hurricane while in South Florida. At least they would have the sunny days at the shore later that summer.

Both of my parent's families were in the midst of a transformation from the traditional Italian family with parents who were first generation Italian Americans to the mainstream, modern American family that was breaking away from the old traditions. With immigrant roots, there was nonetheless a heavy expectation to transcend this base and assimilate into America culture, and not only to make this transition but also to achieve and accomplish more than the previous generation. Anthony showed great promise, and with his beautiful Frances at his side, family and friends imagined they'd go far, such as a big, beautiful house in the better Main Line suburbs among the Wideners, Biddles, and Strawbridges. Perhaps Anthony would move up to one of the bigger investment houses in New York—Drexel Burnham, Bear Stearns, Bankers Trust—and they'd eventually live in Scarsdale or Short Hills or Oyster Bay. Everyone knew they would do well, but just how well?

⮜⁂⮞

My parents had met everyone's expectations as a young couple. My father had a growing career and my mother was a busy stay-at-home wife with a young child. Their success afforded us the opportunity to spend summers in Ocean City, New Jersey, at a rented beach house. My mother and father finished putting away the clothes and groceries, and only then did we finally walk to the beach together. I loved this first excursion to the beach, me sandwiched between my parents and holding both their hands. Every few steps they would pull me high into the air and I would squeal in delight. We staked out a nice area close to the ocean. After pitching the umbrella in the sand and laying out the beach blanket and some snacks, my mother said, "Okay, Anthony, let's take Kristin to the water."

"Are you ready, little girl?" Dad asked, clutching my hand. My mother trailed behind us with a camera.

She asked a passerby to snap a picture of the three of us at the ocean's edge. He took the photo. It was 1973.

This picture was taken right after the Premier Theater had opened and before my father started distributing *Deep Throat*. Walking around the beach that summer, no one would have suspected he was on the verge of a lifelong career in porn.

# 3

# *Arrested*

On July 10, 1974, my father arrived at his office as usual. He walked quickly across W. E. Hutton's big trading room to reach his desk in time for the opening of the New York Stock Exchange. Just as the stock prices began streaming across the ticker board at the front of the room, he draped his brown suit jacket over the back of his chair and slid into his seat. He readjusted his striped tie to settle in for a busy day.

Dad was taking notes from the ticker board and drinking a steaming cup of black coffee when he was called into the reception area. He assumed it was a client dropping by. Instead, he was greeted by two unsmiling men wearing drab gray suits. One of them flashed a badge and said, "Good morning, Mr. Battista. I'm from the FBI."

My father's friendly demeanor collapsed to a disconcerted look of confusion.

"Anthony Battista," the agent continued, "you're under arrest for conspiracy to violate federal obscenity laws by transporting the film *Deep Throat* to Memphis, Tennessee."

For a moment, my father didn't say anything. Finally he managed to utter, "I don't understand. I've never been to Memphis."

The FBI agents did not respond. Instead they read him his rights and made motions to put him into handcuffs. The receptionist looked horrified and quickly disappeared to inform someone about what was transpiring. Trying to maintain an air of professionalism, my father raised his hand to halt them from moving any closer and said, "I have several appointments today with clients. I need to cancel them if this is going to take a while."

The lead agent hesitated, but he agreed that my father could make a few calls. They escorted him to his desk.

"Hello, Mrs. Shapiro?" my father said to one his most faithful clients. "I'm very sorry, but I'll have to cancel my appointment today. Some unexpected things have come up." Then he finished in a relaxed tone, "Yes, next week would probably be fine. I'll call you."

As he put down the receiver from the last call, the agent placed one hand on my father's shoulder, then used the other to secure the handcuffs to his wrists.

"Is this really necessary?" my father muttered.

"Afraid so, sir," the FBI agent responded, and he guided my father down the hallway.

In the office's reception area, a sea of curious onlookers had gathered. Everyone gawked like this was the scene of a terrible car accident. Co-workers, bosses, and secretaries whispered to each other, "What could he have possibly done?"

As he was escorted to the elevator, my father found himself raising his voice more and more. "This isn't right! I didn't do anything wrong! I didn't do anything wrong!"

Many thoughts ran through my father's mind. *Is this some kind of joke? Will I end up in jail? What will Frannie say?* All he'd wanted was to earn some extra income. He didn't think he had done anything illegal. My father cursed under his breath. His dreams of prosperity and success were crumbling by the minute.

When they were outside the building, the agent removed the cuffs and said empathetically, "I'm sorry we had to do this here. Now we need to take you to the FBI Office." My father acknowledged the agent with a nod and slumped into the back seat of their awaiting car.

That day, my father was booked like a common criminal. The agents were calm and professional as they asked him to empty everything from his pockets. Then they searched his wallet and asked him questions about his address, his job, and the names of family members. He was fingerprinted, leaving black ink all over his fingers.

"Do you have anything to get this stuff off?" he asked, showing his hands to the booking officer.

"Sorry, I don't," the guy responded curtly.

"So what happens now?" my father asked another FBI agent.

"We have to take a picture, then there's a hearing with Judge Naythons to set bail or decide to hold you."

"Hold me? For what?"

"Sir, you've already been told the charges against you. I can't discuss it further."

"How long will this take?"

"The hearing should be by lunchtime."

My father was held in a cell for hours, giving him time to envision what serious jail time would be like. He was nauseated by thoughts of losing his freedom and of being confined to such a small, terrible space. Visiting his wife through glass walls, missing the mundane day-to-day activities of his normal life, and being separated from family was all too much to process.

If this craziness went beyond 5 p.m., he knew he would have to call someone. His brother, Gabe, would be the best option because he knew it would be impossible for my mother to come downtown with a child in tow. And there was no way my father would expose his wife and child to any of this until he could sort out the details.

Time passed slowly. It was excruciating. Finally, an officer appeared to take him to the hearing room. "You're up," he said to my father.

Standing in a courtroom, Dad stared up at a judge who had appeared from a side room to preside over his fate. After determining bail and noting that my father was not a flight risk, Judge Naythons declared in a low but booming voice, "Anthony Battista, you are hereby released on $10,000 bond upon agreement that you will report to Memphis, Tennessee, for a forthcoming trial for transporting obscene material over state lines. You are free to go." The judge lowered his gavel with a hard crack that made my father shudder.

And just like that, my father was standing in the bright sun outside the FBI Office in downtown Philadelphia. Staring at his ink-stained hands, he knew he needed to go back to the office and explain to his boss that this was all a mistake. He hailed the first taxi he saw. On the ride, he tried to relax by gathering his thoughts for the many conversations he anticipated having later that day with colleagues and family. He was determined to remain calm. He firmly believed he had done nothing wrong.

Arriving at W. E. Hutton, he buttoned his suit jacket and adjusted his tie, as he did every day before work, and he walked through the trading room with his head held high. He smiled and nodded at co-workers, only to hear snickers behind his back. "Wasn't he arrested today?" he heard someone say.

He cordially knocked on his boss's door.

"Come in."

My father cracked open the door. "Do you have a minute, George? I just want to clear up what happened this morning." He launched into his defense. "I'm going to get this all sorted out. It's silly really, um . . . I am distributing this thing part time, but it has nothing to do with my job here . . ."

"Anthony, please don't go any further."

At first, my father thought this sounded promising. But then George went on to say, "Look, you're a helluva broker, but we just can't keep you on. We had to report you to the stock exchange and your stockbroker's license has been suspended. I'm sorry. I'm deeply sorry." George picked up the phone and dialed. "Yes, Anthony Battista is back. Can you come down to escort him out?"

Keeping a dignified composure, my father said, "Well, I appreciate all the opportunity, George, and I hope in the future we can work together."

George stood up without saying a word and waited with my father in the hall until security and a human resources official could help him clean out his desk. They watched him collect his things and hand over his office keys. Everyone around him tried to stay focused on preparing for the close of the market, but they couldn't help noticing the drama unfolding in front of them.

No one approached to bid my father a proper farewell. No one offered him a handshake. The stock market closing that day was the last one my father would ever witness from inside a brokerage house.

~~~

That evening, my father looked like anyone else boarding the subway car at the Walnut Street station—just another employee making his way home after a long day. But inside he felt dread. He decided the best thing to do was not to panic. He knew that if he lost control of his emotions, then everyone around him might fall apart. So he rehearsed the scene over and over as to how exactly to tell his wife about the day's events. He decided to tell her the truth, but not make it appear like it was any big deal. He would do what he did best: convince his family that everything would be all right.

Dad arrived home at the normal time. Before opening the door, he took a few deep breaths. When he finally entered and my mother saw the flushed look on his face, she asked him what was wrong. At first he declined to answer, trying to gather his thoughts. Then he sat at the kitchen table and he calmly confessed to her that he had been arrested and fired.

My mother slowly nodded her head, not really comprehending as he recounted the insane events of the day. Being arrested sounded so bad to her. Really bad. But he was home, just like always, taking off his tie, and getting a glass of water from the sink to sit and watch her finish preparing dinner. Her mind was blank and confused.

"What does this mean?" she finally asked. "You were arrested for something that happened in Memphis?"

"I know, crazy, right? It has to be some kind of mistake. I think it'll all get sorted out."

Then he showed her his ink-stained hand and moved toward the sink to wash it. "Will you look at this," he said. "Do you think soap will get this out?"

"Oh, Jesus, Anthony. They fingerprinted you?" my mother said, slightly alarmed.

"It's just part of the process, Frannie."

"And you got fired? What did your boss say?"

"George didn't have a choice, since this is, you know, a federal government action. He was very nice about it."

My mother rubbed her eyelids and shook her head. "So do we need a lawyer?"

"Yes, probably. I think Tony Arnone will help."

"And what are we going to do in the meantime?"

"We'll be fine, Frannie. Don't worry," he said, hoping to put off any further questions until he had answers to give her. "I'll talk to Tony Arnone tonight."

"And what about the beach house? We're supposed to go in a few weeks . . ."

"We're still going to the beach house, Frannie. I promise."

My mother nodded.

"I have to go see Mom tonight," he added. "I don't want her hearing this from the news."

"Is this going to be on the news? Gosh, I better call my mother, too."

Though she was shaken by the revelation, my mother trusted my father when he said everything would be fine. After all, he wasn't in jail—he was home for dinner.

Then, like any good Italian wife, she quickly shifted gears to address a very important issue. "You must be hungry," she said. "I made chicken cutlets for dinner." My father nodded approvingly, happy for the tableau of family life to be playing out again, and my mother busied herself setting the table for dinner.

A few minutes later, I joined them for dinner as usual, not knowing the events of the day.

After dinner, my father drove to Drexel Hill where his parents lived. My father stood at the entrance to the kitchen and he heard his mother whistling. She looked up from the sink where she was washing dishes and, with a soapy hand, she adjusted her glasses, which were sliding down the bridge of her nose. She was surprised to see him on a weeknight because his visits usually came on Sunday afternoons. Immediately she asked, "What's wrong?"

"Where's Pop? Something happened at work and I want to tell you both at the same time."

Grandma Emma quickly dried her hands on her apron and ran her fingers through her short gray hair as she sat down at the kitchen table. "Your father's in the cellar messing with his wine barrels," she said. "Just leave him be. Tell me what's going on."

After listening to my father's story, Grandma Emma looked him deeply in the eyes for a long time.

Finally she asked, "Anthony, did you take anything that didn't belong to you?"

"No, Mom," he replied emphatically.

She sat silently for a moment. A pensive expression emerged on her face as she thought back to her determination for my father to attend college and to move beyond the blue-collar roots of his family. His arrest was certainly frightening. But she decided then and there that it wouldn't ruin her plans for her son.

In a very resolute voice, she said, "Then don't let them beat you."

For my Grandma Emma, things were very black or white. She knew about the theater in Orlando and certainly didn't find anything appealing or redeeming about pornography. And although she was hearing about distributing this movie for the first time, she decided it was not like her son had robbed a bank or murdered anyone. Her husband and parents had immigrated to this country for a better life, and she was proud that both of her sons had found good opportunities. Anthony was a college graduate and a businessman trying to earn extra money; wasn't that what the American dream was about?

Relieved, my father said, "Thanks, Mom."

"You go on home now to your family," she said, waving him off and appearing not the slightest bit concerned. "I'll deal with your father. We'll take this as it comes and pray on it."

My father gave her a hug and a kiss on the cheek, and he left.

But Grandma Emma had a sinking feeling in her stomach. The notion of her good boy being arrested made her sick. It also confused her (as it had confused my dad) that the charges had something to do with Memphis, Tennessee, where he had never been. Maybe this was just some terrible misunderstanding. She removed her rosary beads from the kitchen drawer and said a few Hail Mary's in the quiet of the kitchen. The hum of crickets poured through the open kitchen windows. She made the sign of the cross when she was finished, stood up from the table, then yelled downstairs for my grandfather, "Antonio, get up here! I got some news from your oldest son!"

Before my father returned home, my mother called Grandma Maria. My mother hadn't told anyone in her family about my father distributing *Deep Throat*, so the news was a shock. And since Grandma Maria was always suspicious that people were hiding things from her, it was tough for my mother to convince her that my father's arrest was not a big deal.

"What is he doing, Frannie?" Grandma Maria asked suspiciously. "Selling *Deep Throat*? Is that that dirty movie I've heard about?"

"Don't jump to conclusions, Mom. Anthony says everything's going to be fine. If it was that terrible, he'd be in jail."

"I can't believe you didn't tell me about this, Frannie. What the hell's gotten into him?"

Later that night, my father sat down on the back steps of our house and lit a Kent cigarette. Looking at the swing set he had recently installed for me, he thought of the day's events. Had getting involved with *Deep Throat* really been worth it? At that moment, it certainly didn't seem like it. He felt he had made a terrible mistake. He was letting his family down. He had worked so hard for his stockbroker's license, and in an instant, it was gone. What was he going to do? What the *hell* was he going to do?

Dad loved being a stockbroker and, sitting there on the back steps, he remembered fondly how in 1968—the same year he married my mother—the job had found him by a strange twist of fate. After college, he had bounced around to different jobs, the worst being when he was an inventory control analyst for General Electric on the NASA contract that successfully launched the first monkey in space. That job consisted of billing the government for office supplies, and it was like watching paint dry. Hating the drudgery, he abruptly quit one day. This impulsive act ended up being a fortuitous decision because it led him downtown to have lunch at a hot dog cart.

It was a warm spring day and by chance, while strolling in Center City after eating his hot dog, my father stopped in front of the Francis I. du Pont building on Broad Street. He marveled at the spacious lobby with the stock ticker board streaming up-to-the-minute stock prices, and he admired the men in dark suits who anxiously glanced at their watches while waiting at several elevator banks.

My father stepped inside to get a closer look.

While standing in front of the reception desk, a secretary with short, dark hair and very red lipstick peered over her reading glasses and asked my father, "Sir, are you here to fill out an application for the stockbroker position?"

The question broke his trance. He responded *yes* without even thinking about it.

By the end of the day, he was a stockbroker in training.

He went through the rigorous training program, with daily trips to New York City, and he prepared tirelessly for the stockbroker's license exam. He passed the test a week before he married my mother.

But that was six years earlier. Now it was 1974 and he had been fired from W. E. Hutton. His stockbroker career was over.

In addition to these thoughts of self-pity and sadness, my father also felt angry and unjustly accused. *What's the big deal about this movie?* Then, in a moment of ironic levity, he thought, *Life is like the stock market.* He had gambled and lost. As much as you try to time the market and pick the right stocks, business, just like life, can be unpredictable. He would never have anticipated being arrested or losing his job for distributing some stupid movie part time.

For the first time in a very long while, Dad didn't have work the next morning. The hustle and bustle of work life had ended abruptly, which left him feeling both purposeless and determined at the same time.

He stubbed out the cigarette and walked inside to call Tony Arnone. The FBI agents had told my father that afternoon that several others had been arrested at the same time in different parts of the country and he knew that Tony had to be among them.

"What do you say, my friend?" Tony answered.

"Well, I hear the same thing that happened to me today, happened to you. How long did they keep you?"

Tony laughed morosely. "Not too long. Bobby was arrested. Everyone else, too. Yeah, these pricks came to my office on University Drive, showed me some papers, and arrested me. They took me to the federal courthouse in Fort Lauderdale."

The two discussed the details of the day at length and they decided that whatever happened, they would try not to upset their wives.

"I got fired today, Tony," Dad went on. "My license is suspended. I don't know what I'm going to do. The warrant said I violated obscenity laws in Memphis, Tennessee? I distribute in the Northeast. I don't understand. *Deep Throat* has been playing in Philly for almost a year."

"I don't know any more than you," said Tony. "Look, we'll figure something out. *Deep Throat* is still hot. You can still distribute and make money."

"Okay, thanks," said my father, realizing he might not have any other source of income besides distributing and the Premier Theater.

"Look, I gotta go," Tony said. "I'll talk to you tomorrow. We're not going down without a fight."

Dad hung up the phone and realized, all at once, that he was exhausted. The news of his arrest would hit the newspapers the following morning, and he needed to be prepared for calls from friends and family.

And he needed to figure out the rest of his life.

$$\sim \!\! \infty \!\! \sim$$

A few weeks later, my family headed to Ocean City, to our beach house we rented every summer. It was already paid for, so my parents decided there was no reason not to go. At least we could keep the normalcy of our lives just a little bit longer. And this year, for once, my father could spend more time at the beach, like my mother had always wanted him to.

Though our beach vacation provided an opportunity for my father to plan and reflect quietly, it was also punctuated by the harsh realization that nothing afterward would be the same. The normalcy we so valued would slip away as soon as we returned home and my father began distributing *Deep Throat* full time.

# 4

# *The Golden 33*

While we were on vacation that summer, my father aggressively primed his *Deep Throat* client base, conducting business by telephone from the beach house. This was, after all, one of the only ways he had to earn money, and he managed his enterprise with a briefcase full of legal pads to record the bookings and Uncle Coke as his on-the-ground contact. And somehow, it all seemed to be working.

His plan was to distribute *Deep Throat* for as long as the movie was popular. And he realized he would need more income than *Deep Throat* could provide long term because no one would be clamoring to hire someone with a federal indictment on his résumé.

Tommy Rizzo, one of my father's clients and owner of the Locust Street Cinema, had become a good friend. And Tommy was sympathetic to my father's situation.

"Man, I'm telling you, this country is going berserk!" Tommy said in a phone call to book *Deep Throat*. "I can't believe you were fucking arrested. You can't trust the government. Look what we know about Nixon! *That* prick should be thrown in jail, not someone like you."

Tommy was a tough, down-to-earth guy from South Philly. He was also Italian and easily identified with a man's obligation to be his family's breadwinner.

"Yeah, it's all a bit surreal," my father said. "I'm still trying to figure out what the hell I'm going to do."

"Anything I can do to help, just ask."

"Thanks, Tommy."

Tommy hesitated for a moment, then took a chance. "You know, Tony, a lot of people are getting into the theater business. And I've been thinking about diversifying. I am converting the theater into a bar, featuring live shows and topless go-go girls."

"Oh, yeah?"

"People want more in-the-flesh entertainment, especially now since *Deep Throat* is hot. I need an investor and a partner, and I think maybe you and I would work well together."

"Uh . . ." my father stammered. "But I don't know anything about the bar business."

Tommy chuckled. "No problem. I do. I just need a partner and someone to keep the books. I suck at that shit. We could make a lot of money."

"Well, I'll think about it," my father said.

"Sure, think about it. I'm opening a small back bar on Labor Day weekend. Just call me in a few days and let me know where your head is at."

❧

Most of the next day, my father thought about Tommy's offer. He had no interest in running a strip club. But he trusted Tommy, who was both one hell of a nice guy *and* didn't take crap from anyone. Tommy's street smarts paired with my father's college-educated practicality . . . it *would* be a good combination.

*If the government says I'm a pornographer,* my father thought, *then maybe that's what I should be.*

*And I bet I'd be damn good at it, too.*

That afternoon, my father was sitting in the beach house kitchen, reading the newspaper and mulling over his options. It was a bright, sunny day, and a hot ocean wind poured through the lace curtains above the sink. When he heard me and my mother return from the beach, he opened the screen door to greet us.

"It's just too hot, Kristin. We need a break," my mother said as I complained about coming back to the house. (I could spend hours at the beach, unfazed by sand, sun, or saltwater.)

Mom lifted the porch hose and sprayed off my feet and legs, then turned the hose at her own feet as I ran inside to watch television. My father saw me run through the kitchen and got up and greeted Mom in the yard. He took the hose and rinsed the chairs and umbrella.

As he came back into the kitchen, where my mother was now sitting at the table drinking iced tea, he said, "Man, it's hot out there."

"Yeah," she said, wiping sweat off her forehead. "We have to figure out what we want for dinner."

"How about pizza? It's too hot to cook. I could pick it up."

"That would be great," my mother said, relieved at the idea of a no-fuss meal.

My father poured a glass of water from the jug in the refrigerator, then joined my mother at the table.

"So, Fran."

"Yeah?"

"Remember last night when I told you about Tommy's offer to open a club?"

My mother looked up. "Sure. Sounds pretty weird, Anthony." She took a sip of her tea. "So this Tommy Rizzo is one of your clients?"

"He's the owner of the Locust Street Cinema. He's been showing *Deep Throat* for a couple of months."

"Do you trust him? Is he a good guy?"

My father shrugged. "He seems trustworthy. I like him. And he always pays on time for the film."

"But Anthony . . ."

"What?"

"Do you really want to run a club?"

"No, but . . ." and my father shook his head. "But Fran, we need to do *something*."

"And are the girls going to be totally naked?"

My father paused. "I think just topless," he said.

She stared out the window and shrugged her shoulders. "Well, I guess if you need to give it a go, do it."

My father was surprised that there wasn't more of a debate. He reached across the table and squeezed my mother's hand.

"Okay," he said. "I'll go get pizza around five. Then I'll call Tommy to tell him I'm in."

⌘

My father called Tommy Rizzo that evening and agreed to invest $15,000, which was only a portion of the money he'd saved from his *Deep Throat* earnings. A few days later, he returned home to Upper Darby alone to see the club for the first time. His absence from the beach house was, for my mother and me, reminiscent of all those times he'd left for work during our summer vacations in years past . . . only now it was for a *much* different job.

He was greeted home by rain and gray skies, which fit the metaphorical cloud hanging over my family and the problems that awaited him in Philly. He pulled up the driveway, shut off the car, swung open the heavy door of the Thunderbird, and lifted himself out of the front seat. He bounded up the front steps, two at a time, to escape the rain that was starting to come down harder.

He unlocked the front door with a jiggle of his keys and said to an empty room, "Well, I'm home." It was humid and smelled like the air in the living room had been trapped inside for a long time. He immediately turned on the air conditioner unit in the window and took off the Phillies' baseball cap he wore to keep what little hair he had from frizzing up. He sat quietly on the couch for a moment and then realized he should call my mom to tell her he made it home.

*This trip home was certainly under different circumstances*, he thought. No more lunches with wealthy clients and the wheeling and dealing of trying to time the market with a great stock buy. He missed his co-workers and had not talked to anyone since his arrest. He hoped a working relationship with Tommy would be easy. His new life as strip club owner was about to begin and the potential to make money could far exceed his expectations. He decided he would defy everyone's preconceived notions by making this venture a great success and at that moment he needed to seize the opportunity. At least he knew now he wouldn't be trapped in an office aging before his time, like the older stockbrokers he worked with at W. E. Hutton. The broker business could run a person into the ground. In a way, he had gained freedom to do something extraordinary even though he was facing jail time. He brought his bag upstairs, and then he called my mother.

⚬⚬⚬

The next day, my father headed to the Locust Street Cinema, which was located at 1233 Locust Street in a seedy part of downtown Philly among other straight and gay afterhours clubs and bust out joints—places like the 2-4 Club, Sisters, Woody's, and All in the Family. Many of these establishments offered illegal gambling opportunities and the drug trade was notoriously rampant. My father parked his car a few blocks away and he double-checked that he'd locked the doors. He knew this wasn't the nicest part of the city and walking toward the club down a street strewn with garbage and rundown buildings was a stark reminder that he no longer worked in the business district of Center City.

He reached the bar and pushed open its paint-flecked door, which was slightly ajar.

"Hello, anyone here?"

There was fresh construction everywhere and dust hung in the air. Finally, he heard Tommy's voice from the far corner of the room:

"Hey, Tony! That you?"

"Yeah! Where are you?"

"Behind the bar. Come on back."

My father eased through the room and found Tommy fiddling with some shelves that would eventually hold drink glasses. Tommy popped to his feet and reached out to shake my father's hand. "Welcome!" he bellowed. "Glad you could make it!"

Tommy's slim, muscular frame was covered in drywall dust and sweat. A cigarette pack was rolled up in the sleeve of his white T-shirt and, as he talked, he ran his fingers over his slick, black hair, neatly coiffed into a classic ducktail.

"Looks like you've a lot going on," my father said. "You sure it's going to be ready for the opening at the end of September?"

"Yeah, no problem," Tommy said dismissively. "If you're a little behind, that means you're ahead of the game. And anyways, my days as a contractor are coming in handy."

"Oh, yeah?"

"Absolutely. And like I said, the back bar on the St. James Street side will bring in some money, since the cinema is closed. Anyways, let me show you around."

Tommy lit a cigarette, and so commenced the grand tour of the transformation from theater to bar.

All the theater seats had been ripped out and the centerpiece of the room was now a large, elongated stage. Stairs had been built from the second floor above, so dancers could descend directly onto the platform. The stage was encircled with a bar. At least thirty stools lined the service area and there was standing room available as well.

The second floor hosted a small area of tables for two, all with views of the stage. The DJ booth and sound system were also on the second floor, and mirrors would soon be installed on the right and left walls to give the entire room a bigger appearance—and, of course, to give patrons additional views of the girls on stage.

The back bar—connected to the main room by a narrow passageway—faced the cobblestones of St. James Street. This space had a much smaller stage area as well as a bar that took up the right side of the room, with tables and bar stools against the opposite wall. The ceiling here—as in the main club—had beautiful stained glass that revealed the deep history of the building as a reputable residence or business. The back bar area looked like it would fit about forty to forty-five people, which was cozy, but the main bar area had the capacity for at least a hundred.

"You do all this yourself?" my father asked.

"Pretty much, and hired some friends."

"I'm impressed. The only tool I have at home is a hammer and I only use that to hang pictures."

"Thanks," Tommy said, and he took a mock-bow. "So, are you going to be here for the back bar opening the Saturday of Labor Day weekend? It'd be a good way to promote the opening of the main bar at the end of the month."

"Sure," my father said. "My family's still at the beach, so I'll just come in and go back at the end of the weekend. Oh, I almost forgot, here's the check for my part."

Tommy's face beamed with a wide grin and again he shook my father's hand. "Beautiful, beautiful. Congratulations, Tony. You're officially a bar owner."

"I guess so," said Dad, smiling back and shaking his head in bewilderment. "By the way, what are we calling this place?"

"No clue. I was thinking Locust Street Bar or Tommy's Place. But now that we're partners, let's think of a name together. I need to place some advertisements about the opening soon as possible, so call me with some ideas. Sooner rather than later, okay?"

That night, before heading back to Ocean City, my father stopped at Johnny's Pizzeria across the street from his new bar to grab a slice. It was a small countertop service place with two tables that barely fit in the corner next to a refrigerator full of sodas. He ordered two pieces of pepperoni pizza, then left, shoving the first piece into his mouth with the help of the edge of a paper plate. He ate half the slice, then threw the rest away. It tasted horrible.

He later learned that making pizza wasn't Johnny's primary business. Instead, this little joint was a cover for the pills Johnny's sold—Dilaudid, Black Beauties, Quaaludes—that would accompany a slice, for the right price.

⚖

On the drive back to the shore, my father thought about a name for his club. It needed some kind of allure and sex appeal, even if the club wasn't in the nicest part of town.

"So how did it go?" my mother asked as soon as my father walked in the door of the beach house.

"Tommy's doing all kinds of construction, and there seems to be a lot to do. I hope we're ready in time. We're opening a small back bar first, and the main club's opening at the end of September."

"So, that's it?" my mother prodded, annoyed by his short answer.

"What else do you want me to tell you, Frannie? It's not in a great part of town, and we need to name the place."

"Well, that's interesting," she said genuinely. "What names are you thinking?"

"I don't know. Maybe something to do with the address, 1233 Locust Street? The Golden 33? I don't know. The building is nice, but the neighborhood is shitty, so I'm not sure how golden it is."

"The Golden 33," my mother said slowly. "It sounds a little corny, Anthony."

"Who cares if it's corny? It's a strip club."

My mother turned the name over in her mind: *The Golden 33*. It might actually be clever—sort of ironically high class. At the same time, she wondered if the girls who would work at the club would be clever, too. A sexy woman who would flaunt her naked body might also be very persuasive and manipulative. Could any red-blooded male—that is, her husband—resist such an enticement?

Only time would tell.

On opening night of the Golden 33, over Labor Day weekend in September 1974, my father arrived in the early evening to settle into his new job. The back bar had come together nicely and the main area would be finished in a few weeks. The decor had working-class appeal—stark and simple—since it was thought patrons would be too busy looking at tits and ass to notice much else. Tommy Rizzo had placed Help Wanted listings as well as advertisements about the opening in the *Philadelphia Daily News*. He'd hired about ten girls to wait tables and dance topless. All of which took pressure off my father, who was happy for Tommy to manage the staff.

"Tony, let me introduce you to some of the girls," Tommy said. "Here we got Chelsea, Veronica, Wildflower, and Maggie. Girls, this is Tony, your new boss."

"Helllooo," the girls said, almost in unison, and with flirty winks and tosses of their hair.

It was hard for my father to not notice how young and pretty some of the girls were. Others were just okay-looking. He responded in as professional a manner as possible. "Hello. Nice to meet you ladies."

Tommy interrupted the friendly greetings and announced, "Girls, customers should be coming in by 9 p.m. You know who's greeting and who's dancing first, so get your asses ready!"

The girls giggled and dispersed to prepare, one whispering, "Tony looks kinda cute" and another, "I like a guy in glasses."

Besides dancing and waiting tables, the girls' main jobs would be to make friendly conversation and extract money from patrons by asking if they would like some company. The Golden 33 was a "bottle club," which meant that the bar only sold glasses with ice and Coke or club soda (for the outrageous price of $5 each), while customers brought their own liquor. Girls were paid in tips but also by commission for how many "set-ups" they sold. They kept track of that number by collecting the swizzle sticks served with each drink. Along with the set-ups, the girls sold bottles of grape soda for $100 each, along with their extra attention, to good customers.

The girls at the Golden 33 all had similar stories. Wildflower—whose real name was Kathy and who would prove to be great at collecting swizzle sticks—was a tall, nineteen-year-old brunette from Baltimore. She had started go-go dancing at age sixteen before moving to Philadelphia with a boyfriend. When that relationship didn't last, she transitioned from go-go dancer to stripping to make more money. Her youthful appearance gave her a deceptive aura of innocence. She was a great talker and she became happily animated if any customer complimented her stage act. "Aww, honey, you just know I'm having the best time," she might coo while accepting a $50 tip. "I love that you appreciate it."

It was hard sometimes to tell if the girls were entrepreneurial or had lost their way in life. The girls who struggled might be addicted to drugs, be in bad relationships, and haphazardly show up for work. When these problems arose, Tommy promptly fired them.

It was almost opening time and the girls were moving around the bar for last-minute preparations; they were either topless or wearing decorative pasties on their breasts, and all of them wore shimmering G-strings. A high-fidelity sound system with massive speakers blasted "Free Bird" to create a sultry atmosphere. The girls had all selected pulsing disco numbers for their dance routines when the time was right to change the mood of the bar.

James, the bouncer, who also worked at the All in the Family lounge, was stationed at the front door. He was an intimidating African American man who stood about six-foot-six. At three hundred pounds, he was all muscle and my father described him as a gentle giant who watched over the girls and who was the stabilizing force at the Golden 33. All the rowdy crowds that came in from Kensington, Cherry Hill, and the surrounding New Jersey suburbs thought twice about causing trouble under James's watchful gaze.

My father took his place behind the bar and he noticed there were a couple of bottles of bourbon and whiskey next to the club soda and tonic water.

"Tommy, what's with these bottles? Don't we need a liquor license?"

"Nah, we don't need it," Tommy responded nonchalantly. "We won't sell enough alcohol to make it worth our while to get the license. Besides, with the naked girls we probably wouldn't get a license anyway. I just got a few bottles to give good customers a nip here and there. Isn't a big deal."

My dad accepted Tommy's word, then tried to enjoy the beginning of his crazy new venture. They had a decent crowd that first night and even though my father was exhausted by the time they closed—since he wasn't used to the late hours—he was eager to count the proceeds. He'd set up a small office with a safe in the front of the building near to what would become the cashier's area, where he did the evening's accounting. It was easy for the girls to change in the upstairs rooms, then stop by the office to get paid for their swizzle sticks on their way out.

Tom hauled in envelopes full of cash from the bar and plopped down in a chair next to the desk. "So how do you think we did?" he asked.

"I'll tell you in a minute," my father said as he set to work with his calculator and yellow legal pads. One-by-one, the girls paraded through his office to collect their money and all of them seemed pleased with the evening's profits. They even commented on how the clients hadn't been too disgusting, and they were all very chatty, despite the long night they had just had.

"So, Tony, you married?"

"Got a girlfriend?" asked another.

"I love your cute glasses!" said a third.

"Yes," my father replied. "I'm married and we have a four-year-old daughter."

"Too bad all the good ones are taken."

"Hey, Tony, you want to get a drink with us later?"

"Come on. It'll be fun!"

"Not tonight," he said. "I'm real tired. Maybe some other time."

"We'll hold you to it."

"Bye, cutie."

Once they left the room, Tommy playful ribbed my father. "Not a bad few pieces of ass, eh?"

My father blushed a bit. "I guess not." He was flattered by the attention of these attractive women but he quickly shifted his focus back to the money. "Three hundred dollars the first night. And about $100 gross profit," he said with relief.

This business showed promise of making money.

~✦~

By their second day in business, Dad was serving whiskey to a few people who requested it. There was a good crowd that night, even better than the night before, and customers were moving about and talking and laughing and staring at the scenery. Then, at about 10 p.m. a nondescript man in a blue shirt sauntered up to the bar and asked for a whiskey and soda.

My father served the guy.

A second later, the man's voice boomed, "You're under arrest for serving liquor without a license!"

Everyone ran for the door.

"What do you mean?" my father yelled at the man. "We don't serve that much alcohol, so we don't need a license!"

"What planet are you from, pal?" the officer said as my father was handcuffed. "Let's go!"

A few more cops entered the bar and soon they were clearing out the rest of the patrons.

My father, Tommy Rizzo, and two girls from the club were arrested that night and taken to "The Roundhouse," that is, police headquarters in downtown Philadelphia, next to the Benjamin Franklin Bridge.

My father and Tommy were booked and taken to the men's holding cell; my dad was nervous but he said he would have been a lot more scared if Tommy hadn't been with him. This wasn't at all like when he'd been arrested a few months earlier. At the federal courthouse, he wasn't held long and he had felt relatively safe. Now he was in a disgusting city jail that smelled like urine and he was being treated like all the other scurrilous characters—drug addicts, pimps, and violent criminals—who were being held that night.

Tommy, on the other hand, seemed totally comfortable in these surroundings. He sauntered around the cell with an air of confidence and a "don't-fuck-with-me" attitude.

The cell had concrete walls and one long metal bench. Five people were already there when they arrived. There was a pay phone in the cell that my father stared at for a long time, wondering when he should call my mother. He knew she'd be worried if he didn't call her by morning.

Tommy stretched out on the bench. "Anthony," he said, "you realize we're going to be here a while, right? There's no way we'll get a judge to set bail over a holiday weekend. You hanging in there?"

"I don't know," my father muttered through exhaustion. "Do you maybe think a liquor license might have been a good idea?"

"Well . . . hindsight *is* 20/20," said Tommy in a matter-of-fact way. "What are you going to tell Frannie?"

My father sighed. "I really don't know."

When it was finally morning, my father gathered the nerve to call my mother, looking sheepishly back at Tommy with a here-goes-nothing expression.

"Fuck, man," Tommy said. "It's like a Band-Aid. Don't be a pussy and just rip it off."

My father plunked a dime into the pay phone and dialed.

It was about 7 a.m. My mother was startled awake by the ringing phone and answered in confusion. All she could hear on the other end was the echoing conversation of two stoned guys in the cell who wouldn't be quiet.

"Is that you, Anthony?" she said. "Where are you? What's all the noise in the background?"

In the most apologetic tone he could muster, my dad finally said, "Frannie, I'm sorry to tell you this, but I'm in jail. We were selling liquor without a license. I'm okay. I just wanted you to know where I was. I'm here with Tommy and we can't get a bond hearing until Tuesday."

The line was silent.

"Frannie, you still there?"

"I'm here," my mother replied. "Do you want me to call anyone?"

"No, don't. As soon as we get a hearing, we'll be out of here. So I'll be here until I'm not." He took a deep breath. "I'm sorry."

"Just get out as quick as you can, okay?"

Then she hung up.

My father sat back down next to Tommy and looked around the room. In one corner was a passed-out drunk with a bloody eye. He was young, probably a college student, but his preppy clothes looked wrinkled and grimy, as if he'd rolled around in the street. On the other side was a thin African American man who was sitting with his elbows on his knees staring at the floor, deep in thought about his troubles. Two other men—the bickering stoners from earlier—were still acting like they were hanging out on the street corner, laughing and yelling in riotous conversation about nothing. My father wished they would shut up.

He shook his head, then shifted into planning mode. "Tommy, who do you know that could pick us up? I don't want to call my family."

"Nah, I'll call Wildflower," Tommy said calmly. "We could pay her back right away for posting bail on Tuesday and she'll give us a ride back to the club. I need her to check if someone locked up anyway."

It sounded like an easy solution. Tommy stood up from the bench, gave my father a wink, and dialed.

"Tommy! Oh, my god!" Wildflower screamed on the other end of the line, so loud my father could hear her across the room. "Are you calling from jail? We all just got the hell out of there when the cops started swarming!"

"We're okay, sweetie, but we need a big favor. As soon as we get a bond hearing on Tuesday, can you bail us out and pick us up? I promise we'll pay you right back as soon as we get to the club."

"Sure thing, baby! Just let me know when to come get you. I'll stay close to the phone."

⤙⤚

Tommy and my father spent Sunday and Monday in jail until a hearing on Tuesday morning. Spending the long weekend in the same clothes, sleeping on a hard bench, and eating crappy tuna fish sandwiches had worn on my father's last nerve. It also gave him too much time to think.

There were all kinds of characters who shuffled in and out of the holding cell, and all of them seemed eager to share their problems or to ask the question, "What are you in for?" Tommy, who was chatty, made conversation with anyone to pass the time.

My father, who wasn't chatty, just listened to their stories about the "old lady" who was nagging them, the fight they were in to "defend" themselves, or various strange traffic violations. As he listened, he wondered about the fine line between himself and them. To him, these criminals looked pathetic, troubled, and going nowhere. But somehow he had ended up just like them, at The Roundhouse.

On a positive note, he and Tommy got to know each other better and talked about their plans for the Golden 33 including the specialty acts they could book, redecorating, and cover charges once the club became better known.

Finally, on Tuesday morning, Wildflower appeared in front of the police station to pick them up, having already posted bail. A few minutes later, she dropped them off at the club.

"I would give you guys a hug," Wildflower said, "but you smell."

"Hilarious," Tommy said groggily.

They were both hungry, exhausted, and desperately in need of showers. My father drove home to Upper Darby and slowly climbed the steps to the front door, noticing what a beautiful, sunny day he was going to miss because he needed to get some sleep. The house was empty. He went to the kitchen, opened the refrigerator, grabbed a container of cold pasta, and ate it quickly standing up.

A moment later, he let out a heavy sigh. He should have spent the weekend at the shore with his family, not at a bar, and certainly not in jail. But he knew he had no choice but to make this current situation work. He couldn't pull out of the Golden 33 now. He still needed to earn money.

He went upstairs to take a shower and get some sleep. He had to drive to the beach to get my mother and me later that day. Our summer vacation was over.

~∾∾∾~

One afternoon a few weeks later, my mother paced around the main bar of the Golden 33. It was her first time in the bar and she was looking everything over from top to bottom. Her arms were crossed but every once in a while she would uncross them to run her fingers over the highly polished bar.

"What do you think?" my father asked.

"Well . . . It's a beautiful building. The open brick walls and stained glass. This is a great space . . . despite the neighborhood."

My father smiled. "You know, Tommy and I were thinking of ways to improve the joint. Maybe a jukebox and pinball machines in the front."

"I guess," Mom said, again looking thoughtfully around the room. "Do you think women will come here?"

"A few, but not many."

My mother nodded. "Well, I could help clean before the opening. And I could decorate. Maybe some tablecloths and curtains. And the ladies' room I'm sure could use some help."

My father was taken aback. "Wow! I love the idea of you doing stuff like that around here."

"Okay then. I'll help," she said smiling, and she placed her arms around my father's neck. She took a deep breath. "I think this place is going to be a big hit."

~∾∾~

My mother was right. Within a few months, the main part of the club had opened and the Golden 33 was a thriving business, without a liquor license. My father adjusted to club life, working six days a week from 7 p.m. to 3 a.m. And, as promised, my mother decorated the ladies' bathroom with pretty yellow curtains framing the small window and wallpaper depicting little naked women. She loved that her husband was now a successful entrepreneur and she enjoyed thinking that she was helping him even though, unbeknownst to her, there was a seedy side to running the Golden 33.

The neighborhood's drug scene had carried over into the club, not unexpectedly, but not welcome either. And reluctantly, Tommy and my father became more intertwined with the lives of several troubled girls who worked there. Not to mention, law enforcement always wanted them out of business, vendors hesitated to work with a tits-and-ass club, and local government officials demanded bribes. It was not an easy business to run.

The Golden 33 operated in cash to make paying vendors and bribing officials easier. They didn't even have a checkbook. In the basements and living rooms of row homes in South Philadelphia, Tommy and my father would attend meetings with city officials. Over biscotti and coffee, hefty envelopes of cash were exchanged for building licenses and assurances that the Golden 33 would remain open.

Unfortunately, after a few months, Tommy grew tired of the weekly demands of $200 from local police to ensure security at the Golden 33.

"The captain's going on vacation," said a black-clad officer who was paying a visit to the club one evening.

"What the fuck do I care?" Tommy shot back.

"Tommy, look, we got a good thing going. Just pay us and I'll be on my way."

"Fuck you!"

The police officer shrugged. "Okay, fine. When your scumbag customers want to kill each other, we're not going to come rushing."

"Get the fuck out, you worthless piece of shit!"

A few weeks later, Tommy would regret his gamble when a huge brawl broke out at the club after several jerks from the New Jersey suburbs had gotten drunk and started harassing the girls. And even though James, the bouncer, tried to step in, the situation got out of control quickly. Tommy knew my father didn't have a clue how to fight, and as chairs started breaking, he yelled, "Tony, get out of here! Go across the street with the girls!"

My father escaped the club with a few of the girls and stood on the corner feeling helpless. At that moment, four bouncers from other clubs came running up the street to help. My father watched through the window as Tommy decked a guy with a good shot to the jaw, then opened the door to kick him onto the street. James could take on two to three guys at once and, with the help of the other bouncers, they finally got the situation under control.

That night, the Golden 33 was nearly destroyed. Broken glass lay everywhere. Tables and chairs had been toppled and splintered. There was nothing to do but clean up. My father had a business to run. The bribes paid to the cops would resume.

꧁꧂

It was many years later when I was a teenager that Grandma Maria, my mother's mother, said to me, "You know, I went to the Golden 33 once."

"So . . ." I stammered after I'd recovered from my amazement. "Did you just show up at the club one night? Go with Grandpa?"

Grandma Maria threw her head back and laughed. "Ha! Your grandfather would *never* go into a place like that. And your father never even knew I was there."

"So this was like a secret mission?"

"Well, the club was getting popular and I had to see what was going on over there."

"Of course you did, Grandma," I said, covering my face and laughing.

Grandma Maria went on to tell me about the Thursday evening in the fall of 1974 when she made her clandestine visit to the Golden 33. She made dinner for my grandfather after work, as usual, then told him she was going to run an errand. She had hoped he wouldn't question her. But she was wrong.

"What kind of an errand?" he pressed, squinting and studying her face.

"Well, I'm . . ." she hesitated. Finally, she blurted, "I'm going up to Anthony's club, okay?"

"Now why would you do that?"

"I need to see what this is place is all about. It's driving me crazy. I won't be long."

"Wait, Mary. No good can come from this."

"Listen to yourself, Frank. You sound like a gangster movie. I'll be back around midnight."

"Mary . . ." Grandpa Frank said, but then he shook his head, knowing that arguing with her was useless.

She covered the top of her head with her best silk scarf and she wore sunglasses and a trench coat with a wide collar that she would pull up around her neck.

She took the bus to Locust Street and immediately after stepping onto the street, she became hyper-aware of her surroundings: the drug dealers, the seedy bars with loud music pouring out. She tightened her grip on her umbrella like it was sword.

A few minutes later, when she came within a few blocks of the Golden 33, she hesitated. *How am I going to get in here without Anthony noticing?* she thought. She also realized how strange it would be for any older woman to go into a strip joint alone. She leaned against the wall of a building and lit up a cigarette. She needed a moment to work up her resolve. As she smoked, she noticed a decent-looking gentleman walking up the block and, just as he crossed her path, she said, "Excuse me, sir, can I ask for your help?"

"Sure, I guess," the man said.

"Can you escort me to the Golden 33 on the next block?"

The man stared blankly. "Lady, I'm happy to help but . . ."

"I'm sorry. I should explain. My son-in-law owns the place and I don't want to go in alone." She was speaking in her most appealing, damsel-in-distress voice. "My husband wouldn't come with me. He doesn't approve of the visit. But I just want to see my son-in-law's place of business."

"Well . . ."

"Please, sir. It would make it so much easier to be escorted by a man."

He stared at her blankly. "Sure," he finally said. "I can at least make sure you get inside okay."

"Really?"

He smiled politely and extended a bent arm. "Shall we get going?"

"Thank you so much! By the way, my name is Maria."

"I'm Henry."

They strolled the rest of the distance to the bar and casually walked in. Grandma Maria paid the cover charge for both of them and they went up to the second floor and found a small table.

"Wow," Henry said. "This is some place your son-in-law has." He was bug-eyed and almost too embarrassed to look around at all the topless women moving around him.

"You got that right," Grandma Maria said furtively—her elbows were on the table and she was sort of hiding within her coat. Thankfully, she didn't see Anthony anywhere.

"Henry, can you get us a couple of club sodas from the bar?" she said, handing him a ten-dollar bill.

Henry darted off to the bar and at that moment the club suddenly shifted to a disco number, which signaled that a dancer was about to appear on stage. Grandma Maria watched as a young blonde with pin straight hair descended the stairs in nothing but a G-string and with her delicate areas strategically covered in body paint. A clever flower decoration enhanced her full, perky breasts; petals were painted around the nipples and a vine snaked around her waist.

The dancer strutted across the stage and leaned over several men sitting below her, fondling herself into a faux-aroused state. The male customers mindlessly passed her dollar bills. Her high heels clicked across the stage until she reached a brass pole. She wrapped her leg around the pole and tossed her body in a circular motion to elongate her figure and make her breasts bounce.

Everyone, including Grandma Maria, followed her every move.

When the blonde finished her dance routine, she hopped off the stage and circulated the room. She stood close to the men seated at the bar, asking how their evening was going and if she could get them another set-up. She also gently touched their shoulders and even, much to my grandmother's amazement, hopped up on the bar to let them lick or finger her for an additional tip.

Grandma Maria was slack-jawed and disgusted. But she was also intrigued. This club reminded her of her own father's bootlegging days when he had owned the South Philly Bar and Grill. One moment she was thinking about how these girls were far too young for all these gross, lascivious men, and the next moment, she noticed that the place was packed even on a weekday night and that there was a ton of money changing hands. She glanced at the customers, all of whom seemed totally relaxed and basking in the attention from the dancers. Then she looked at Henry, who had returned with their drinks, and who was now sitting bolt upright in his chair.

"Maria!" he said abruptly. "I'm sorry. I have to go home to my wife. You gonna be okay?"

"Sure, honey. Thank you so much and nice to meet you."

"Likewise," he said without looking at her. Then he nodded quickly and left.

Now that her escort was gone, Grandma Maria knew she didn't have much time left to sit and watch. Besides, she'd seen everything she needed to see and she didn't want to be out too late in this neighborhood. So, a few minutes later, she raised the collar of her coat as high as possible and she slipped downstairs and out of the club.

When she arrived home, Grandpa Frank was watching the evening news on television in the living room and Kitty, their pet ocelot, was rolling around on the floor to greet her.

"So what did you see?" Grandpa Frank asked urgently. For being against the visit, he certainly seemed curious now.

"Oh Frank, I feel nauseous," she said, and she slumped onto the couch and began to cry. "It was terrible."

"What do you mean?"

"Those girls . . . they're all so young. It reminded me of when Dolores and Frannie were that age, which wasn't so long I ago. I just couldn't imagine them . . ." but her voice trailed off.

"Mary, this thing Anthony's doing is temporary," Grandpa Frank said, moving closer to her on the couch. "He's not going to do this forever."

"What's going to happen to our baby, Frank? Who is this man she's married to?"

"I don't know," he said, shaking his head and falling back on the couch.

Kitty jumped to his side, pressed her body against his leg.

They sat in silence. There was nothing left to say. Then they went off to bed.

# 5

## *Honeysuckle Divine*

The Golden 33 did very well through the fall of 1974, but my father knew it was time to push the envelope to capitalize on the club's early success.

A few of the dancers were developing fan bases, such as Ginger, who was skinny and lithe and who had perfected a particularly popular dance to the extended version of "Free Bird."

To cash in on the growing following of Ginger and the other girls, my father and Tommy Rizzo increased weekend cover charges. Tommy also hired a Baltimore booking agent with a track record for bringing in crowds. Stripper acts like Silver Sunshine—known for her theatrical performance, complete with flower props and skimpy attire to match, to Eric Clapton's "Let It Grow"—was hired for $200 to $300 a week. Baltimore was becoming known for its wild strip clubs and the talent was ripe to bring to Philadelphia.

But the act Tommy wanted most was Honeysuckle Divine.

While setting up the club one evening, Tommy pitched the idea to my father.

"Honeysuckle Divine is incredible. She performed once at the Locust Street Cinema. She's expensive, but she's dynamite. She has a comedy act that features . . . um . . . well, how do I say this? She does some amazing things with her pussy."

"I think I've heard of her," my father said. "But what kind of things?"

"Well, here's one of her promotional photos."

In the photo, Honeysuckle was shown spreading peanut butter on her vagina. She was plain-faced and older looking (meaning in her mid-thirties) and her body was soft and flabby. She had straggly blonde hair and didn't look like any of the other girls featured at the Golden 33.

"She's not very attractive," my father said flatly.

"Yeah, but her show is something people want to see," Tommy insisted. "She's got this bit where she smokes cigarettes with her pussy. She asks audience members for a light, then makes crude jokes like, 'After sex, your pussy deserves a cigarette, too.' It's raunchy, what's happening between her legs."

"Holy shit," my father said, laughing heartily.

"She's the real deal, my friend. A little strange, maybe. She does other things like blowing out candles with her pussy and shooting Ping-Pong balls out of it. So, what do you think?"

"Well, she certainly isn't sexy. But she is attention-grabbing. No one is doing anything like this in Philly. Let's do it."

Tommy laughed and clapped my father on the shoulder. "I knew you'd get it! I even got something else to sweeten the deal. Al Goldstein at *Screw Magazine* needs a venue to film Honeysuckle for his *Screw on Screen* film. I told the agent we could do it here. It'll be great publicity."

My father didn't object to this, so Tommy hired Honeysuckle Divine for a string of shows in December 1974, and he agreed that the *Screw on Screen* crew could film in the club for a few days before the live event.

≈≈≈

When Honeysuckle Divine arrived in town that December, she stopped by the club and strolled casually through the door. Her patchwork cap and denim vest with matching bell-bottom jeans looked comfortable, not sexy, as if she wasn't at all interested in making an impression.

"Nice to see you again, Tommy," Honeysuckle said, greeting him with a hug.

"Great to see you, too. Welcome to the Golden 33."

She looked around the place, nodding approvingly. "Shit, Tommy, you did a lot of great work redoing the place. And I almost forgot about the stained glass in the ceiling." She was looking straight up and smiling widely under the green light from the windows. "Maybe it's a sign from God that I'm meant to be here. I feel right at home, like I'm in church."

Honeysuckle—whose real name was Betty Jane Allsup—was from Washington, DC and before becoming a famous provocateur, she had been a nun-in-training at the Grey Nuns of the Sacred Heart in Yardley, Pennsylvania. (So yes, though it's hard to believe, she was sincere in praising God.) Her strict Catholic upbringing had made it easy for her to start down the path as a nun. But in the end, she believed everyone has her calling and she had realized that a life of celibacy, with no freedom of expressing herself, was ultimately not for her.

She did, however, believe that her act was divinely inspired, though she'd also gained inspiration from a *Screw Magazine* article about a French performer, Le Pétomane. In the late 1800s, Le Pétomane had created a stage act around the amazing things he could do with his anus, such as passing gas on cue and blowing out candles. He had appeared at the Moulin Rouge in 1892 and he had performed for princes, kings, and dignitaries. So, as far as Honeysuckle was concerned, she was following in the footsteps of history as well as God's plan for her life.

Even though Tommy knew all about this, he was always taken aback by Honeysuckle's religious references. Still, he kept the conversation going.

"Yeah . . ." he stuttered. "The new set-up is working out well. Anyways, the film crew is setting up. Feel free to get acquainted with them. And I know how particular you are about your props, so I'll let you figure out where you'd like to store them backstage. If you need help, let me know. "

"Thanks, Tommy," Honeysuckle said, smiling serenely. Then she held up a *Screw Magazine* T-shirt. "Look at this, I'm going to wear it for the filming."

Tommy nodded. "Clever."

"You bet. Think we'll have a big crowd for the opening?"

"Absolutely. I advertised and all the customers have been talking about it. But I should tell you, I'm hearing rumors about cops possibly trying to bust the show. News people are calling, too."

Honeysuckle laughed dismissively. "That's ridiculous, Tommy. I'm not afraid. God is on our side."

Honeysuckle got to work with the *Screw on Screen* crew. She was serious about her craft, offering solid direction for camera set-up and walking through every step of her act before shooting. And she was the consummate professional; she was always on time, never took drugs, and never got involved with troubled men. Honeysuckle understood that her vagina and her act were a small business and she wasn't going to let anything get in the way of her business's success.

The filming went well but, because of the rumors that the cops might try to bust the show, my father opted not to attend Honeysuckle's opening night. Her pending appearance had made the local evening news several times. Tommy was interviewed on camera, where he proudly took credit for featuring Honeysuckle Divine at the Golden 33.

All the publicity worked. On opening night, the club was packed and there was a line snaking around the block for the next show later that evening. They planned to run the show four or five times, clearing out the club every forty-five minutes to set up for the next performance.

Honeysuckle began her first act. She walked out on stage in bizarre fashion by sticking out her tongue and awkwardly leaning against a side rail to grab her breasts. She was wearing crotch-less stockings, and nothing else. Then she lifted up her leg and highlighted the real star of the show with her forefinger for everyone to see. "Hello, Philadelphia!" she called out. "You know, people ask how I got the idea for such a dirty show and I just tell 'em it was divine intervention. I sneezed while I was fucking this guy and he was like, 'Ohhhh that feels good.' So it gave me the idea for this act!"

Honeysuckle pulled a cart onto the stage—the kind of cart my Grandma Maria might have used for shopping at the Ninth Street market. Honeysuckle's cart contained various paraphernalia:

Ping-Pong balls in individual plastic bags, peanut butter and jelly, cream cheese, Jergens lotion, and a mop.

She started her shtick by taking the mop and inserting its handle into her vagina to simulate sex. "Oh, I just *love* doing housework," she said, eliciting laughs from the audience. Then she showcased her unusually strong vaginal muscles by mopping the floor of the stage. "To all you guys out there who might wonder why your wives are so tired at the end of the day, this is probably why."

Honeysuckle then spread a plastic tablecloth at the edge of the stage and opened her legs in preparation for the Ping-Pong ball routine. "I always like to play a good game of Ping-Pong after I clean house. Who wants to play?" She inserted a ball into her vagina while lying on her side and lifting her leg, her knee touching her ear. "Hey, you over there! Catch!" Honeysuckle pointed her crotch in the direction of a spectator and launched the ball.

With incredible arc, accuracy, and distance, the ball sailed through the air and hit the bewildered man in the face.

After that, she got the crowd participating in a game: she asked them to guess which ball she could launch the farthest and most accurately, based on a location selected by an audience member. There was also a trick she did shooting multiple balls in quick succession, like a machine gun.

"Now, is anyone hungry?" she asked coyly.

A few eager Chinese tourists seated in the front row enthusiastically raised their hands.

"Well," Honeysuckle said, "let me make you a peanut butter sandwich."

She inserted peanut butter in her vagina with her fingers, like a tampon, and then it pulled back out. Honeysuckle took a plastic knife and spread it on bread. She offered the sandwich to her Chinese fans and one of them happily ate it.

"Now that's what I call eating some pussy!" Honeysuckle exclaimed happily.

The crowd collectively gasped and cheered.

The grand finale of her show was her Jergens lotion routine. She poured about half a bottle of lotion into her vagina, then squirted it high in the air as she pretended to orgasm.

The audience was enraptured. It was odd, funny, and disgusting . . . and everyone loved it. After she took her final bow, Honeysuckle was cheered with a hearty standing ovation. She autographed Ping-Pong balls as she was leaving the stage, like a football player who had just won the big game.

But exiting the stage, she was immediately confronted by a police officer. The man flashed a badge and placed her under arrest for open lewdness.

"What do you think you're doing?" Tommy said angrily, running up to Honeysuckle and the officer.

"Who are you?"

"I'm Tommy Rizzo. I own this place"

"Just the guy I'm looking for," the cop said. "You're under arrest for conspiracy of open lewdness."

"You're full of shit!" Tommy screamed, drawing the attention of the departing crowd, all of whom started to boo and hiss at the officer.

⤜ೋ⤛

Honeysuckle and Tommy were arrested on obscenity and the public lewdness charges, and Honeysuckle's remaining shows were canceled. This was the beginning of a court battle for Honeysuckle, Tommy, and my father that would drag out for two years. During the proceedings, exhibits of Ping-Pong balls would be presented in court and ultimately they—my father, Tommy, and Honeysuckle—were found guilty on all charges brought against them. They appealed the decision.

While on appeal, Honeysuckle's ACLU lawyer, Joel Molofsky, and the Golden 33's lawyer, Michael Seidman, who was a local expert on obscenity cases, secured an injunction for Honeysuckle to continue performing at the Golden 33. Until her act could be deemed "obscene" by the courts, Honeysuckle needed to earn a living. While in town for shows, she worshipped every morning at St. John's the Evangelist

Catholic Church, where she prayed to win this case and for the strength to forgive those who railed against her.

Because of the all the publicity generated from the arrest, Tommy and my father were able to charge double the normal cover rate whenever Honeysuckle performed at the Golden 33. They even started running afternoon shows. She was more popular than ever and people came back multiple times, dragging their friends along and sharing with them valuable lessons, such as sitting in the back row to avoid squirting lotion and errant Ping-Pong balls.

My father appreciated Honeysuckle Divine's unique genius—how she had turned her body into a business—and he said she was the most memorable part of owning the Golden 33.

Finally, after much legal wrangling, the case against Honeysuckle Divine and the Golden 33 was dismissed and all charges were dropped on June 22, 1976. Her act was declared "not obscene" because she didn't actually perform sex acts on stage. She was just guilty of being disgusting.

# 6

# *The Pornbroker's Wife*

"**M**om! Come quick! Daddy's on TV!" I shouted one afternoon while playing in the living room. When I heard my father's voice and then turned around to see his face on the screen, I was excited. My mother turned off the stove and rushed into the living room. There, she saw her husband on television, wearing a brown suit and standing in front of his new theater, The Lane, located at 16700 North Board Street in a mostly African American neighborhood. Behind him, an angry crowd shook signs that read, BOYCOTT THE LANE! and proudly shouting, "Hey, hey! Ho, ho! Porn-o-gra-phy has got to go!"

In February 1975, my father had leased and reopened the old RKO Theater, which had been vacant for five years. Steve Fox, who was head of the Fox Theater chain and had worked with my father to show *Deep Throat* in all of his theaters, had partnered with my father to open The Lane. Their only features would be porn movies like *Deep Throat* and *The Devil in Miss Jones.*

"I'm here today with Anthony Battista, owner of The Lane Theater. Mr. Battista, what inspired you to open this theater?" asked the Action News Live reporter.

"Well, *Deep Throat* and *The Devil in Miss Jones* are very popular right now. This rundown theater needed a new life, so we thought this was the perfect opportunity to showcase these movies."

"What do you say to the people in this neighbor who seem outraged and want The Lane Theater closed?"

"We are not hurting anyone," my father answered quickly and confidently, his breath visible in the cold air. "And there's nothing shown outside of the theater that could be offensive. All consenting adults are welcome."

"You're facing federal obscenity charges in Memphis, Tennessee, as one of the leads in distributing *Deep Throat* nationally. Do you think this is going to help your case?"

"I have broken no laws in Pennsylvania and I have never been to Memphis, Tennessee. The federal government is on a witch hunt and the American people will see that this upcoming federal case is an attack on free speech and a waste of taxpayer money."

My mother sighed; she was worried about what our family might think about the interview. My father sounded intelligent as always, but the scene behind him was concerning. The picketers looked angry. Was it possible that some of them might retaliate against him or his family in some violent way?

She leaned forward and turned down the television volume. A moment later, we heard my father enter through the front door.

"Daddy, what are you doing here?" I said in astonishment. "Aren't you supposed to be in the TV? Was the interview outside our house?"

He smiled, lifted me off the floor, and gave me a hug. "The interview was recorded earlier today, little girl," he explained.

"You sounded good, Anthony," my mother said.

"Really? I'm not one for being in front of a camera."

"You were fine. Now, can you help me with dinner?"

Back in the kitchen, she said, "Anthony, do you think opening this theater was good idea? Don't you have enough to deal with already? Those picketers . . . they looked crazy."

He shrugged. "It's fine, Frannie. They have the same right to express their opinion as I do to open the theater. Besides, it's good publicity."

"You are being so calm about this," she said, sighing. "My family isn't going to understand. And your family's not going to be too happy about it either."

"My family doesn't judge me," Dad said.

My mother gave him a puzzled look. She sensed that not everyone in my father's family was okay with what was going on, even though his parents didn't outwardly express any negative opinions and his brother appeared neutral on the situation. Then the phone rang. My mother answered and heard Grandma Maria's voice. And, weirdly, she also heard several heavy clicking and crackling noises.

"We saw Anthony on the news," Grandma Maria said through the interference. "This doesn't look good."

"Mom, hello . . . can you hear me? I think something's wrong with the phone."

"I hear you, Frannie."

"Okay . . . Mom, can I call you later? We're about to have dinner."

"You better call me back. I need to have a conversation with you about this. I'm worried."

"Don't worry, Mom. Really."

My mother hung up the phone. "And here it goes," she said.

My father was looking through the mail and didn't acknowledge my mother's comment.

"That was my mother," she went on. "And I think there's something wrong with the phone. There was some kind of interference, like a clicking sound. Maybe I should call the phone company?"

My father's ears perked up when she mentioned the clicking noises. "What did your mother have to say?" he asked.

"She's upset about the TV interview, obviously."

Then the phone rang again, and again my mother answered it. This time it was my father's Aunt Millie.

"Frannie, is everything okay? Uncle Joe and I just saw Anthony on the news."

"Everything's fine," my mother said in an exasperated voice. "Anthony's right here. Let me put him on." She handed the phone to my father.

That evening, in rapid succession, more calls came in from family and friends, and my mother was growing more and more irritated. Finally she said, "Am I *ever* going to get dinner on the table with all these interruptions?"

We lived near most of our extended family, so grandparents, aunts, uncles, and cousins from both sides were always involved in our lives. This was especially true of both of my grandmothers, who at times wreaked something close to havoc in our house. Grandma Emma, for example, would sometimes drop by unannounced, look through my mother's kitchen cabinets, and declare, "Frannie, my son doesn't eat this stuff!" Grandma Maria and my mother spoke daily regarding how my mother cleaned her house, cooked, raised her child, and "handled" her husband. Both my grandmothers were a smothering presence in my mother's life, and my mother didn't feel comfortable confiding her worst fears to them. Worrying them would be worse for everyone, she reasoned. So her only recourse was to maintain the pretense of a normal home life, which was becoming harder and harder to do.

❧

"Dinner's ready!" Grandma Emma called from the kitchen one afternoon in the early spring of 1975, signaling the beginning of another Sunday afternoon meal with my father's side of the family. Aunt Rose—the wife of my dad's brother Gabe—and her sons Stephen and Christopher were also in attendance, though Uncle Gabe was living in Italy for work.

I was four-and-a-half years old.

Aunt Rose and my mother brought out the first course of steaming cavatelli pasta with grated locatelli cheese, as well as crusty Italian bread we used to soak up the extra gravy in our bowls. Everyone sat down, settling in to prepare for hours of eating the decadent meal.

"*Salud*," said Grandpa Antonio, making a toast with his glass of homemade red wine.

"Rose, have you heard from Gabe?" said Grandma Emma.

"Yeah, Mom. He's gonna call you. G. E. is keeping him busy."

"Doesn't mean he should wait so long to call his mother."

"He'll be home for a visit next week. We'll see him real soon."

My cousins and I were squirming in our seats, wanting to escape outside to play. My mother ordered us to eat, while my father and Grandpa Antonio inhaled their food.

"Anthony's club is doing very well," my mother chimed in with pride. "You should come see it sometime, Rose. I decorated and found the perfect wallpaper for the ladies' room."

A disapproving look flashed across Aunt Rose's face. Rose, who was from a working-class, no-nonsense family in West Philly, had been vocal about her disapproval of my father's business. She couldn't fathom visiting the club. While Uncle Gabe was in Italy, she was on her own with two small children. Not to mention Aunt Rose and my mother didn't have much in common besides the Battista brothers. My mother was soft-spoken, the opposite of Rose's abrasive, independent nature. They weren't friends in the way sister-in-laws could or should be.

"I have better things to do with my time," Aunt Rose finally replied.

At that, my mother's face fell, and her controlled and graceful façade immediately cracked. Many times, she'd overheard Aunt Rose and Grandma Emma whispering in the kitchen behind her back about how they thought she was a spoiled wife. So far, she'd bitten her tongue. But all the tension that had been building culminated in this moment. She simply snapped.

"You bitch!" my mother screamed.

Then she emptied the contents of her wine glass into Aunt Rose's face.

Everyone at the table was stunned silent.

The wine soaked Aunt's Rose's dark hair and dribbled down the front of her shirt.

"Are you crazy?" Aunt Rose screamed. Then she grabbed a bowl of hot pasta and hurled its contents, which landed squarely on at my mother's chest and lap.

I saw that Grandpa Antonio's eyes had grown as big as saucers.

I glanced at my mother. Her face was twisted and unrecognizable.

Then she lunged across the table toward Aunt Rose.

I ducked under the table with my cousins and huddled into a ball to block out the chaos above me, but I didn't cry. Stephen was screaming at the top of his lungs, and tears streamed down his face. Christopher looked bewildered, yet somehow thoughtful, as he cocked his head to one side to listen to what was happening above. We heard breaking glasses, then saw another whole bowl of pasta spill onto the dining room floor. We watched my mother's feet rush away from the table and my father chase after her. A moment later, my father returned to the room, picked up a chair, and in frustration flung it across the room.

The room fell silent again. My cousins scurried out from under the table and huddled to Aunt Rose's side. I slowly crawled out and went over to Grandma Emma, who was crouched over the floor picking up the ruined pasta and putting it into her apron. She was fighting to hold back the tears.

"Grandma, are we still going to eat?" I asked.

"I don't know, sweetheart. I just don't know," she responded quietly.

At that moment, Aunt Mary—my Grandpa Antonio's sister—and her husband Uncle George entered the house. "*Mio Dio!*" Aunt Mary said. "What happened, Emma?"

"The girls just had a fight, Mary."

"Jesus Christ! Has everyone gone crazy?" Aunt Mary cried, giving the sign of the cross. Then she bent over to help Grandma Emma clean up.

Later that afternoon, my cousins and I were sent to the backyard, where my mother and Aunt Rose were sitting together on a bench, crying and apologizing to each other. We lined up in a neat row in front of them.

"We want you all to know everything is okay," Aunt Rose said to us, though she was still visibly shaken. "We're not mad at each other anymore."

"We've apologized and made up. Everything's fine now," my mother said.

I noticed that the sleeve of my mother's orange shirt was ripped off and that she had gravy stains down the front of her clothes. Aunt Rose looked equally disheveled, with red wine stains on her outfit.

*Everything is not fine,* I thought.

But they were holding each other's hands, both as a sign that they had forgiven each other, and also, I realize now, in the hope that their children wouldn't be scarred for life. Then they both gave us hugs and apologized for their behavior.

The incident became family legend, and as family legends often go, it became funny as time passed. We all laugh about it now.

But the truth is, it wasn't funny at all.

～◯～

I never slept past 7:00 a.m., so my mother always got up early and let my father sleep in because he usually got home around 4:00 a.m. One morning, she padded down the stairs in a robe and fuzzy slippers and found me on the living room couch watching TV. My toys, which I'd brought down from my room, covered the floor around me. I was a self-sufficient and quiet child and didn't readily acknowledge her presence or show an interest that she had appeared in the room.

"Are you hungry?" my mother asked quietly.

"Nooooo," I said. I was never hungry.

"You're going to have to eat soon," my mother insisted. "You have to get to school."

I was enrolled in preschool at the neighborhood Jewish synagogue, which was within walking distance from our house. It was the perfect school for me because my mother didn't drive and I was happy to learn "The Dreidel Song" and all about Jewish history. This environment also helped coax me out of my shell since I was a very shy child. My Grandma Emma wasn't at all thrilled about me attending a Hebrew school, but since my father had promised her that I would start Catholic school in kindergarten, her discontent was quelled.

My mother entered the kitchen to make coffee and squeeze fresh orange juice. It was cold outside and frost covered the windows. But the days had become longer recently and my mother was happy spring had officially arrived on the calendar despite the chilly morning. As the grinding noise of the juicer filled the kitchen, she made a checklist in her mind of the groceries to pick up later after she dropped me off at school.

By 8:00 a.m., our morning routine was in full swing. My mother was stationed at the stove making scrambled eggs, while I sat at the table complaining about how I didn't want to eat. I was an Italian mother's worst nightmare but luckily this was my only challenging quality; I was generally a well-behaved child.

"Good morning, everyone," my father said as he entered the kitchen.

"You're up early," said Mom. "You want some eggs?"

"Sure," he said as he poured himself a huge cup of coffee. "Remember when we first got married and your eggs were served floating in a pool of bacon grease.?" He was smiling and trying to get a smile out of her. "You're a much better cook now."

"Ha, ha, very funny," she said, still focused on cooking breakfast.

"What have you got going on today?" he asked.

"The usual. Take Kristin to school, shopping, and I might clean up around here. What about you?"

"I have to be out of here soon to go with Tommy to some meetings. Then I'm just going to stay downtown to open the club."

"Oh . . . so you'll miss dinner." She kept her eyes on the eggs she was cracking into the frying pan. "Well, okay."

We ate breakfast together, then separated for the day.

Sometimes, in the afternoons, my mother would watch reruns of Julia Child's *The French Chef*. I loved to listen to Julia's funny accent, with its buoyant cadence as she pronounced, "Welcome to *The French Chef*! Today we're going to cook . . ." My mother and I would watch the show on the small black-and-white TV in the kitchen as Julia held up a whole fish or beat the counter with her kitchen tools in reckless abandon. My mother would race around the kitchen, pouring ingredients together and trying to keep up with Julia's instructions. Or she would frantically write down cooking tips for later reference.

Despite my mother's passion for cooking, she had lost a lot of weight that year. She was down to 115 pounds for her five-foot-eight frame. She had also been recently diagnosed with ulcerative colitis, so she just couldn't eat that much. To top it all off, I was such a picky eater that whenever my mother went to the trouble to prepare one of Julia Child's creations for dinner, I never appreciated it. Instead I daydreamed, often out loud, about eating Oscar Meyer bologna on Wonder bread, like the happy kids in the TV commercials.

After I went to bed, my mother would wander the house straightening up, drinking tea, and watching TV. With her husband away, it was too quiet for her most evenings and her mind would wander to what might be going on at the club. Was it busy that night? Did the girls flirt with my father? Did he flirt with them? Did anyone care about the decorations in the ladies' room?

And what would happen if my father ended up in jail again?

≈≈≈

More than a year and a half had passed since my father had first started distributing *Deep Throat* in the fall of 1973. It was around that time my mother distinctly remembers him carrying large film canisters through the back door for the first time.

"Help me," my father grunted as he placed some canisters on the kitchen floor. Then he rushed back outside toward his car in the driveway. My mother followed him and found his trunk full of films. They worked together to move all the film canisters to the upstairs' guest bedroom.

Over the following months, this bedroom would become "distribution central" for *Deep Throat* in the Philadelphia area. Films were stacked on the floor, against the wall, or stashed under the bed, and stacks of cash were piled neatly on the desk, ready to be sorted for the Perainos. My father carefully accounted for all the money and the films, and both my mother and I knew never to touch anything in that room.

≈≈≈

The Golden 33 and *Deep Throat* had altered our lives. My father awaited the Memphis trial, the details of which my mother didn't know much about, and the phone calls at home from Tommy Rizzo and theater owners and the club girls had become more and more frequent. My mother had a gnawing suspicion my father was cheating on her. It was the kind of suspicion you felt in your bones that tugged painfully at your conscience. But she explained it away with rationalizations.

*I'm a good wife and mother.*

*He wouldn't risk his family.*

*I'm not ugly.*

*He won't find someone else more attractive.*

*Anthony is just doing his best to provide for the family.*

But still . . . something bothered her.

"Anthony, can't these girls call Tommy to ask these questions?" she asked one night. "I thought he managed the staff. And anyway, you'll see them tonight at the club. Can't it wait?"

"Frannie, it's about money and commissions. Tommy doesn't answer those questions."

"Fine. But what was that call just now about?"

"That was Veronica. She's already at the club and wanted to ask for a raise on her commissions before opening." My father removed his glasses, set them on the kitchen table, and rubbed his temples. "Frannie, it's hard being a business owner. There's always something that needs to be done. Always someone asking a question. There's never any time off."

How could my mother argue with that? She had no idea how to run a club or a business. Things were stressful enough without her complaining, she thought. And she had no proof of infidelity.

"I just wish you'd tell me more about the club," she said, her voice beginning to crack. "I don't know how you spend your nights."

"It's boring, Fran."

"How boring? I'd like to know."

My father looked at her directly. "It's paying vendors and dealing with the dancers. It's things you shouldn't have to worry about. "

My mother rolled her eyes.

"Okay," my father said. "I'll tell you one thing."

"What's that?"

"We have to pay the cops to leave us alone."

"What?"

"To ensure the cops will come if we have trouble in the club, we have to pay them off."

Suddenly, my mother was furious. "Crooked cops? I'm going to call the news stations!"

"Frannie, don't you dare!" my father said, immediately regretting that he'd mentioned anything. "*This* is why I don't tell you things. If you call reporters, it draws more attention, and then the local authorities will push harder to close down the club. How would I earn a living? Don't you see? They could throw me in jail."

My mother realized there must be many things going on that she didn't know about. Though she wasn't sorry she'd pressed for answers, this news about the cops' extorting my father was unsettling. And what was more unsettling was that her questions were always answered with so few words. Now she knew why. My father often said he just wanted to protect her so she wouldn't worry. But his plan of creating a utopia at home, by any means necessary, was only making matters at home worse. And the dismissals of her persistent concerns often led to bitter arguments that forced me to run out to the backyard to escape.

"These girls keep calling!" I heard my mother scream from upstairs while I was playing in the basement, and I immediately put my hands to my ears and started crying. My father's muffled voice and heavy footsteps followed after my mother's screams.

"Calm down, Frannie! Please!"

"I will not calm down! Something is going on! I know it!"

"Frannie, nothing's going on."

"Just get out, Anthony. Get out!"

"I will not leave my own home. Maybe you just need to go to your mother's for a while."

"No! No! No! Get out!"

Uncontrollable sobs followed and in the chaos of the argument, the walk-out basement provided my escape to the backyard. As soon as I left the basement, I noticed how much quieter it was. I pushed open the fence, sat by the rocks on the side of our house near the driveway, and played with my Cher doll.

A few minutes later, I caught the eye of a neighbor who was on her way out. I quickly turned away and focused on beating the dirt with a rock.

"Hey, what are you doing out here?"

I turned around to find a beautiful teenage girl, about sixteen years old, with long, straight, brown hair parted down the middle. She wore bellbottom jeans, and she was staring at me with concern.

Suddenly, I burst into tears.

"My parents are fighting," I managed.

"Oh, no!" the pretty girl said. "Why don't you come next door and we'll play for a while. You shouldn't be alone outside. What's your name again? I'm Tina."

I had seen her coming and going from her house, but our families had never gotten to know one another. I sniffled and gripped the Cher doll tighter. Finally I said, "My name is Kristin."

Tina took my hand and led me to her house. As we entered the back door to their kitchen, Tina called out, "Mom, come quick!" Tina's mother Marie appeared in the kitchen doorway.

"Hey, there," Marie said. "I know you. You live next door."

"Mom, I found her crying, and she said her parents are fighting."

"Would you like to stay and play for a while?" Marie asked kindly.

I nodded my head, grateful for the reprieve from my house.

"Okay, Tina, why don't you play with Kristin here at the kitchen table, and I'll make a snack. Then I'll go tell her parents where she is."

Just then, there was a furious knocking on the front door. Marie rushed to answer.

"Marie, have you seen my daughter?" I heard my mother say in near hysterics. I looked toward the front door. Tears and mascara streamed down my mother's cheeks.

"She's here," Marie said. "Calm down. I was just going to come over to tell you. Tina found her in the side yard. I don't know what's going on over there, but your daughter is scared to death."

"I'm so sorry to bother you, Marie. My husband and I, um . . . we got in an argument . . . the next thing we knew . . ." My mother was breaking down. "We didn't know where Kristin was. Can I see her please?"

"Pull yourself together first," Marie said softly. "She's fine to stay here for a few hours until things settle down."

"Oh, thank you. Again, I'm sorry to bother you."

Marie and my mother appeared in the kitchen as Tina was playing with me and my Cher doll. I looked up at my mother. "So you want to stay here to play?" she asked me as cheerfully as she could.

I gave her an icy glare. "Uh huh," I said, then looked back at my doll.

"Okay, I'll be back later to pick you up."

Over the next few months, I would retreat to the backyard many more times during my parents' arguments, in the hopes of catching Tina's gaze. But whenever I would see her, or any of her family, they always looked away, apparently not wanting to be involved in our problems. And each time they averted their eyes, I felt more alone.

⟋⟍⟋

The Lane Theater closed in the summer of 1975 despite my father's efforts to run mainstream movies like *The Sting* as well as live stripping acts and popular porn titles. But the outrage in the neighborhood simply scared customers away, and nothing my father tried could create a loyal customer base like the one he still enjoyed at the Golden 33. On top of that, my father was growing weary of distributing *Deep Throat*. The trials in Memphis were coming quickly, scheduled for March of 1976. Perhaps, if he were no longer distributing the film, it would help his case.

The good news was the Golden 33 was still doing very well, and the Premiere Theater in Florida—despite local authorities' efforts to shut them down—was also bringing in a good income. The Premiere was the only establishment of its kind in central Florida to see popular porn movies like *Behind the Green Door*, *Deep Throat*, and *The Devil in Miss Jones*.

Despite the stable income, mounting tensions between my parents surfaced again and again. One night in the fall of that year, my mother was drinking wine at dinner to calm her nerves, which was unusual. "So, Anthony, the trial is soon. What's been going on?" she asked.

"Well, Tennessee is an extremely conservative state. The jury probably won't be sympathetic to a bunch of Italian outsiders. But I doubt this will lead to any convictions. It's just silly to be indicted for a movie." My father took a bite of his dinner, chewed, and swallowed. "You know, I may need to be in Memphis for the trials. I don't know how long it's going to last."

My mother abruptly stood up. She took her plate to the kitchen sink and dropped it with a crash. Then she grabbed the wine bottle and poured herself another glass.

My mother returned to the table and sat down. "So, you're saying you won't be here?" she asked in a loud voice. "What else is new?"

"You can come to Tennessee to visit," my father said calmly. "And Kristin can stay at your mother's."

"Why should I come? I'm sure you won't be lonely." My mother leaned back in her chair and took a big gulp of wine.

"Don't start," my father said, his calm beginning to fade. "I don't know why you have to break my balls. I'm doing the best I can to bring money in and battle these assholes trying to put me in jail. None of this was my choice. I didn't do anything wrong."

"I never thought you did anything wrong, Anthony," she said. "For Christ's sake, I supported the club from the beginning. But you have to go and mess around with these other women. Am I not pretty enough? So little respect for me, Anthony, these other women. How many are there?" Tears were streaming down her face. "Answer me! How many others are there?"

"Frannie, you sound crazy."

The word *crazy* hung in the air. It was the only word my mother heard. And my father's silence after uttering it just made her angrier.

"I'll show you crazy," she said, starting to shake slightly. "Just tell me the truth!"

Then she threw her wine glass at my father.

He ducked. The glass sailed toward the kitchen window behind him. I heard the sound of shattering glass, and I ran up to my room.

My mother wept as she leaned against the kitchen counter. "I'll show you crazy . . . I'll show you crazy," she repeated over and over.

My father just took a deep breath. Then he left for the club without saying another word.

My mother stood in the kitchen trying to calm herself down. Minutes later, as she regained her senses, she realized what a mess she'd made. The glass she'd thrown had not only broken the window but also shattered all over the floor. She wiped her tears, grabbed a broom and a dust pan, and started sweeping.

Her body felt heavy, and every muscle was sore. She was so tired lately but just couldn't sleep.

She hoped Anthony felt guilty. But she suspected that he didn't.

❧

The next morning my father was in the kitchen when I got up. He greeted me cheerfully. "Good morning, little girl."

I was surprised to see him, but I was happy he was there. It seemed like a special treat. He served me a bowl of cereal and started making coffee. I sat at the kitchen table, slowly spooned cereal into my mouth, and watched as he inspected the broken window. He pulled out masking tape from the kitchen drawer and secured a piece of cardboard over the missing window pane. Then he noticed how I was thoughtfully watching him work on the window.

"We'll fix it, no problem," he said with a weak smile.

My mother appeared in the kitchen. "Good morning," she said quietly. "Anthony, do you want some breakfast?"

"Sure," he answered politely. "I'm going outside to get the paper. I'll be right back."

On his way to the front door, he hoped my mother would not start another argument. He had a full day, plus another long night at the club ahead of him.

My mother was quiet as she cooked breakfast and as she heaped eggs onto my plate.

"Mom, I don't want these," I protested, since I'd already eaten cereal.

"Just eat some," she encouraged gently, trying to be motherly.

I picked up my fork and pushed the eggs around my plate, pretending to eat. My father had returned and was now reading the paper at the table. He ate in silence, then announced he had to head to the bank and then to the club to meet with Tommy to go over the month's receipts. "I won't be home for dinner, Frannie," he said. "With my afternoon schedule downtown, it doesn't make sense to come all the way back home for dinner."

"Okay, see you tomorrow," my mother said nonchalantly.

My father nodded, but I saw a concerned look on his face. "Be good," he said to me as he left the table, and he kissed me on the top of my head. I was disappointed he was leaving. He leaned in and kissed my mother on the cheek but she barely reciprocated the affection.

〜⌒つ〜

The following Tuesday, my mother invited my grandparents for dinner. She had resolved to get past the terrible argument and had asked Grandpa Frank to fix some things in the house.

When they arrived, I ran to the door to greet them.

"There she is!" Grandpa Frank said, hugging me. "Have you gotten bigger since the last time I saw you?"

"No," I replied giggling.

My mother came to the door and kissed both her parents on the cheeks. They removed their coats and placed them on the edge of the couch and Grandpa Frank set his tool box down in the living room.

"Come on back to the kitchen," my mother said. "Dinner's almost ready."

The table was set and my mother finished frying the cutlets and gave the chicken soup a stir.

"Everything smells good, Frannie," Grandma Maria said. "Did you make your own bread crumbs for the cutlets?"

"No, they're store bought. Come on, sit. Let me serve."

"Isn't Anthony going to eat with us?"

"No, Mom. He's at the club."

As my grandmother sat down, she caught sight of the cardboard covering the window pane. "Frannie, what happened to the window?"

"Is that what you need fixing?" chimed in Grandpa Frank.

"Oh yeah . . . we had an accident, and the window broke," Mom said casually as she ladled out the soup with tiny little meatballs and escarole.

Grandma Maria was immediately suspicious but for the rest of meal we just spoke about the news or about other family members or about how I liked preschool. My father wasn't mentioned at all.

After dinner, my grandfather measured the windowpane so he could order the replacement glass. Meanwhile, Grandma Maria cornered my mother in the living room. "So how did the window break?" she wanted to know.

"I got angry with Anthony about the club and lost my temper. I threw a wine glass at the window. It was a dumb thing to do. His hours are just crazy and he's never here. It's making me a little crazy."

Grandma Maria was furious. "I swear, Frannie, he's killing you. I hear it in your voice. Every time I see you, you look worse. When are you going to leave him?"

"I am *not* leaving Anthony," my mother said emphatically.

"Frannie, you can come home any time. The third floor of the house has plenty of room for you and Kristin. I can fix it up real nice."

"I don't need to move back home, Mom."

"Coming to fix broken windows, and Anthony never being here . . . this is not the sign of a happy home. And Frannie, I think he's cheating on you, too."

My mother shook her head violently. "I don't want to believe that, Mom. I ask him if there are other women but he denies it."

"Of course he does! He wants that trash at the club and to keep you, too."

"I don't want to talk about this anymore."

Grandma Maria took a step back. She looked up at the ceiling, then back at her distraught daughter. "Fine. Just remember that you're my baby and you can come home whenever you want."

Both Grandma Maria and my mother's sister, Dolores, had urged her to leave my father. But the thought of returning home to South Philly with a small child didn't seem like a reasonable option for my mother. When she'd lived with her parents, she had only wanted to escape and live her own life. In her mind, moving back would be admitting some kind of defeat. And she knew filing for divorce would only make Anthony's case weaker in Memphis. She wasn't happy, but she certainly didn't want her daughter's father in jail.

The following week, my Grandpa Frank arrived alone with his toolbox and a glass panel in hand to fix the broken window.

"Thanks for coming, Dad."

"No problem," said Grandpa Frank as he pushed his eyeglasses back up on his nose. His once dark, wavy hair had gone gray and now only framed his ears and neck. My mother noticed her father had been wearing the same style of clothing for years. His tall frame and broad shoulders were accentuated by his uniform: a buttoned-up cardigan over a blue short-sleeve dress shirt, a tie, charcoal gray pants, and black lace-up dress shoes.

Grandpa Frank went about his work, pretending this was just a regular fix-it visit. He'd never asked any questions about how the window had broken. He did, however, notice my mother looked too thin and tired. He fixed the window, then stepped back to admire the finished product.

After lunch with my mother, Grandpa Frank returned to South Philly. He wished that things for his daughter could be fixed as easily as that window. When the trials were behind my father and this nonsense at the Golden 33 was over, Grandpa Frank wanted peace restored to his family. He liked my father, whom he thought of as a good, smart Italian boy. And besides, no marriage was perfect.

# 7

# *Grandma Maria Sees* Deep Throat

"Kristin, did I ever tell you that I saw *Deep Throat?*" Grandma Maria said to me.

It was a few days before Christmas of 1985. I was fifteen years old. Grandma Maria and I were sitting alone at the kitchen table eating pizzelles and honey cookies, and our conversations had turned, once again, to our family's *Deep Throat* past. I was still a young woman but I'd already learned that every time I was alone with Grandma Maria, I would learn something new and strange about my family. But this latest revelation, I never expected.

"Oh, my God!" I replied. "No you didn't! You have to tell me this story."

Grandma Maria laughed. "So you didn't think your old grandma would see a movie like that?"

"I'm just surprised, I guess. Why would you see it?"

"Your dad got me the tickets," Grandma Maria said, and she dunked a honey cookie into her coffee.

"Really?"

"I didn't ask him for the tickets. Just one night your father calls me up and says, 'Mom, my film is playing at the President Theater on Twenty-third Street and Snyder Avenue. I'll get you free tickets.' It was just up the street and it was free, so I thought why not."

I understood how, with her Depression-era frugality, Grandma Maria could never turn down anything free. And at the time, it must have seemed that everyone except her had seen *Deep Throat*; it was a major cultural event of that decade. So I shouldn't have been surprised. But still, the thought of her watching a porn flick was just unfathomable. Maybe it's because no child ever wants to believe that her grandmother, or parents for that matter, has any sexual curiosities. I also wondered why my father had offered the tickets in the first place. It must have been to preemptively indulge her unstoppable need to know everything.

"Well," she went on, "I didn't want to go alone, so I asked my friend Ida Shultz to go with me."

"Ida?"

This was the first time I had heard my grandmother mention a girlfriend and it seemed out of the ordinary, since I knew my grandparents didn't socialize much or have a large circle of friends.

"She was my best friend from my neighborhood," Grandma Maria explained. "She married a German man who was nice, but at the time, it was highly scandalous. Italians just didn't marry outside of our kind. Ida died about ten years ago of cancer. Poor Ida, I loved her, and I didn't see her much when she was sick. Your grandfather never let me see her much after we were married."

Grandma Maria spoke in a bitter tone and tears welled up in her eyes. But I knew my grandfather was just being painted as the scapegoat, since I knew he couldn't stop her from doing anything. Rather, I think it was hard for Grandma Maria to admit that she'd just become busy with life and family and that seeing friends had become more difficult.

Before Grandma Maria got to the juicy details of the story, I imagined two ladies in their early fifties watching *Deep Throat* with the raincoat-and-couples crowd, and I likened it to when my best friend, Kelley, and

I tried to sneak into see the R-rated film *Purple Rain* when we were fourteen years old.

Best friends, I knew, were your companions for mischief.

࿇

"Mary, are you crazy?" Ida said. "Do you know what kind of people go to this type of movie? Perverts! That's who! What if someone sees us?"

"Don't you have any sense of adventure?" my grandmother prodded. "It'll be fine."

"I know plenty about adventure, Mary, and this isn't adventure. It's purely disgusting."

"Please, Ida. I don't want to go by myself. I have to see what my son-in-law is doing."

After some debate, Ida finally said, "Okay, I'll go. I can't believe how you talk me into these things."

They agreed to meet in front of the President's Theater at 8:00 p.m. on the following Thursday night.

Grandma Maria arrived home from work at the Beaumont Birch Company, where she was a receptionist, and she prepared dinner for my grandfather and for Kitty, the ocelot. Kitty received a bowl of raw chicken while Grandpa Frank got a simple meal of eggs and asparagus. As Grandma Maria cooked, Kitty jumped on the countertop. If Kitty became too persistent, my grandma would have to coax her in a kitchen cabinet where Kitty liked to sleep while Grandma cooked. Kitty had once nabbed a whole raw turkey just before Thanksgiving dinner, so Grandma Maria knew not to turn her back, even for a moment.

Grandpa Frank emerged from his basement darkroom after a day of retouching and developing photographs. He shuffled into the kitchen, ready for dinner.

"Frank, I'm going to see that movie Anthony is showing at the President's Theater tonight."

Grandpa Frank gave a double take. Then he raised his voice, "Mary, do you really need to see that movie?"

"Yes, I'm going to see *that* movie." She rolled her eyes. "Ida's going with me. It's fine. Don't get all riled up."

Grandma Maria was accustomed to her husband's small outbursts. When she married him at age of fifteen, Grandpa Frank's raised voice had been intimidating. But as she had matured, she'd realized it was all hot air.

"Don't you want to know what your son-in-law is up to?" she went on, keeping her eyes on Kitty and the cooking. "Honestly Frank, you are the most uninquisitive man. Your family was always like that, even when your sister Annie was sleeping with that married guy."

Grandpa Frank looked down at Kitty, who was now under the table, for sympathy. But all he saw staring back was a wild cat looking for scraps of meat—another symbol of his wife's determination.

"Mary, I don't want you wandering around the streets at night."

"I'll have my umbrella and mace," she interrupted calmly. "I'll be home by midnight."

Grandpa Frank shrugged. A moment later, he muttered, "I'm going back to finish retouching," and he retreated to his sanctuary of the dark basement.

After dinner, Grandma Maria freshened up by reapplying red lipstick and powdering her face along her square jaw line and prominent nose. To tame her thick brown hair, she pulled it back into a tight ponytail. Then she put on a black turtle neck sweater and a trench coat with matching beret. She stroked Kitty goodbye.

"I'm leaving, Frank," she yelled down into the basement

"Okay, Mary! Be careful!"

It was beginning to rain, but she didn't mind because she had her trusty umbrella, which on more than one occasion had doubled as a weapon. The night air felt slightly cool and crisp as she walked up Broad Street, weaving in and out of people who were walking too slow. Grandma Maria always walked fast and with purpose, not only because she was impatient to get to wherever she was going, but also because she wanted to avoid being a target for a mugger.

A couple blocks from the house, she lit up a cigarette. She only smoked at work and when she went out and avoided smoking at home so she wouldn't have to hear a lecture from Grandpa Frank.

When she arrived at the theater, she was relieved to see Ida already waiting for her under an awning next to the ticket booth. Ida waved and adjusted the rain cap covering her short dark hair. Standing up to make her short stature appear taller, she looked the same as when she was schoolgirl. Her black pencil skirt and blouse were perfectly pressed and she wore a silk scarf around her neck.

"It's about time you got here," said Ida, looking around nervously.

"I'm so glad to see you, honey," said Grandma Maria. She gave Ida a big hug.

A moment later they were standing at the ticket booth. "My son-in-law left tickets for me to see a movie featured here tonight. My name is Maria Parrotto."

The man in the booth smiled wryly as he handed her the tickets. He then stroked one index finger over the other in the "shame-on-you" hand gesture.

"Enjoy the show, ladies," he said.

Ida looked at the man strangely and hesitated before stepping into the lobby. But Grandma Maria quickly hooked her arm around Ida's and dragged her through the door. The lobby looked like an ordinary movie theater with Hollywood movie posters of upcoming films, deep red carpets, and the smell of fresh popcorn. Once inside, Ida looked like a teacher studying the space in academic curiosity, while Grandma Maria played the grinning, mischievous student, up for anything.

"Are you sure this is a good idea?" Ida whispered.

"Of course it is! Let's hurry, the movie's already started."

They entered the dark theater. All around them, men sat alone in various seats. There were also a few giggling couples. Then Grandma Maria and Ida looked up at the screen and saw a huge penis.

"Oh my . . . Mary . . . I don't think we should stay," Ida gasped, and she stood there motionless, too paralyzed to move.

"Yes, we *should* stay," Grandma Maria hissed. "We walked twenty-five blocks to get here, and we're *going* to see this film."

"Okay," Ida said as Grandma Maria hustled them into a pair of seats. Ida glanced again at the screen, sort of covering her eyes with her hand. "Mary . . . let's sit near the back."

Throughout the film, Ida interjected repeatedly, "Oh, my God!" and "I don't believe this!" It was impossible not to stare. And just like that night in the strip club, Grandma Maria was both horrified and curious.

The blowjob scenes almost made her gag. *How can a girl actually do that with her throat?* she thought. She questioned if any of it was real. She also felt sad that our society had come to such a place that a movie like this was acceptable, even praised.

When the movie ended, they were greeted outside by pouring rain. Both of them let out a big sigh of relief. Then they just looked at each other and exploded into laughter.

"Well, Mary, thanks for an experience of a lifetime," Ida said, still laughing as they said goodbye.

As Grandma Maria crossed Twenty-third Street, she saw a young man she knew from work. John was a single twenty-five-year-old and he was hanging out with some buddies on the stoop of a brownstone. John recognized Grandma Maria immediately and his eyes widened.

"Maria! Did you just see *Deep Throat?*"

"I certainly did, honey!" Grandma Maria called back, and she proudly gave him a wink. "See you tomorrow at work."

But as she walked home, worry settled in. What her son-in-law did for a living was disgusting and she believed it may even be damaging to her daughter's soul. She couldn't understand why her daughter didn't feel the same way. How could her own flesh and blood see this movie, and the club, and not think it was degrading to women?

When she arrived home, Grandpa Frank had already gone to bed. The house was quiet and dark with the exception of a small light in the kitchen. She found Kitty lying across the dining room table. As she stroked Kitty, she murmured about the disgusting movie she had just seen. Then she went up to bed.

The next morning at work, John stopped by Grandma Maria's desk.

"How's it going, Maria?" John asked nervously. Then he leaned in and whispered, "Hey, can I ask you something?"

"Sure, honey. What is it?"

"Is it true that the clitoris is in the back of a woman's throat?"

Grandma Maria covered her mouth and chuckled. But given this young man's bravery for even asking the question, she tried to be kind.

"No," she said sweetly. "That's not true."

"Are you sure?"

"I'm positive. I think you should go to the library and get some books about sex. I think it would help."

"Yeah, maybe I should do that," John said with a confused look on his face.

*Men are so dumb,* Grandma Maria thought as she shook her head in disbelief.

# 8

# *Goodnight*

"Mrs. Battista, I'm sorry to keep you waiting," Dr. Jacobs said. "Please come back to my office." It was the fall of 1975 and the first time Mom was going to see a therapist.

Dr. Jacobs escorted her to his office which was a quiet space brimming with natural light. The hardwood floors were shined to a high gloss and a couch and two comfortable-looking chairs were positioned near the window where potted plants in macramé holders hung from the ceiling.

My mother settled on the edge of the couch opposite Dr. Jacobs. He was in his mid-thirties, wore glasses, and had an approachable face framed by curly brown hair. She liked him immediately, and the diploma on the wall behind him—a PhD in psychology from the University of Pennsylvania—impressed her. She had been overwhelmed searching through the Yellow Pages for a counselor or psychologist among the many names ending with PhD, MA, or MD and knew she'd been lucky to find a reputable therapist.

She hadn't told anyone except my father that she was in treatment. She didn't want people to think she was crazy.

"I see you graduated from the University of Pennsylvania. I used to work in the billing department over at the hospital," she said.

"It's a great hospital. I've been at the U of P in outpatient services and in my own private practice since I graduated." Then, after a brief pause, he asked, "So what brings you here today, Mrs. Battista? And may I call you Fran?"

"Sure."

"Okay, good. You can call me Mark."

"Okay, Mark." Then, without warning, my mother began to cry. "I'm sorry, um, I don't know why . . ." She took a tissue from her purse and blew her nose. "I guess I've just been under a lot of stress lately."

"I'm sorry to hear that, I hope we can talk about that and get to know each other today."

As my mother began her story, she watched Dr. Jacobs's reaction carefully. Was there judgment behind his friendly smile about what her husband did for a living? Or was he as understanding as he seemed?

"Well, that's certainly not a typical job," Dr. Jacobs said after she'd finished. "Can you describe what happens when you try to talk to your husband about your suspicions of his infidelity?"

"He just denies it," my mother said. "I believe him, but then I have my doubts. I guess I just really *want* to believe him."

"What makes you have these doubts?"

She shifted on the sofa. "I don't know. It's mostly just a gut feeling. When I ask questions about his work, he hardly tells me anything. And the girls from the club call the house a lot. I don't like that. I know my husband's a catch for any girl at that club, so they're probably pursuing him. My mother and sister think he's cheating, too. They say I should leave him."

"So you're quite close to your sister and mother?"

"Yes, we're very close. I'm the youngest in the family, so they look after me."

Dr. Jacobs nodded. "Birth order is very influential in how people function in a family. We should definitely explore this further."

"I talk to my mother every day. And I see my parents weekly. My sister lives in Connecticut, and we talk at least two or three times a week by phone. Everyone has an opinion about my life. And with all the input, I sometimes get frustrated and confused. Then I scream and throw things. The last big argument, I threw a wine glass at Anthony."

"You threw . . ."

"It missed him. It broke a window in the kitchen."

Dr. Jacobs nodded again. "I think *your* opinion of Anthony is the only one that matters."

"I guess so," my mother said, though she only half-heartedly believed it.

"That last argument sounded very heated," Dr. Jacobs said. "Does that happen a lot?"

"More than I would like."

They went on to talk in more detail about my parents' relationship and how different family members influenced my mother. Then after nearly an hour, Dr. Jacobs looked at a small white clock on his desk.

"Fran, I'm afraid we're out of time today," he said. "If you'd like to come back once a week for a few months, we could focus on developing better communications skills and how to assert yourself. I get a sense that expressing yourself and making decisions is difficult for you. I'd also like to meet with both you and your husband for at least one session, if that would be okay."

"I'm not sure Anthony will come. But I'll ask him."

"Asking is a good first step," he said with a smile.

My mother made a standing weekly appointment with Dr. Jacobs, then left the office. Later, on the EL train home, she realized that even though she had spilled her guts, she wasn't feeling any better. She hadn't expected to be fixed in one session but she'd hoped to feel at least a little relief. Still, she liked Dr. Jacobs and she believed her transformation back to a happy housewife would come in time.

～∽৩৩৩৩～

"Dr. Jacobs is very smart," my mother said to my father over an early lunch at our house. "He suggested I see him once a week, so I set up some regular appointments."

"Good," my father said. "I'm glad you went and that you liked him."

"He also offered to see us both for a session. What do you think?"

"We could do that," he said without hesitation. "So you think this guy knows what he's doing?"

"It was just one session, but he seemed good."

A few weeks later, my parents arrived together at Dr. Jacobs's office. In the waiting room, my father was reading the *Philadelphia Inquirer*, and my mother was subconsciously fiddling with the handles of her handbag when Dr. Jacobs appeared.

Then a few moments later, my parents sat next to each other on the couch opposite Dr. Jacobs.

"Anthony, I'd like to take this opportunity to get to know you and to have Fran talk about how she feels things are going at home. She's told me about your club and I understand that there's a pending federal trial. I'm sure it's all been very stressful."

"Dr. Jacobs, um . . . I mean Mark . . . I know it hasn't been easy for my wife. But she *has* been supportive. So I want to be supportive, too. That's why I'm here. I hope these sessions help her."

Dr. Jacobs smiled. "I'm so pleased to hear all that, Anthony. It's very important that you've come in today. So, to get our conversation started, Anthony, I'll ask you, how do you think things are going for Fran at home?

My father took a deep breath. "Well, as evident with us being here, I think it's been hard for Frannie. She seems isolated and doesn't have friends that live close by, and I'm not home as much as I'd like to be. She also has full responsibility of taking care of our daughter. Luckily, I've been doing okay financially."

"Fran, do you want to describe what it's been like *for you*?" Dr. Jacobs asked.

"Well . . . just like Anthony said, I just wish he was home more. But I know he has to work."

"Please go on."

My mother shook her head, looked off at the floor. "Mark, I don't know what else to say."

"You don't seem to be vocalizing your feelings," Dr. Jacobs said. "I think this could be making you feel more depressed. You're in a safe environment here. You can say whatever's on your mind."

My mother's eyes began to swell with tears.

"I just wish Anthony was around more," she finally burst. "And . . . and . . . I feel so unimportant sometimes. The girls at the club get more attention than I do and I . . . I . . . I wonder if he's having affairs with some of them."

My father sighed. "But I'm not with any other women, Fran."

"Anthony, why do you think your wife thinks this?" Dr. Jacobs asked.

"I just think she feels insecure about me being around strippers. And I can understand that."

Through clenched teeth, my mother said, "I think something else is going on."

"Frannie, I don't know how many times I have to tell you that that isn't true."

My father looked the picture of sanity, while my mother began to fall apart. He sat calmly with his hands folded in his lap, while my mother looked away from him, started to tremble, and dabbed her eyes with a tissue.

"Anthony, Fran may be having these feelings, in part, because you're both in an extraordinary circumstance. Your open communication will be the key to helping her get through this. I'd also suggest you both try spending some quality time together."

My mother was in a daze. She'd expected Dr. Jacobs to take her side; instead, he remained neutral throughout the session. Again, my mother wondered if her suspicions about Anthony cheating were unfounded and if her psychological troubles were more about her deep-seated insecurities. She started to blame herself, yet again, for the state of their marriage, and she became resigned to the possibility that things may not get any better. As far as she could tell, therapy seemed to focus on how my mother coped with her current situation, not on the acknowledgment of how her circumstances may have caused her to feel depressed.

On the way home that day, my mother stared out the car window at the shops and tall buildings passing by. Her hands felt cold and numb, just like she felt on the inside. She rubbed them together, trying to create warmth.

"Thanks for taking me to the session," she said in a monotone voice.

"You're welcome," my father said, smiling and hoping he'd never have to see Dr. Jacobs again.

✧

A few weeks after that therapy session, my mother woke up at 5:00 a.m. and realized my father wasn't home yet. Maybe he was just late. She rolled over and tried to go back to sleep but she just couldn't shake her restlessness. Finally she rose, wrapped herself in a robe, and headed to the kitchen to make some tea. On the way, she peeked into my room to make sure I was still asleep.

She called the Golden 33, but the phone just rang and rang.

As she sat at the kitchen table, her hands gently cupping her mug, she stared at the ticking clock—5:30 a.m., 6:00 a.m., 6:30 a.m. Her thoughts raced. *Maybe he's been in a terrible car accident? Mugged? A bar fight?* But, of course, the most pervasive image in her mind was that he was with another woman.

At about 7:00 a.m., my father finally came home.

He looked disheveled and bleary-eyed, and he seemed surprised to find her in the kitchen.

"Did you just wake up?" he said. He reeked of alcohol and his clothes were damp and sandy.

"Why are you home so late?" my mother asked harshly, looking at him up and down from head to toe. "You look like you've been rolling around in sand."

"I gotta . . . get . . . some sleep. Goodnight, Fran."

"Goodnight!?" my mother screamed. "Anthony, where have you been!? Anthony!" She followed him into the living room as he began climbing the stairs. She stood at the foot of the stairs and continued to yell after him.

"Anthony!"

My father didn't respond.

After this incident, my parents didn't speak for days. My mother contemplated getting another life, maybe even a job. But first she had to know what was happening; what her husband was up to. So, after breakfast one morning, about a week later when I was at school, she questioned him again.

"Anthony, why did you come home so late the other night?"

My father stared at his bacon and eggs, his fork now frozen in his hand. "I told you. I stayed to help Tommy do some restocking and to finish counting the night's receipts. We stayed late and had a couple of drinks, too."

"I called the club. There was no answer."

"We must not have heard the phone, Frannie."

"But why were you all sandy?"

"I wasn't."

She scowled at him while he continued to eat his breakfast.

Later that morning, she arrived home with her arms filled with grocery bags. She went to the kitchen to unpack them and was surprised to find my father.

"Anthony, I'll ask one more time," she said with determination as she set down the grocery bags. "*Please* tell me why you were home so late the other night."

"Don't start this again!" he snapped. "I've already answered your questions. I'm tired and I have a shitload of stuff to do today."

"Who were you with?"

"I was with Tommy! Please stop. You sound crazy again."

"I'm calling Dr. Jacobs. He should know about this," my mother said, as she slammed her hand on the kitchen counter.

"That's not a bad idea," my father said. "I think you *should* call him."

My mother went to the living room to find Dr. Jacobs's card in her purse. When she returned to the kitchen, she picked up the wall phone and dialed.

"Hello, Mark. I'm so glad you answered. I have to talk to you. Anthony came home late the other night and . . . and . . . um . . . um . . . I just don't think he's being honest about where he was," my mother rambled breathlessly.

"Fran, please try to calm down," Dr. Jacobs said.

My mother described her recent confrontations with my father.

"Fran, it's hard for me to say anything, not knowing the context of your interactions. You're too emotional right now to make sense. Can we table this discussion until our next session?"

"Okay, I guess . . . but in the meantime, could you prescribe some sleeping pills? It might calm me down."

She heard Dr. Jacobs sighing into the phone.

"What is it, Mark?" she asked.

"Fran, I'm concerned that you're asking for pills. That isn't a healthy way to deal with your feelings. I'm also afraid that, in your current mental state, pills might be more hazardous than helpful."

"I just need to sleep," she protested urgently. "Please. It is nothing more than that."

"Fran, I'm a psychologist. Not a psychiatrist. I can't prescribe pills. And even if I could, I don't recommend it in your agitated state. I should tell you that I've been considering your case and I've come to the conclusion you may need more medical supervision. I'm going to refer you to a colleague, Dr. Ross. He's a psychiatrist."

My mother started to cry as she said, "I don't want to see another doctor, Mark."

"I don't think my counseling will be enough to help you. We'll talk about all this in our next session."

"I thought things were going well," she sobbed into the phone.

"I'm sorry, Fran, but for you to get better, I think seeing Dr. Ross might be necessary. Please take down his number and we'll continue this conversation next week."

My mother pretended to write down the number, then hung up the phone.

My father was standing in the doorway. He'd heard the entire conversation, and my mother now looked at him with bloodshot eyes. Her face was streaked with tears.

"I'm going to lie down now before I go to pick up Kristin from school," she muttered. She left the kitchen and slowly climbed the stairs. *There is no one who can help me now*, she thought.

Later that afternoon, she called her physician, Dr. Romo, whom she had only seen once, and she easily got a thirty-day prescription for Nembutal.

～⌾～

My mother's side of the family gathered at our house for dinner that Christmas—my grandparents, my mother's siblings and their families. I got loads of presents, including a Barbie townhouse with an elevator, which my cousins wrecked after my father had stayed up all night assembling it.

My father loved Christmas. We always had a huge tree in the living room that touched the ceiling and holiday music was on most December evenings.

The holiday season provided my mother with a much-needed reprieve from the day-to-day arguments with my father. She busied herself pulling together a fabulous Christmas dinner that started with an antipasti of olives, provolone cheese, and soppressata, was followed by our traditional main meal of ravioli and gravy with meatballs and sausage, and ended with cannolis and Italian rum cake for dessert.

In the kitchen after dinner, Grandma Maria, Aunt Dolores, and Aunt Nancy helped serve dessert and wash dishes.

"Frannie, you're looking too thin," Aunt Dolores said, standing alongside her sister at the sink.

"Dolores, I'm fine," my mother said with a weak smile. "It's the colitis. I just can't eat a lot."

"I think with what's going on with Anthony and this health issue are taking their toll," said Aunt Dolores, referring to my mother's hospitalization earlier that year for dehydration.

"Dolores, we can talk about this later," my mother said, giving her sister a stern look.

My mother tried to act as if everything was okay, but Aunt Dolores sensed the truth. Since she lived in Connecticut, it had been frustrating for Aunt Dolores to try to decipher what was happening with Mom. But her conversations with Grandma Maria and my mother gave her enough of an idea. Aunt Dolores sighed and left the kitchen to serve a plate of fresh cannolis and rum cake with coffee. She realized she would not solve this big family problem today.

The evening ended with hugs and kisses and with the children high on sugar and excitement. As my mother closed the door after the last of the family members had departed, she realized that the same problems from before Christmas had not magically disappeared.

"I am going to get Kristin to bed," she said in a whisper to my father. "Can you put some dishes away in the kitchen?"

"Sure. It was a nice holiday, wasn't it Fran?"

"Yes, it was. I love the bracelet you gave me. But I think we went overboard on the presents for Kristin."

Jewelry was my father's way of making things better and it often temporarily stopped some arguments.

"I'm glad you liked the bracelet," he said. "And maybe we did get too many presents for Kristin. But I don't care. She's our only daughter."

My mother nodded but didn't look him in the eye, then walked up the stairs without another word.

⋘⋙

Two days after Christmas, my father was at the Golden 33 and my mother was sitting alone in our living room, crying. She'd held it together long enough to tuck me safely in bed but the rest of the night had seemed to go on forever with so many thoughts swirling through her head.

*I can't stand the other women.*

*I must be unworthy of love.*

*Why is the one person I love never here and chooses to spend time his free time working?*

*Anthony's family hates me.*

*I want to stop feeling this pain.*

*Maybe everyone would be better off if I wasn't here.*

*My life is a total failure.*

*I just don't want to live anymore.*

My mother went upstairs to the bathroom. She opened the medicine cabinet and grabbed the bottle of Nembutal. Then she went back downstairs to sit on the living room couch, where she opened the bottle and counted the pills. There were thirty in all. Would that be enough? She had no idea. But she'd heard that taking pills in large quantities was like "falling asleep and never waking up." It seemed easy. And thirty did seem like a lot of pills.

Maybe this would show Anthony how much pain she was in. Nothing else seemed to get through to him.

She struggled to gain the courage to swallow the pills and, for help, she pulled out a bottle of Wild Turkey. She took big, throat-burning gulps of the liquor. Then she poured the pills into the palm of her hand and popped them to the back of her throat, five at a time, washing them down with more Wild Turkey. It took several gulps, but they were all down within sixty seconds.

Then the panic set in.

*If I'm gone, who's going raise Kristin?*

*My mother will be devastated.*

*I'm scared to die.*

*Will Anthony survive the trials without me?*

My mother ran to the Yellow Pages and looked up the suicide prevention hotline she'd seen on TV. She found the number and quickly dialed, but the line was busy. She hung up, dialed again, but still the line was busy.

Time was running out.

Not knowing what else to do, she called Uncle Jerry's house. Aunt Nancy, Uncle Jerry's wife, answered and realized my mother was in deep distress and quickly went to wake Aunt Dolores, who was staying at her brother's for the holidays, to take my mother's call.

"Dolores, um, I did something bad . . . I need help," my mother wept.

"What, Frannie? What's going on?"

"I . . . . I . . . I took some pills."

"Oh, my God, Frannie. I'm hanging up to call the police. Stay awake! I'll call you right back!"

"Oh God, Dolores, what did I do?" sobbed my mother.

After she called the police, Aunt Dolores furiously searched for the number of the Golden 33. She found the number and called but no one at the club knew where my father was. Next, Aunt Dolores called my father's brother Gabe.

"Gabe! Frannie has taken a bunch of pills! I called the police but I can't find Anthony at the club. Someone's got to get over there right away to stay with Kristin so Frannie can get to the hospital."

Uncle Gabe bolted out the door to find my father.

At the same time, Uncle Jerry left immediately on his way to our house. He sped over the suburban streets with hazard lights on . . . he ran stoplights, all in the hopes of reaching my mother in time.

In the meantime, the police arrived at our house.

My mother was in a heap on the couch, fighting intense grogginess, when she heard knocking at the door.

"Upper Darby Police!"

She managed to stand and look through the peephole. Two uniformed officers were there. She decided that she wouldn't leave me alone in the house. She didn't want to leave with the police.

"Officers, what's going on here?" my mother said rudely, like she'd just been awakened from sleep.

"Ma'am, we got a call that you were in distress and had taken some pills. We're here for a wellness check. Are you okay?"

"I'm fine, thank you very much. I have no idea why you got that call."

"Are you here alone, ma'am?" the other officer asked, trying to peer around my mother to see inside the house.

Again, my mother tried to feign frustration. "Officers, please. My daughter is sleeping upstairs. My husband works nights but he's on his way home."

"Okay, ma'am. Sorry to bother you," the first one said. "If you need anything, please call us."

My mother thanked them and quickly shut the door. The phone rang a few seconds later and she answered it.

"Frannie, why are you still there?" Aunt Dolores asked in horror.

"I don't want to go with the police, Dolores," Mom's speech was starting to slur.

"Oh, my God, Frannie! Stay awake! Anthony and Gabe or Jerry should be there soon."

Aunt Dolores stayed on the phone with my mother until the men arrived.

My father bolted through the back door into the kitchen with Uncle Gabe right behind him. He found my mother with the phone to her ear and her head face down on the kitchen table.

"Frannie! Frannie! Wake up!" My father grabbed the phone receiver. "Dolores? I'm here. Gabe will stay with Kristin. I'm taking Fran to the hospital."

"Call me as soon as you get there. Jerry is on his way —"

But my father had already dropped the phone.

"Gabe, search the garbage cans for the pill bottle," my father barked as he lifted my mother into a standing position and began walking her around like a ragdoll.

"You're finnnally . . . heeere," my mother stammered.

"We're going to the hospital, Fran, right now! What did you take? What did you take?"

"Umm, some stuff there . . ."

Uncle Gabe overturned the garbage can onto the kitchen floor. "Here it is, Anthony!" he said, handing over the empty bottle of Nembutal.

My father carried my mother down the back steps toward his car, and Uncle Gabe helped him ease her into the front seat. Then my father ran around to the driver's side, jumped in, and fired up the engine.

"Fran, why did you do this?! Why did you do this?!" my father yelled.

That was the last thing Mom heard before everything went black.

# 9

## *Lock Down*

The morning after my mother's overdose, I woke up and headed straight for the Christmas tree to play with my unwrapped presents, which still littered the living room floor.

"Good morning," said my Aunt Dolores.

I frowned at her. I had no idea why she was there. "Aunt Dolores?" I said hesitantly. "I want my Lite-Brite."

"Okay, let's get it out," she said, and she got down on her knees to help me pull out the box. "You want breakfast soon?"

"No."

"Okay. That's fine. Let's plug this in and set it up."

The glare from the Lite-Brite set was so exciting—I couldn't wait to pick my stencil to create a new glowing picture.

"You should do the white pegs first," instructed Aunt Dolores. I knew that she was a teacher so I listened obediently. Then she walked into the kitchen, where I saw my father sitting at the table drinking coffee. I played with the Lite-Brite and wondered when my mother would be getting up. Then I heard whispers from the kitchen.

"Frannie is stable for now," my father was saying. "They pumped her stomach and they want to keep her for a few days."

111

"Maybe I should take Kristin to Connecticut," Aunt Dolores whispered. "She can play with my girls and just relax. She'll have a lot of fun."

"No," my father said flatly. "I want her at my mother's."

"That makes no sense. You work all the time and Kristin will be bored at your mother's. There aren't any kids to play with."

"I am *not* sending Kristin to Connecticut. I can see her every day at my mother's."

Though I couldn't see Aunt Dolores's face, I could tell from her voice that she was growing angry. "Anthony, I can only imagine what's going on here based on what my mother tells me and my conversations with Frannie. I just don't know how my sister got to this mental state, and against my better judgment, I won't tell my mother about this. Not yet. Not until Frannie is out of the hospital."

My father nodded emotionlessly. "Frannie will be home in a few days. There's no need to worry your mother."

An icy stand-off followed between my father and aunt. But because they both wanted to help my mother, and me, they decided to silently tolerate each other and to provide a united front.

My father walked into the living room and sat down on the couch to watch me play with the Lite-Brite.

"Little girl?" he said quietly.

I looked up at him.

"Mom is in the hospital for a few days. I'm gonna take you to Grandma Emma's while I'm at work."

"Can't I go with Aunt Dolores? I want to see Donna and Laura."

I had overheard the conversation, so I tried to appeal to my aunt with a sad expression. But Aunt Dolores, who was standing in the doorway, was powerless to sway the outcome. So she just shook her head no.

"Grandma Emma wants to spend time with you, and you're going to have a good time with her," my father said.

I shrugged my shoulders, just to be agreeable, but I felt uneasy about my mother's absence. I didn't understand what my father was saying about the hospital. I barely understood what a "hospital" was.

All I knew was that she'd put me to bed the night before and now she was gone.

"Daddy, was mommy's stomach bothering her again?" I asked.

"Something like that, little girl."

"Anthony, I'm going to my brother's," said Aunt Dolores. Then she hugged me goodbye. "You'll come for a visit to my house real soon, okay? I'll see you later."

I grabbed her tightly, not wanting to let go.

Later, my father helped me pack a few of things for my trip to Grandma Emma's house. But on the car ride there, I protested, "Why can't I go with Aunt Dolores?"

"Grandma Emma really wants to see you," my father said, his voice turning stern, and I noticed that his eyes were red with exhaustion. "There'll be no more discussion about going to Aunt Dolores. Do you understand?"

I looked away from him and nodded.

When we arrived, Grandma Emma clapped with excitement and reached out to hug me. "There's my little chickadee! Do you want some ice cream? I have cups of vanilla and chocolate in the freezer just for you."

My father left shortly thereafter to go to the club, and my grandmother and I went upstairs to make up my bed and to give me a bath. She presented me with a rosary of blue and silver beads that were fun to spin around with my fingers. As I laid down on one of the beds, I stretched the rosary apart with my knees until it broke in two. The broken beads fell to the floor with a loud clatter.

"What happened to the rosary?" Grandma Emma asked.

"I dunno? I was just holding it."

My grandmother just smiled and took what was left of it back. I'd expected her to be angry, but she didn't seem to be upset at all.

When my mother awoke in the hospital, she felt like she was looking through a dark tunnel. Everything around her was hazy. She could only see a faint light at the end of the tunnel where she was barely able to distinguish Aunt Dolores sitting at her bedside.

"Frannie? Frannie? Do you know where you are?" her sister asked her.

"Hmmmm, I guess so. Hospital?"

"Yes, you are."

"So I guess I'm not dead."

"No, you're fine. You were very lucky."

"Where's Kristin?"

"At your mother-in-law's."

My mother nodded slightly, then drifted back to sleep.

Aunt Dolores had stuck to her word and had not told Grandma Maria what had happened. She had also began investigating an inpatient psychiatric program at the University of Pennsylvania Hospital, knowing that my mother wouldn't recover without more help. She didn't take my mother's actions lightly, and since she was traditionally the problem solver in the family, she easily took over in absence of anyone else. My father was overwhelmed with what to do next and seemed open to suggestions.

Meanwhile, over the next few days, my father and Grandma Maria played a game of cat-and-mouse by phone regarding my mother's whereabouts.

"Anthony, is Frannie there?"

"No, Mom. She's out shopping to return some Christmas things," my father said, calling her "Mom" as he always did.

"Well, please have her call me back. She has been out a lot lately."

"You know it's the holidays, Mom."

"Yes, Anthony, I know that."

There were many more calls and my father made various excuses, from shopping to doctor appointments. Grandma Maria began to suspect that something was wrong—and what was most suspicious was that my mother wasn't calling her back.

꧁꧂

My mother was discharged two days after the overdose. When she arrived home with my father, Aunt Dolores was there waiting. I was still at Grandma Emma's. The living room was a mess, with many things out of place, but my mother was too tired to care. She settled in at the kitchen table with a glass of water.

"I want you to consider going to an inpatient program at the University of Pennsylvania," said Aunt Dolores. "They have very good doctors there who can help you feel less depressed."

"But I don't want to do that," my mother said.

"I don't think things are going to improve unless you go."

Mom teared up. "But how long would I have to be there?"

"About two weeks. Though four weeks would be better."

"That's too long. It's just too long. I have to be at home. Where will Kristin stay?"

"At my mother's," my father chimed in from the doorway. "She's been fine there the last couple days, and she can stay there while you're at the hospital."

"We don't want you to hurt yourself again. I think you need help," Aunt Dolores insisted.

"And we can afford it, Frannie. Money's not a problem," said my father.

It took the entire day to convince her. Uncle Jerry arrived and urged her to go and Aunt Dolores continued to make a good case: if my mother took the time, she could feel much better and be better able to take care of me.

"Okay, I'll go," my mother said softly later that night. A bowl of soup sat in front of her that she hadn't touched. Tears were rolling down her face. It was hard to argue with her older sister and brother and her husband, and she was still groggy from the overdose.

"That's good, Frannie," Aunt Dolores said with relief. "You're making the right decision. I'll deal with Mom. Anthony's been telling her you've been shopping or out. But I'll tell her what really happened."

My mother was glad that Aunt Dolores would break the news, but she worried about the repercussions of having kept all this from Grandma Maria.

My mother was organizing some things to check-in to the inpatient program when the phone rang.

"Frannie, is it true?" Grandma Maria wailed. "Were you in the hospital because you took some pills?"

"Yes, Mom, but . . . um . . . I'm okay. I'm going to this program Dolores found."

"Yes, she told me. Oh, my God! You don't sound like yourself, Frannie."

"Uh . . . I'm just tired."

"What is that husband of yours *doing* to you?"

"I don't know, Mom," my mother said, her voice sounded detached and she gazed out the window of her bedroom.

"Anthony lied to me! That dirty rat! And your sister didn't tell me anything! That's it! I'm coming up there right now!"

"Mom, please don't!"

But before my mother could finish her sentence, she heard the dial tone. There was no time to convince Grandma Maria not to come. She would arrive at our house in about half an hour. My father appeared in the bedroom doorway.

"Who were you talking to?"

"My mother. She says she's coming over."

"Let's go out for a ride, Frannie. You'd like to get out of the house, right?"

❦

Grandma Maria was enraged and frantic when she hung up the phone. "Frank! Frank, come upstairs!"

"What's all the screaming about?" Grandpa Frank said when he reached the kitchen door.

"We're going to Frannie's. Now. Let's get in the car. I'll explain on the way," Grandma Maria said while grabbing an umbrella.

My father tried his best to get my mother out of the house as quickly as possible but she was groggy and slow moving. He was escorting her down the front steps when he saw Grandma Maria and Grandpa Frank pull up in front of the house. Grandma Maria jumped out of the car, slammed the door, and started running toward them. Grandpa Frank followed behind, barely keeping up.

"My baby, my baby!" Grandma Maria said as she scurried up the driveway. She embraced my mother, then shot my father a horrible glare. "You bastard!" she sneered. "What did you do to my daughter?"

"Mom, I'm just taking Frannie out for a bit."

"I'm tired," my mother said, sounding a little drugged and still gripping my father's arm for support. "We're just going for a ride, Mom."

Grandma Maria protested but my father opened his car door and began easing his wife into the front seat of the car.

"Frannie, you're not going anywhere with this man!" Grandma Maria cried. "You're coming home with me." She grabbed my mother's arm and began pulling her out of the car.

"Whoa, whoa! Stop it, Maria!" my father said. "I'm just taking Frannie out for a drive. She wants to stay with me."

"Oh, no she doesn't! Get your hands off my daughter!" She started beating my father with her umbrella.

"Mary, stop hitting Anthony," Grandpa Frank pleaded weakly from behind the fray.

"Mom, I'm going with Anthony," my mother said, her voice barely coherent but powerless to stop the struggle while leaning back in the passenger seat.

"My daughter is drugged, you bastard. What did you do to her?!"

My father fended off Grandma Maria, pushing her away to close the passenger door. She lost her balance and fell on the ground. Then, Dad got into the car and peeled out of the driveway, leaving my grandparents behind.

Grandpa Frank helped Grandma Maria off the ground and steadied her onto her feet.

Grandma Maria was not beaten yet. "Frank," she said, "I'm calling the police." She marched over to our neighbor Rosie's house and knocked on the front door. When Rosie answered a moment later, Grandma Maria said, "Can you please help me? I need to use your phone? Anthony is abusing my daughter."

"I heard all the commotion," Rosie said. "Are you okay?"

"No. He just took away my daughter. And he pushed me hard to the ground, too!"

Two police officers were waiting when my parents returned from their drive. My father stepped out of the car, left it running, and approached one of the officers.

"Sir, did you have a confrontation with Mrs. Maria Parrotto?" the officer asked.

"Yes," my father said gravely. "But it was just an argument. Everything's fine."

"Ma'am, are you okay?" the other officer asked my mother, leaning down and looking at her through the car window.

All my mother could do was cry. A few moments later, the officers arrested my father for assault and domestic violence, and, without protest, my mother watched them put him in the back of a squad car. My grandparents stayed with my mother the rest of the day to make sure she was alright, and then eventually left her to rest.

⁓⁓

Later that evening, Grandma Maria arrived home and called Aunt Dolores. "Dolores, I saw Frannie today. She looked awful and drugged. She didn't even look like herself."

"I know, Mom. She's still recovering."

"And Anthony pushed me so hard to the ground when I tried to get to Frannie. He forced her into the car." Grandma Maria was weeping as she spoke. "I think he's abusing her. I called the police and they arrested Anthony."

"He pushed you? He's been arrested? Oh, my God! My friend Rachel is a judge at Delaware County Court. I could talk to her about Anthony."

After a few phone calls, Aunt Dolores successfully had my father held in jail overnight.

⁓⁓

As my father awaited his bond hearing, he made one phone call. "Mom, please drop these charges," he said to Grandma Maria.

There was a long, frigid silence. Finally, Grandma Maria replied, "Absolutely not. Drop dead, Anthony."

"This isn't going to solve any problems. It'll only make things worse."

"I'm going to do whatever I can to stop you from ruining my daughter's life."

The stand-off went nowhere and finally my father hung up. He made bail the next day. My mother had not pressed charges for domestic violence and assault. All the chaos seemed unimportant to her and she was unable to negotiate what was going on around her through her depressed haze. She was preparing to check into the hospital for treatment within a few days.

My father drove my mother to the University of Pennsylvania Hospital located in Center City. They met Uncle Jerry and Aunt Dolores in the main lobby, which was filled with visitors and hospital workers bustling about. They all escorted my mother up to the floor where she would check into the inpatient program. Since she would be voluntarily signing papers to commit herself, family members were at the ready to ensure that she wouldn't back out of the plan. My mother signed on the dotted line and then said goodbye to everyone. I was still safely at Grandma Emma's.

"I hope you're right about this," my mother said, hugging Aunt Dolores and crying.

"It can't hurt, Frannie. It can only help."

Mom hugged her brother. "You'll be out of here before you know it," he said.

Then Mom hugged my father. "I'm so sorry," she whispered into his ear.

"It's okay. Just get better. Listen to the doctors. I'll visit and bring Kristin, too."

My mother was turned over to the hospital staff who quickly escorted her to the locked ward. She looked behind her, gave a weak wave to my father, and then disappeared.

⁓

My mother's first night at the hospital was spent acclimating to the rules of the program. She would have limited access to the outside world, with few phone calls allowed, and monitored visitations only with approved family members. Different types of therapy sessions would be conducted: one-on-one sessions with a psychiatrist, group sessions with other patients, and family sessions with my father or with Grandma Maria and Grandpa Frank (but not all of them together).

Claire, my mother's neighbor in the clinic, was an affable woman who was being treated for Anorexia Nervosa. She was also severely depressed. "Welcome," Claire said as my mother was settling in. "It's nice to meet you."

My mother noticed Claire's skeletal frame, gaunt cheeks, and thinning hair, and she realized that she'd finally met someone thinner than herself. Claire appeared to have lived on the ward for a long while. Photographs covered the walls of her room and she had many personal items from home—blankets, sheets, and piles of books. Mom's room had single bed, a simple dresser, and a small square window with iron bars on it. She unpacked a few things and placed them in drawers, and she tried to get comfortable in her new surroundings. But sleeping here, she knew, would be difficult.

The next morning, my mother approached the nurses' station and asked, "Can you have someone make up my bed?"

"This isn't a hotel, Mrs. Battista," a nurse said coldly without looking at her. "You'll make up your own bed."

"Oh," my mother said in a surprised voice. "I didn't know that."

"And you'll have to hurry to the cafeteria. Breakfast is only served for thirty more minutes."

"And after breakfast I see Dr. Shelton, right?"

"Yes, Mrs. Battista. Here's your schedule for today," the nurse held out a piece of paper. "You better get dressed. You're not allowed to stay in pajamas all day."

The routine at the clinic quickly became apparent. My mother's morning session with the psychiatrist lasted an hour and was followed by a group session. Later was lunch, a late afternoon therapy or family session, then dinner. Visiting hours were in the late afternoon and the evenings ended very early, with lights out by 10 p.m.

As my mother recalled, the group sessions were what most helped her put things into perspective. As crazy as she felt, almost everyone else there seemed to be in much worse shape than she was. Many of the patients were getting daily electric shock treatments and it was horrifying for her to see them groggy and forgetful afterward. And Claire had been at the hospital for more than six months, fiercely battling her anorexia, but it seemed like she was nowhere near winning the war. Her accounts of how she felt fat every time she looked in the mirror—despite *actually* looking like a Nazi concentration camp victim—broke my mother's heart.

Also in the clinic were self-cutters, manic-depressives, and severe agoraphobics for whom even a glimpse of the Philadelphia sky was devastating. And there were several patients who had tried to commit suicide multiple times. Seeing all the suffering around her, my mother began to think she wasn't nearly as sick as some . . . but she did come to realize exactly how depressed she felt.

Even so, after a few days on the ward, my mother had become a social butterfly. She often sat with other patients, listened to their problems, and shared stories. Everyone liked her. She'd always been good at interacting with others. Her sessions were going well but she was still depressed and felt that being separated from me and locked up wasn't helping her. She asked every day if her time there could be shortened. She didn't want to stay the entire four weeks. She was there by her own choosing and she thought there was no reason for her to stay longer than she needed or wanted to.

She received a phone privilege and she called Grandma Emma's house to speak to me.

"Hi, Mom!" I said excitedly. Since she was calling, I thought she must be feeling better.

"Hello, so . . . how have you been doing?"

"Fine. I'm eating ice cream."

"That sounds yummy."

"It is! When are you coming home?"

She sighed into the phone and I could hear the sadness in her voice. "Pretty soon, Kristin. Are you being good for Grandma?"

"Yes."

"That's just great. I'll see you soon. Daddy is bringing you for a visit tomorrow."

"Okay . . . bye, Mommy!"

I went back to busily coloring in the other room and started a new picture of me and my mother holding hands together in front of our house with the dogwood tree in the background. I had missed her and felt like she had been gone a long time. I still did not fully understand why she was sick but I believed what Dad told me—she just needed some rest and would soon be as good as new.

I then overheard my Grandma Emma abruptly shattering the cheerful nature of the phone call. Although I couldn't hear everything she said, she seemed very angry on the phone. Everyone had seemed so mad lately and I figured if I could be on my best behavior, maybe this would help.

"Frannie, everything's fine here. But I have to say, it's awful what you've done."

My mother was stunned silent.

"You need to pull yourself together," Grandma Emma went on. "If you ever pull a stunt like this again, they're going to take Kristin away from you."

My mother slammed down the phone and started screaming. "My babyyyyyyy! I need to get out of here!"

Her wail was deafening, and nurses quickly came rushing into her room.

"Mrs. Battista, please calm down. Who were you talking to?"

"Just leave me alone!"

"Mrs. Battista, please," the nurse said, now holding my mother's hands. Then the nurse screamed towards the nurse's station, "Someone get me a sedative *now*! And call Dr. Shelton right away!"

My mother sobbed uncontrollably. "You can't take away my baby . . ." she repeated over and over, until finally a nurse gave her an injection. My mother felt a rush of warmth and immediately lay down to sleep. This incident was a setback and she knew she might not get home as soon as she had hoped.

Later, Dr. Shelton requested Grandma Emma come in for a session. But she refused. He also discussed with my father and Grandma Maria the prospect of starting electric shock treatments for my mother. My father was willing to authorize whatever the doctors recommended, but Grandma Maria absolutely refused to allow the treatments.

"Don't you touch a hair on her head, or you'll have me to deal with!" she threatened.

The conversation about electric shock did not go any further.

⁓ᘓᘔᘒ⁓

The next day, my father picked me up at Grandma Emma's. I wore a nice dress, tights, and my black Mary Jane shoes. I didn't know what to expect at the hospital and I was nervous. I wondered if my mother would look sick. My father was quiet on the drive to the city and when we arrived at the hospital, we first stopped at the gift shop.

"Pick out something to bring to Mom," said Dad.

I looked through the entire shop, wanting to pick something really nice and special to make my mother feel better, then gravitated toward the big glass refrigerators packed with beautiful flowers.

"I like this one, Daddy," I said, pointing to a slender vase with a few red roses.

"Okay. Let's get this one and go visit Mommy."

I gripped them tightly with one hand and held Dad's hand with the other as he escorted me on the elevator. I wanted to see my mother but hoped she looked like herself. We arrived at her floor and walked down a long, highly polished white hallway. The sound of my heels clicking against the floor reverberated around me until we reached a set of locked metal doors. My father rang a bell and the doors buzzed open. Inside the ward was the big round nurse's station, a common area with a TV, several simple-looking couches, and big windows with a view of the city.

We headed through the common area, then down another long hallway, and finally we stopped in front of a door. I hid the flowers behind my back. My father squeezed my hand and then he pushed the door open.

I saw my mother seated in a chair facing us. Her face was sad and pale and it scared me

"Hi, Frannie," my father said in a near-whisper. "Look who's here to see you."

I came in right behind my father. As I approached my mother, I awkwardly twisted the vase from behind my back and the flowers and water spilled all over the floor.

"Oh . . . I'm sorry . . . Hi Mom," I said meekly, so sad I had ruined the flowers.

"Don't worry, Kristin. Here, let me pick these up," my father said, scrambling on the floor to shove the flowers back into the vase.

I covered my face with my hands.

"Well, hi there," my mother said, fighting back tears. "You look so nice, Kristin." Then she looked at my father and said in a low voice I could barely hear, "Anthony, I just . . . can't do this . . ."

I didn't know what to say or do. I must have ruined the visit.

"Okay, Frannie," he said as he set the ravaged flowers by the window. A moment later, my father had led me into the hallway. "Just wait here for one minute," he said. My father stepped back into the room. I felt like crying and overheard some whispering, then he reappeared. "Let's say a quick goodbye to Mom, okay? She's real tired."

I was marched back into the room, and all I could think to do was to wave, a gesture my mother barely acknowledged. Then we left, and Dad drove me back to Grandma Emma's house. On the way home, it seemed to me like my visit had been a disaster and she didn't seem like she would be home anytime soon. I had ruined everything. If only I hadn't dropped the flowers.

⚬⚬⚬

A few weeks later, my mother was discharged from the hospital, but her doctors recommended that she and my father separate for a while. It was decided that my mother and I would travel to Aunt Dolores's home in Connecticut for a peaceful, two-week stay. There was a ton of snow in New England that year, so my older cousins—Donna and Laura—took me sledding every day in the backyard. It was great fun, but during our snow antics I would glance toward the house and see my mother watching us from the window. I worried about her and it was too heavy a concern for someone of that young age. Whenever I waved at her, she always waved back, but she never moved from that seat until I'd returned into the house. Her motions of helping me take off my coat and boots were quiet and deliberate, as if she were in deep thought contemplating the next steps of her life. And I was helpless to do anything to ease her pain.

# 10

# *The Memphis Trial*

In late January 1976, our house was in exactly the same state my
mother had left it before going to the hospital—like a snapshot of our
lives before her overdose. Open Christmas presents lay at the bottom
of the stairs and stacks of folded laundry and holiday decorations were
arranged on the dining room table. My father hoped that my mother's
time in Connecticut would be a respite, both for him and for her.

But in the beginning of February, he would have to fly to Memphis
to attend pre-trial hearings, and the respite would be over. He was
incredulous that he was about to stand trial simply for distributing
a movie. And even though he'd stopped distributing *Deep Throat*
in November of the previous year, that wouldn't stop the legal
proceedings. Nothing would, it seemed.

My father also needed a lawyer. So far, he had received counsel from
Tony Arnone's lawyer, Robert "Bob" Smith, a hotshot First Amendment
attorney from Atlanta. But Bob had recently advised my father that
he needed his own representation. The time to go to Memphis was
quickly approaching and there was much left to do.

As Dad put away Christmas decorations, his mind wandered back
to the hectic events of the last few years. He had feelings of sadness

and regret, of course, but also the pleasure of some successes, at least financially, and of so-far surviving this whole ordeal. He recalled a 1974 trip to the Peraino's office in Florida, when Bobby DeSalvo had revealed how a good gesture to support Tony Arnone's growing adult theater business had gone terribly wrong and had altered my father's life—an event that had been more and more on his mind lately.

"I still can't figure out why just a few of the distributors were indicted and not everyone," my father said that day to Bobby, who was busy sorting the Philadelphia proceeds. "It's not like I was the only one."

"Well, not everyone has a prime spot at the top of this venture," said Bobby looking thoughtfully at my father with his grayish-blue eyes.

"What?"

"Anthony, Tony Arnone is your best friend. The two of you are business partners. And you started the AMMA Corporation together, am I right?"

"The AMMA Corporation? How is the AMMA connected to *Deep Throat*?" My father shook his head, confused. "Tony and his cousin asked me sign as the president of that company years ago to help them open new theaters in Florida."

"And why would you do that?" Bobby asked, glancing up with one eyebrow raised.

"Because I lived in Philadelphia and they said it would make opening the theaters easier for them and more difficult for Florida law enforcement to shut them down."

"So you're saying . . . you don't know what the AMMA is used for today?"

My father stared blankly.

"Anthony, the AMMA Corporation was pulled off the shelf for our little venture here," and Bobby made a sweeping hand gesture at the piles of cash.

"When did that happen?" my father asked.

"About a year and a half ago, I guess."

"But why . . . why didn't Tony tell me?" my father stammered, rubbing his forehead, his mind beginning to race. "I was just trying to help him."

Mom's family in Wildwood, New Jersey, around 1953. From left to right are her older sister Dolores, her mother Maria, my mom, her father Frank, and her older brother Gerald.

olores, Gerald, and Mom about 1952 at
1e Jersey shore.

My dad with Kitty the ocelot around 1967.

Mom and Dad's wedding day on June 1, 1968.

My parents, Frances and Anthony
Battista, in 1969.

My grandparents, Emma and Antonio
Battista, around 1968.

Grandpa Frank with Kitty about 1968.

Grandma Maria with Kitty about 1970.

Me and Mom in front of our house in Upper Darby, Pennsylvania, around September 1976.

Me and Dad at the beach in 1971.

My parents enjoying a trip to Hawaii in 1973.

At the beach with Grandma Maria in 1973.

Me at age five in 1975.

Celebrating my third birthday with Grandpa Frank.

Me and Mom on Christmas Day in 1975.

In front of our house in Plantation, Florida, in 1978.

Dad and his brother Gabe around 1979 in Gaithersburg, Maryland.

Gabe and Rose Battista.

Dinner at the Plaza Hotel with *Deep Throat* distributors and producers in the fall of 1973. Georgina Spelvin is bottom far right and Bobby DeSalvo is top right.

ANTHONY BATTISTA
LANE THEATRE OWNER

interview of Dad when the area neighbor-
od protested against the Lane Theatre in 1975.
andpa Frank took this picture while watching
e coverage live.

Me and Dad in front of our house in Plantation, Florida, around 1979.

Dad, Mom, Grandma Maria, and me at my high school graduation in 1988.

Mom and Dad at my graduation from Florida State University in 1992.

Me, my husband Brian, and daughter Grace in 2013 at the FSU versus Maryland game in Tallahassee. Go Noles!

"Hmm . . . well, let's wrap up what we're doing here," Bobby said, shrugging his shoulders dismissively. "How about we go to the bank to take your name off the accounts," he offered, sensing my father's anxiety.

Later that afternoon, the two of them left the office to head to American National Bank.

"Little fuckers," said Bobby under his breath as he turned the key in the ignition.

"What are you talking about?"

"You see that church across the street?"

"Yeah."

"Look at the corner. The sedan parked there. We're being watched by the FBI."

"Jesus Christ!" my father said as he turned around and squinted against the sun. He saw a light blue car parked on the side street next to the Covenant Presbyterian Church. Two men were sitting in the front seat.

"Are you being followed in Philly?" asked Bobby.

"I don't think so."

"You probably are."

Later, after their business at the bank, Bobby and my father returned to the office.

"Thanks for your help, Bobby."

"No problem. Hey look, one piece of advice."

"What's that?"

"You think Tony Arnone is your friend?"

"Yeah?"

"I'm here to tell you, he's not. Just keep that in mind."

Bobby's voice was foreboding and my father nodded in acknowledgment of the warning. He didn't want to believe that Tony had intentionally set him up. But the AMMA Corporation's connection to *Deep Throat* might explain why my father had been dragged into the federal case. It was, as far as he could tell, the only explanation.

After that day, my father realized he had willingly signed papers to be the president of the AMMA Corporation. And he knew that blaming

Tony would not solve his immediate problems. Tony's omission about the use of the AMMA Corporation for *Deep Throat* angered him, but it would still be best, my father decided, for them to stick together.

≈≈≈

My parents spoke every day while my mother and I were in Connecticut, but they didn't discuss the events that had led up her overdose. The immediate crisis was over and neither of them was capable at the moment of resolving any underlying issues. My father was distracted by the trials, so he didn't let his mind dwell on the fact he had almost become a widower.

My mother just wanted to go home and not cause any more turmoil.

"How's Kristin?" my father asked during one of their many evening phone conversations.

"She's fine," my mother said. "She's having a good time with her cousins."

"I'm glad. Frannie?"

"Yes?"

"When do you think you might be coming home?"

"I think in a few days. I want to be in my own house."

"Good," my father said, sighing in relief. "I'm glad. It'll be good to have you both home. I'm just sorry that I'll have to leave so soon."

"We knew this was coming," my mother said quietly. "We don't have a choice."

When we arrived home a few days later, we fell immediately back into our regular routine, almost as if nothing had happened. The feelings of the past—and fears about the future—were put on hold. We all seemed to be collectively holding our breath. My father compartmentalized certain areas of his life; he resolved to stay focused on surviving the next bump in the road and nothing more.

≈≈≈

While sitting alone in our kitchen one morning, my father picked up the phone and dialed Memphis information to find an attorney. After a few calls, he reached Brett Stein of Finely, Stein & Kuhn Law

Offices, who quickly agreed to take his case. Brett's firm, my father would learn, had a solid reputation for taking cases that other lawyers considered to be underdogs.

"Mr. Battista, my partner Phillip Kuhn and I will meet you at our offices when you arrive for the pre-trial hearings," said Brett.

Brett hung up the phone, and then he strode purposefully toward Phillip's desk, the thud of his cowboy boots echoing through their small office space.

"We just got a new case!" Brett said triumphantly.

"Yeah? What's it about?" Phillip asked, somewhat distractedly as he prepared a brief for another client.

"His name is Anthony Battista, a stockbroker from Philadelphia. He's indicted on obscenity charges in that pornography case about *Deep Throat*. The pre-trial hearings will start in a couple weeks in Judge Wellford's court."

Phillip looked up. "That's pretty soon, Brett."

"It's enough time."

"But we don't have experience in pornography cases and we're very busy," Phillip countered doubtfully. "You're crazy for taking this."

"You have a civil rights background, and this case has First Amendment implications. What're you worried about?"

"I just hate it when you spring stuff on me."

"I told Mr. Battista we'd meet him the day before the hearing to discuss his case," Brett said, disregarding Phillip's protests. "He's flying down at the end of the month."

"How long you think this trial is going to last?"

"Maybe a couple of days?" said Brett.

"That's probably about right."

Phillip shook his head and for a moment he worried that Brett may not be able to do much work on this case, given the firm's workload. But then he laughed quietly to himself. He was always ready for a challenge.

Arriving for work a few weeks later, Phillip found a young man standing alone in his office's small waiting area. "Mr. Battista? I'm Phillip Kuhn, your lawyer. You talked to my partner, Brett Stein, earlier this month."

The two men shook hands.

Dad was immediately struck by how much Phillip looked like Abraham Lincoln. The man was in his mid-thirties, with dark hair and a tall, lanky frame. My father would later learn that Phillip had run for Congress in 1972 and that he had been involved with many groups associated with the civil rights movement and was well liked in the black community.

Phillip escorted my father to Brett's office. Brett was seated behind his desk and he immediately rose to greet my father. Brett's cowboy boots, dark Jewish features, and the firecracker pep in his voice all made my father feel right at home. Brett was not a typical southerner, but he had made a home for himself in Memphis. Maybe there was hope yet for my father to win over a Memphis jury.

The men sat down and Phillip opened his briefcase and spread an array of papers out on Brett's desk. They discussed the pre-trial hearings first.

"This pre-trial's just gonna be standard procedure stuff," Phillip said. "Basically, the judge will call on us to acknowledge that you understand the charges against you and that you'll come back to Memphis for the trial. If you don't come back, that will be grounds for throwing you in jail. Got it?"

"Got it."

"Then there will be other procedures discussed about witnesses, jury selection, and how the trial will work," Brett said. "Simple stuff."

"Okay," my father said, relieved by Phillip and Brett's confidence.

The next day, when Phillip and Brett arrived at Judge Wellford's courtroom, about two hundred people were standing around waiting for the proceedings to begin. The courthouse was a massive open space with marble floors, wide columns, and a large wooden judge's bench slightly elevated over the court. Both lawyers thought, *The judge must have a lot of people on his docket today,* but they would quickly realize that everyone was here for one case.

*Deep Throat.*

My father was already there with Tony and Bob and he waved Phillip and Brett over to where they were sitting. Everyone settled into the courtroom's wooden benches.

My father glanced to his right and across the room he saw, for the first time in person, the man responsible for dragging him to Memphis. Larry Parrish, the case's prosecutor and the Assistant US Attorney, was sitting alone with stacks of notebooks at his side. Parrish was famously known as a good Christian, a fundamentalist, and a member of the Evangelical Church. He was outspokenly dedicated to ridding America of pornography. His nicknames were The Memphis Heat, Mr. Clean, and the Smut Raker. His reputation was growing as the most active and successful prosecutor on obscenity and for the fiery speeches he gave to juries.

Despite Parrish's bigger-than-life persona reported by the media, he looked rather ordinary to my father. He wore a simple brown suit and he was not glad-handing the room as one might have expected. Could this be the same person my father had read about and seen on TV? He would soon find out. From what my father had read and seen, Parrish certainly had grandiose ideas about conspiracy and misplaced energy placed on upholding a law that nobody otherwise would probably care about. Parrish had a laser focus on the task at hand—to put my father in jail.

"Phillip, what do you know about Larry Parrish?" my father asked his lawyer.

"Umm . . . well . . . he's an able prosecutor. And a zealot who is infinitely prepared."

Just then, Herbert Streicher—a.k.a. "Harry Reems," the male lead of *Deep Throat*—entered the courtroom with his lawyer, Bruce Kramer, president of the West Tennessee Chapter of the ACLU. Gerard Damiano, the film's director, and Linda Lovelace, Harry Reems's co-star, had been granted immunity in exchange for their testimony for the prosecution. All eyes followed Reems. He was the real star attraction of this trial.

Then Michael Cherubino, Louis Peraino, Sr., and Joseph Peraino, the film's producers, entered the room. They were all dressed in leisure suits and dark sunglasses, and they gathered on the defendants' side of the courtroom.

My father looked around for Bobby DeSalvo. But Bobby was nowhere to be found.

※※※

After the pre-trial hearings, which lasted only a few hours, the courtroom was abuzz about the absence of Bobby DeSalvo. A rumor circulated that Bobby was a fugitive living in the Bahamas.

"Do you really think Bobby DeSalvo is in the Bahamas?" my father asked his partner Tony Arnone.

"I don't know," Tony said, shrugging his shoulders.

"I'm not surprised," my father said after more contemplation. "Why would he want to stand trial?"

My father hadn't spoken to Bobby in at least four months, since he stopped distributing *Deep Throat*, and he had not seen Bobby for nearly two years, since the fall of 1974, when they'd gone together to American National Bank. Before the trial, another rumor had surfaced that Bobby had been whacked by the Perainos in England, where he'd gone to collect money he thought the Perainos owed him. Even if this story wasn't true, my father and Tony knew they'd done the right thing by distancing themselves from the Perainos.

Years later, when I asked my father about Bobby DeSalvo's disappearance, he said, "Bobby didn't have lick of sense. Like Pussy in the TV show *The Sopranos*, no one ever saw him again."

※※※

Phillip Kuhn called my father in Philadelphia just before the trial was set to begin on March 1, 1976. My father planned to drive to Memphis in just a few days.

"Any news?" Dad asked.

"Well, the trial is here. We're ready. But I hear Larry Parrish has developed a witness list of more than five hundred people and he has a truckload of experts lined up to testify. Judge Wellford is going to have a fit."

"Jesus Christ. Who's he bringing in?"

"Just about anyone who may have touched the film before it got to Memphis. And lots of psychiatrists and social scientists."

"This whole thing is ridiculous."

"Well, the judge is probably going to make him cut the list. But this trial is going to last longer than I thought."

My father shook his head. "Well, I will be staying at an apartment with Tony Arnone and Bob Smith. I'm in for the long haul."

"That's good," Phillip said. "But I have to tell you, the government is extremely well prepared. They've been collecting evidence for a long time. The IRS and FBI have had all the defendants, including you, under surveillance for at least a year prior to the arrests."

"I was warned about the FBI," my father said, and he thought back to Bobby DeSalvo's warning. "What do you think our chances are?"

"Hard to tell. Maybe fifty-fifty? But let's see how things go before we come to any conclusions."

My father murmured in agreement.

"Do you think your wife and daughter could make an appearance at the trial? It might make a good impression on the jury."

Dad was adamant. "I don't want them involved. Let's keep them out of this."

My father knew he was lucky that Phillip and Brett were his attorneys. The three of them had established a great working relationship and even though the trial was going to take much longer than Phillip and Brett had originally thought, they had not asked my father for any additional money. This was a relief, since my father had to pay his own legal fees.

〜✿〜

Both of my parents entered my bedroom before dawn on the day my father was to drive to Memphis. Dad knelt by the side of my bed and touched my shoulder to wake me from a deep sleep.

"Honey, Daddy is leaving. I just wanted to say goodbye."

I rolled over and rubbed the sleep out of my eyes. I tried to focus on his face.

"Okay, I'll see you soon," I said sleepily, and I hugged him tight around the neck.

He hugged me back. "I'll be back as soon as I can," he said.

Over my father's shoulder, I saw my mother leaning against the door frame and watching us with her arms crossed. She wore a robe and her curly black hair was everywhere on the top her head. She looked like she wanted to go back to bed.

"Try to go back to sleep," my father whispered to me. "I love you."

"I love you too, Daddy."

As my father left the room, I had a horrible feeling in my stomach. In a short amount of time, I had experienced the absence of at least one of my parents, with the first being my mother's hospitalization and then my father's trial.

I heard my parents whispering in the hallway.

"Don't forget, Tommy will have money waiting for you every week. Just go to the club to pick it up," my father said.

"Okay, I will."

Then I heard all the sounds of my father leaving the house: his footsteps down the stairs, the front door closing, and his Thunderbird rumbling down the driveway. I never went back to sleep. I wondered when I might see him again. In my young mind, it seemed he might be gone forever.

⚘

For my father, Memphis was an interesting, charming southern town nestled along the Mississippi River. The streets oozed with its music history; homages in the form of statues, street names, and restaurant menu items, to Elvis Presley, Aretha Franklin, B. B. King, and other legendary musicians were everywhere. But under the surface, the city still carried its painful past as the place where Martin Luther King, Jr. had been assassinated and where many ugly battles of the civil rights movement had been fought. Some people, my father noticed, still held tight to racist traditions while hiding behind friendly smiles.

My father pulled his car into the parking lot of an apartment complex located in the suburbs just outside the city. He got out and stretched, then grabbed his suitcase from the trunk. He had two more hanging bags he'd left in the car; he'd brought every single suit he owned to Memphis. It had been a long time since he had worn a suit.

My father walked up to the second floor to an apartment that faced a garden courtyard. He knocked, then turned the knob, and found that the door was unlocked. Tony Arnone emerged from the back bedroom.

"You made it!" Tony said. "Good to see you!"

"Likewise," my father said. "When did you get in?"

"Yesterday. Here, I got an extra set of keys for you," Tony said, tossing them to him. "Bob should be coming in tonight."

"This place isn't bad."

The apartment had three bedrooms and one bathroom. It was modestly furnished and, like a typical bachelor pad, sparsely decorated.

As my father unpacked, he caught up with Tony.

"So, what are Bob's thoughts about the trial?" he asked.

"Bob thinks we're outsiders here. We'll be associated with the Perainos and the jury may have an immediate distrust of us because we're not from the south."

"Phillip's saying the same thing," Dad said, feeling grateful that at least his lawyers were from Memphis.

"But people here have been pretty nice," Tony said, "At least they don't *seem* to hate Yankees."

"Good old southern hospitality. While we are here we should at least get some good barbeque."

Tony laughed then asked, "How's Frannie?"

"She's okay. We're working things out. How are Pat and the kids?"

"They're all okay."

They sat together in silence for a moment thinking of their respective homes they had left behind.

"Well, I'll finish unpacking. You want to drive around town later, figure out where things are?"

"Sure, we can do that," said Tony.

On the first day of the trial, Bob, Tony, and my father woke up early feeling like it was the first day of school or the start of a new job. The day my father had hoped would never come had finally arrived. In the kitchen, Bob sipped coffee and read the *Memphis Commercial Appeal*. He was always impeccably dressed and had a flamboyant, big-city style. His Irish good looks, which turned reddish when he drank, matched his sharp wits in the courtroom. He also had a reputation as a ladies' man, and he had a girlfriend in addition to a gorgeous wife.

"We made the papers," Bob said, slightly impressed.

"Let me see that," said Tony. He sat down at the table with Bob.

Dad poured himself a cup of coffee at the counter. "What does it say?" he asked.

"It's just a small article called '*Deep Throat* Trials Start Today.' Our names are listed as defendants," Tony said, and he slid the paper across the table toward my father.

"By the way," Bob said, "you guys both look great. I have to say, the three-piece suits are a nice touch. You need to play the part of the college boys. The government is after the mob here, so don't dress like them. And remember, keep your distance from the Perainos."

~%~

The courtroom was a circus. Members of the press jammed the hallways and the gallery to report on the court proceedings. The media people didn't seem at all bothered that Judge Wellford had banned news cameras from the trial at the urging of Harry Reems's attorney, Bruce Kramer.

My father, Tony, and Bob made their way through the throng of people—most of whom were just there to see Harry Reems—and found their place at the defense table. Phillip was there waiting for my father.

There was still no sign of Bobby DeSalvo.

My father began to sweat a little at the temples. He took a drink of water that he swallowed hard against his dry throat.

"All rise for the Honorable US District Judge Harry W. Wellford," a bailiff called out.

Everyone stood as Judge Wellford entered the courtroom. He was a short and stocky man in his fifties, and he had a very fast gait, like a military officer. He was known to be part of Memphis society and had been a corporate attorney before being appointed to the bench. Most lawyers described Judge Wellford as feisty and as someone who expected strict decorum in the courtroom.

My father took a deep breath. He glanced at Tony. They nodded at each other, ready to begin.

Jury selection lasted for three days. Eight women (each of whom wore Sunday church dresses) and four men were selected, and they were divided evenly between white and black. My father remembers Phillip mentioning that the fewer African American woman on the jury the better, since, in his opinion, they had a reputation for hating oral sex. In any case, my father's chances of encountering an open-minded jury were not great because the pool of candidates had been taken from rural parts of Tennessee, which made up most of this federal jurisdiction.

During opening statements, Michael Pelle, Louis Damiano's attorney, characterized his client and his family as "good Italian boys who grew up in New Jersey that had children to feed," while Larry Parrish, the prosecutor, would counter with claims about the strong-arm tactics used by the *Deep Throat* organization, such as threats and intimidation, and even the suspected murder of a government informant.

Parrish, later in his own opening statement, recounted the early partnership of Gerard Damiano, *Deep Throat's* director, and Louis Peraino to coproduce the film. According to Parrish, Damiano had later sold his interest in *Deep Throat* for $25,000 under pressure to the Perainos.

My father and Tony Arnone slogged through long days in court. One day, they listened to the testimony of Damiano and Chuck Traynor, Linda Lovelace's ex-husband. They both talked about how the various *Deep Throat* players had met and about how Damiano—a one-time Brooklyn hairdresser—had created this cinematic phenomenon, conceiving of the film's crazy plot based on oral sex scenes Linda had performed for one of his other movies.

"Do you consider this movie to have any artistic value?" Parrish asked Damiano under oath.

"Oh, yes. It is not artistic in the sense of Greek tragedy, but it is a comedy, a farce, a social statement of our time. But if I was shooting this film today, I would include less sex and more plot."

"You think that would improve the artistic standard?" Parrish asked.

"By today's standards, yes. But when you take everything into consideration, it's probably the most successful movie ever made." He was alluding to *Deep Throat*'s estimated grosses of $25 million.

In addition to the film history lesson, Parrish repeatedly introduced the testimony of witnesses about the threats of murder and violence in connection with distributing the movie. Judge Wellford finally objected, stating that these alleged crimes were not part of these proceedings. But Parrish effectively argued that every witness needed to tell his whole story in order to avoid perjuring himself. Judge Wellford then allowed some of the testimony about the violence.

Parrish even called Uncle Coke as witness for the prosecution; Uncle Coke was, after all, a theater checker for my father in the Philadelphia area. On his day in court, Uncle Coke appeared wearing a new suit, though he still had all the attitude of a blue-collar working man.

"What is your relationship to Anthony Battista?" Parrish asked him.

"He's my nephew," Uncle Coke responded curtly.

"Did you go to the Johnstown Theater for Anthony Battista?" Parrish asked.

"Yes."

"Did you deliver money and films to Anthony Battista regarding *Deep Throat*?"

"Yes."

After answering only yes or no to an hour-long series of questions, Uncle Coke stepped down from the stand. Then he sat next to my father and said, referring to Parrish, "Boy, this one is stating the obvious, huh?"

The case was reported in the newspaper and on local and national TV almost daily, and everyone was anxiously awaiting the arrival of Linda Lovelace to testify. Unfortunately, she never appeared and was rumored to be hiding in Mexico.

During the proceedings, my father and Tony Arnone's names were brought up repeatedly by the prosecution, connecting them to the national distribution network for *Deep Throat*. Also, my father's title as president of the AMMA Corporation was constantly highlighted.

Because their days in the courtroom were stressful, my father tried to relax by enjoying the nightlife in Memphis. He went out to dinner most evenings with Phillip and Brett or with Tony and Bob. Memphis was an exciting city and it gave my father a chance to indulge in his love for live music. In particular, he liked to frequent the blues bars on Beale Street.

"Tony, we're going to Caroline's," my father said one night. "Come with us?" Caroline's was a friendly country western bar that featured southern rock, like Lynyrd Skynyrd, and great food. It had become a frequent hangout for my father and the *Deep Throat* gang.

"No, I'll pass," Tony said. "I don't like that kind of music." On most nights after dinner, Tony just went back to the apartment.

"Suit yourself."

My father, the other defendants, and their lawyers were treated like local celebrities whenever they went out. And conversations always revolved around the trial.

"Do you think Judge Wellford will allow Warren Beatty and Jack Nicholson to testify?" my father asked one night, referring to Hollywood's intense interest in this trial for fear that actors would now be prosecuted by the law for artistic expression.

"I don't know," Phillip said, taking a sip of beer. "I don't think so, but Tony Bill, the director of *The Sting*, will."

"I hope his testimony helps."

"Wellford is already pissed that this trial has lasted so long," said Phillip.

"I can't believe it's almost the beginning of April. Has it been six weeks already?"

"Yeah, I know. It's been a long haul. Harry Reems loves the media attention though."

My father shook his head and laughed to himself.

"Let me tell you a funny story," Phillip went on. "I was in the elevator the other day with Harry and this reporter from *U.S. News and World Report*. Reems started talking to him about how Hollywood supports him and all the fundraisers being thrown for his legal defense all over the country. The reporter just looked at Reems and said, 'Look, I'm writing for the legal section, not the fucking leisure living section.' I almost died laughing."

"Jesus Christ, that's the funniest story I've heard in a while!" my father said, holding his sides while chuckling.

Then they both stopped laughing—the seriousness of their situation descending on them, as usual, in sudden downpours.

"Well," Phillip said, "this case has a lot of colorful characters, which isn't necessarily good for us. And I think the judge is going to allow a screening of the film. If that happens, it won't be good for us at all."

The following week, on a Monday at 9:30 a.m., a special screening of *Deep Throat* was held for jurors. Defendants, their lawyers, and the prosecutors also attended. In a nine-hundred-seat theater in downtown Memphis, gasps could be heard from jurors viewing the jarring, sexually explicit visuals. It was like nothing any of them had ever experienced.

~⚬~

A few weeks later, on April 30, 1976, a verdict was reached. Deliberations had only lasted twenty minutes, so as the jury foreman—a credit manager at Firestone Tire and Rubber—began to read the decision, my father was expecting a guilty verdict.

"We find the defendants guilty on all obscenity charges and nationwide conspiracy to distribute *Deep Throat* to Memphis."

My father looked straight ahead after the guilty verdicts were read. When it was finished, a burst of energy erupted in the courtroom with loud conversation and people moving about. He turned to Phillip.

"Don't worry," Phillip said steadily. "We'll appeal."

"I know."

Dad looked at the prosecutors. They were congratulating one other and many reached to shake Larry Parrish's hand. He looked pleased— smiling like the cat that ate the canary. This angered my father. Parrish's misguided notion of justice, he thought, was just a waste of everyone's time. He wasn't protecting society, as he claimed, since the viewing of a movie was voluntary. It was also infuriating that while Parrish had claimed he would never argue with what a man does in private, that was clearly what he had done in this trial. Also his prosecution of the case seemed to be colored by his own personal religious views.

Later that day, one female juror member, a waitress, was quoted in the newspaper as saying, "[*Deep Throat*] was the most disgusting thing I had ever seen. People had to be sick to pay good money to see this movie."

⁂

"Frannie, they found us guilty," my father said simply over the phone.

There was a long silence. My father had kept my mother informed about the trial in almost daily phone calls home, so she had been expecting this outcome.

"But this isn't over, right?" she asked.

"No, it's not."

"Okay."

"We're going to appeal. And I'm coming home."

"Well, that's good news."

"The prosecution will decide sentencing in a few weeks. Nothing will happen yet."

⁂

"We've been railroaded!" my father said in frustration as he was packing to return home.

"I know," said Tony. "We never had a chance for a fair trial in Memphis."

"This is a nightmare!"

"Anthony . . ."

"I never would have thought being involved with some stupid movie would turn out like this."

"I don't think it's anything *anyone* could have anticipated," Tony said in a low voice.

My father turned from his packing and stared Tony dead in the face. "You know, I wish you'd have told me the AMMA Corporation was being used to distribute *Deep Throat*. Why didn't you tell me? You and your cousin, Tony De Pra, said you would tell me when you used the company. You used my fucking name. I should have had the opportunity to make decisions."

"AMMA wasn't the reason you were dragged into this, Anthony. A lot of corporations were used to distribute *Deep Throat*."

"But my name was mentioned as the president of AMMA, not yours, a bunch of times."

Tony raised his voice, "Do you think I wanted any of this to happen?"

"I think you wanted to make money! And you didn't think about how it would affect anyone else!"

"Look, you were indicted because we're friends and business partners. There's no proof AMMA is why you were arrested."

"Sure," my father said, disgusted.

"I'd never want anything bad to happen to you or your family, Anthony. How long have we known each other?"

"A long time. Maybe too long."

"Come on . . ." Tony pleaded. "It seems like yesterday Pat and I lived on the third floor of your grandmother's house and we sat next to each other in economics class at Villanova. I was a groomsman at your wedding, for Christ's sake!"

They stood staring at each other for a long time.

Finally, my father's expression softened. "I'm just frustrated," Dad said quietly.

"We're not giving up," Tony replied. "We'll appeal to the Supreme Court if we have to."

Dad was up for the fight, especially if he had someone willing to fight at his side.

This guilty verdict was only the first of many hurdles yet to come.

# 11

# *Let the Sun Shine In*

My father returned from Memphis—after a two-and-half month absence—to an empty house. He set his bags just inside the front door, gazed around the living room, and let out a sigh of relief. He noticed that nothing in the house seemed to have changed. His life was just as he had left it.

"Anthony!" my mother called out a few minutes later as she opened the front door. "Are you home?"

Holding my hand, she guided me inside.

"I'm here!" my father said happily, rushing into the living room.

"Daddy, Daddy, Daddy!" I squealed, jumping up and down. "You're home!"

"How are you, little girl?" he said, picking me up and hugging me like always.

"I'm fine, Daddy."

"You look taller."

"I didn't realize you'd be here this afternoon," my mother said, leaning in to kiss his cheek.

"I'm so glad to be home," he said.

She smiled. "It's nice to have you back." Although her voice was metered and her body tense, my mother was truly pleased that my father was home. But she had grown accustomed to his absence and would now have to get used to his presence.

In many ways, for both of my parents, this was a homecoming with little to celebrate. The guilty verdict meant we were still awaiting sentencing as well as an appeal. Things could easily go from bad to worse.

⤙❦⤚

While we waited for my father's sentencing, decisions in other high-profile obscenity cases—which were being prosecuted simultaneously all over the country—were rapidly changing the legal landscape around pornography. This would ultimately impact the *Deep Throat* case.

For example, in July 1976, Robert Bork, the US Solicitor General from the Sixth Circuit Court in Cincinnati, asked the Supreme Court on behalf of the Justice Department and was granted a new trial in a Kentucky obscenity case (Marx versus the United States). This case convicted theater owners in Kentucky for showing *Deep Throat*. Bork believed, and the Justice Department brief stated, that the convictions in Kentucky had been unfair because the "offenses" had occurred before the obscenity law was changed with the 1973 Supreme Court ruling in Miller versus California, which granted local communities the right to determine obscenity standards. Also in 1973, the definition of *obscenity* had changed from "utterly without redeeming social value" to "lacks serious literary, artistic, political, or scientific value." The Kentucky case was similar to the Memphis case, so it was believed that what happened there might lead to a new trial for those convicted in Memphis.

About this development, Larry Parrish was quoted in a UPI article as saying, "To think the US Solicitor General would even entertain such a thought is the most deplorable thing I can imagine."

⤙❦⤚

"The sentencing is delayed at least until September, which will also push back any new trial for us," Phillip Kuhn said in a phone call with my father a few months after the conclusion of the Memphis trial. "Everyone is waiting for the Supreme Court to weigh in on the Bork brief from the justice department on the Kentucky case. Whatever that decision, it will impact us."

"That's good news, right?" my father asked.

"Absolutely. But even with a new trial, if we can't change the venue, it's very possible we'll end up with the same verdict as before."

My father digested the mixed news. Finally he said, "But the longer this is delayed, the better, right?"

"Well, as things change over time . . . yes, a delay might help."

"I understand," said Dad, his voice both hopeful and somewhat somber. "Well, that's something."

"One problem," Phillip went on. "Larry Parrish is still pushing for the defendants to pay the government for the cost of the trial. They're estimating at about $500,000 for the whole trial but we still have to press for more detail here. It's a ridiculous cost assessment."

My father laughed heartlessly. "Jesus, they're just not going to stop, are they?"

"No, they won't. But it seems to me that this whole case is taking another turn. Really. We have reason to be optimistic."

There were many delays as the Bork brief on the Kentucky case awaited a Supreme Court decision. They finally weighed in on March 2, 1977, and overturned the Kentucky convictions. As a result, in April 1977, Harry Reems's conviction in Memphis was overturned by US Attorney Mike Cody, who had taken over for Larry Parrish when he left the US Attorney's office earlier that year but was retained as a special prosecutor. Cody had agreed with the Bork brief on the Kentucky case that the obscenity standards established by the 1973 Supreme Court ruling should not have been used in the *Deep Throat* case in Memphis against Reems.

But while Reems enjoyed a mighty victory, the convictions for everyone else in the case (including my father) were upheld.

On April 29, 1977, about a year after the verdicts were reached in the trial, my father was sentenced to four months in prison and given a $4,000 fine, while Tony Arnone was sentenced to five months in prison and a $6,000 fine. Both were put on probation and barred from dealing with obscene material. Appeals were filed. A mistrial decision for the distributors' conviction was still possible due to some discovered error in the instruction of the jury, according to my father's lawyers, but it was not at all assured.

Everyone just waited.

～❧～

I didn't realized until I was older that *Deep Throat* was the reason we had moved from Philadelphia to Fort Lauderdale in the summer of 1977, when I was six years old. By the time of my father's sentencing, he had acquired interests in three adult movie theaters in Florida, in addition to still running the Golden 33 in Philadelphia. The Golden 33 had been open for three years, and while it was still flourishing, my parents' marriage had suffered. My father was ready to leave the club behind and make a bold move for our family.

"It's beautiful down here today," my father said cheerfully to my mother on the phone. He was on another business trip to Florida for the theaters, which had become more frequent in the past year. "Eighty degrees and sunny, just like it is every day."

"Oh, sounds nice," my mother cooed back happily. "I wish Philly was that warm."

"If we move here, Frannie, you could be warm all year round. And you'd never have to shovel snow again."

My mother wasn't quite convinced. "I just don't know, Anthony. I might miss the change of seasons. And what about our families?"

"I know, Frannie. I have some hesitations about moving, too. But my business is here."

My mother agreed.

"The Arnones have lived down here a while. They love it. Pat, Tony's wife, could tell you all about it," my father offered.

"Sure, I could talk to Pat."

"I think Florida might give us the fresh start we deserve."

"A fresh start sounds nice."

"Yes, it does. We can talk about this when I get home."

When my mother hung up the phone that day, she started daydreaming about sunny blue skies, pools, and sandy beaches. Living near the beach sounded like being on vacation all year round.

And most enticing of all was that moving to Florida meant my father would leave the Golden 33.

But just as she allowed herself to entertain the idea of moving to Florida, she immediately felt guilty, even terrified, about leaving Philadelphia. She didn't want to move away from her parents. And she knew that living in a brand new place, after a lifetime spent in her hometown, would be difficult.

"Anthony called today from Florida and he still wants to move there," Mom told Grandma Maria on the phone. Then she added hesitantly, "I don't think moving would be a bad idea."

"Well," Grandma Maria said, "I've been thinking, since the last time you mentioned it, maybe moving to Florida would be okay." She had put the turmoil of the past behind her and honored her daughter's commitment to her marriage. Grandma Maria also understood the draw of an unconventional business since her own father had been a bootlegger.

My mother was stunned. "Really?" she said. "But you have said that you didn't want us to go. What changed your mind?"

"Well, honey, Anthony *needs* to get away from the club. He can't run that business forever. And he has the theaters in Florida. It just seems to make sense."

Mom agreed, though she couldn't believe what she was hearing.

"But if you decide to move," Grandma Maria said, her voice beginning to shake, "I'll miss you and Kristin terribly."

When they hung up, Grandma Maria wept. To encourage her youngest daughter to move more than a thousand miles away felt ludicrous. She couldn't believe she'd just done it. But, unbeknownst to my mother, my father had visited Grandma Maria a few weeks earlier and had broached the subject.

"Thanks for seeing me," my father had said on that visit. The two of them were sipping coffee at Grandma Maria's kitchen table. In the last year, they had gotten along fairly well. They held an odd mutual respect for each other and a deep love for me and my mother that forced them to both accept each other as family. In the end, she always liked my father despite their rocky relationship.

"Of course, Anthony. What's on your mind?"

"I'm sure Frannie has mentioned that we're considering moving to Florida."

Grandma Maria eyed her son-in-law closely. "It's too far away, Anthony. You both should be around family."

"I know it's far, Mom. And I don't want to leave my family either. But I have no other business opportunities here. None."

"Well, I can appreciate that, but . . ."

"And I'd like to get away from the club, Mom. I don't want that kind of life . . . working nights, the chaos," my father said bluntly. "And I know Frannie hates it. I really think Florida might be a chance for a better life."

Grandma Maria looked at him skeptically but she couldn't deny the seriousness in his eyes. She also realized there were bigger things to consider, things over which she had no control—like how my father had chosen to earn a living. It had been more than a year since the Memphis trial and over the past few months my parents had been getting along better.

"Leaving the club would be a good thing," she said in a resigned tone.

"But Frannie is *not* going to move unless you're okay with it," my father said. "I'm asking for your support here."

"Okay . . ." Grandma Maria said with a heavy sigh. Then her tone turned more serious: "But, if *anything* bad happens to my daughter and my granddaughter in Florida, I'll kill you."

My father smiled. Then he stood, walked around the kitchen table, and hugged Grandma Maria.

"Okay, Mom," he said laughing. "And I know you mean that, too."

&#8766;

"Okay, let's move to Florida," my mother said one day, completely out of the blue. Her voice was a little giddy

"Really?" said Dad.

"Yes. Really, let's go!"

Dad hugged her. "Frannie, we're going to get a new house with a pool. You'll see. This is going to be a great move for us."

"I think so, too."

Now that my mother was on board, it became her job to prepare me for the move.

"Where's Florida?" I remember asking her one evening.

"It's where Disney World is."

"Disney World!" I said, and I immediately pictured myself prancing around the Magic Kingdom. It was the happiest I had been in a while.

"That's right."

"Are Grandma and Grandpa coming, too?"

"No, they aren't. But they'll visit us soon and then we'll all go to Disney World."

I thought carefully about what my mother had said. "But I don't want to go unless they're going."

"Come here. Let me show you something." On the living room carpet, my mother rolled out a large blueprint of our new house. I got down on my hands and knees next to her and I studied it with amazement.

"Here's your new room," said Mom. She pointed to a large square drawn at the front of the house. It looked much bigger in comparison to the other rooms.

"And here is the family room off the patio," she went on. "And the best part is, we'll have our own swimming pool."

"Really?"

"Yes!"

I looked at the blueprint again. "This is a pretty house!" I said in amazement.

But as our moving date drew closer, my parents grew more conflicted about leaving their hometown. Pat and Geno's cheesesteaks, their favorite Italian stores, and, most importantly, family and friends would soon be far away. My father hoped that we might return to Philadelphia once the case was over; a few years down the line, he would be in a better position to get back into the stockbroker's business without a federal trial hanging over his head.

Our house sold quickly and packing became a heart wrenching endeavor as we willingly upended our lives.

❦

A few weeks before the move, my mother was drinking coffee and reading through the Sunday edition of the *Philadelphia Inquirer* at the kitchen table. The kitchen was in a state of disarray, with cabinets emptied and dishware packed into boxes that scattered the floor. In the newspaper, she found the *Today Magazine* insert, and, as she had every Sunday for the past few weeks, she searched for an article by reporter Jack Smith. Smith had interviewed my father months before and it had taken a long time for his article to be published. That day my mother came across the headline, STOCKBROKER TO PORNBROKER, and saw my father's name in the paragraphs below.

*Hopefully the article isn't as racy as the title,* she thought. "Anthony! That article in *Today Magazine* was published!" she announced.

My father appeared in the doorway. "Let's take a look," he said.

They took turns reading the article at the kitchen table.

"Geez, Anthony. He makes you seem like the porn king of Philadelphia," said my mother when they were finished reading.

"Well, I'm not really. It's just that I'm just a pornbroker with an unlikely background."

"It's all because of the Memphis trial. It's been so highly publicized."

"I guess so. Interesting quote: 'The only difference between selling stock and smut is I don't have to wear a tie.'" My father looked at my mother and chuckled.

"Funny," my mother said half-heartedly.

In the end, my father was unimpressed with the article but my mother read it several more times to absorb every word. There was one mention of "young girls" hanging out in the office at the Golden 33 and quotes from my father about how the government was on a witch hunt—all of which gave my mother a more comprehensive glimpse into my father's work life and his legal troubles than she'd ever had before. He'd never described these things to her in such vivid detail—but he didn't seem to mind describing them to some reporter, and to the entire world.

It also pained her, perhaps most of all, to read about how my father said he didn't have enough time with his family.

After absorbing the article, my mother had an overwhelming feeling that she was ready to leave Philadelphia. Maybe in Florida, they could start over, forget the past, and make up for lost time.

~~~

"Well this is it," my father said as he put his arm around my mother's shoulder. We were standing in the living room and taking one last look around our empty home. The moving vans had taken away all of our furniture and the big boxes, leaving us with only a few suitcases.

"I remember bringing Kristin home from the hospital here like it was yesterday," my mother said wistfully.

My father nodded. "The last seven years have gone by so fast."

I silently said goodbye to my room, to the swing set in the backyard, and to the dogwood tree in front of the house as Dad locked the front door for the last time. I was sad but excited about Florida. We piled into the Thunderbird and pulled out of the driveway. As we left, my mother cried.

"At least you'll never have to deal with the cold weather again," my father said soothingly. "You'll love the weather in Florida. You'll love all of it. I promise."

My mother dabbed her eyes with a tissue and shook her head; she was getting tired of all the reminders about Florida's amazing weather.

That evening, we stayed at Grandma Emma's house, then left early the next morning to begin our road trip to Florida. Grandma Emma put on a brave face while standing outside to see us off, but her sorrow about our departure was betrayed by how she kept wringing her handkerchief with both hands. "I guess we won't be having our Sunday dinners for a while," Grandma Emma said as she began to cry softly.

"We'll visit, Mom," my father said, giving her a hug. He was worried about moving so far away. She had had a few terrible asthma attacks and increasing difficulties in breathing. These symptoms had left doctors puzzled.

Grandpa Antonio shook my father's hand. Grandma Emma squeezed me in a tight hug. My grandmother even gave my mother a hug, despite the fact they had never gotten along that well.

I looked out the back window as we left, and I saw that Grandma Emma's entire body was shaking with sobs.

✺

My mother hated long drives, mainly because my father was so strict with our schedule. He insisted on waking up at dawn to beat the traffic and he only liked to stop for short bathroom and meal breaks. I shared the back seat with our luggage, which left me squished to one side. To pass the time, I waved at people in other cars, read *Highlight* magazines, and slept.

We stopped overnight at a small hotel in North Carolina. After a cozy night's sleep, we left at dawn the next morning, my mother hastily gathering our things and rushing to the car so I could go back to sleep in the back seat. It wasn't until two hours later that I awoke and realized that my Bunny was missing.

"Mom, do you know where Bunny is?" I asked nervously. Bunny was my most prized possession—a pink and white rabbit with a wind-up music box inside of it that played lullaby songs. I took Bunny with me everywhere and I couldn't sleep without him.

"You don't have it?" my mother said. She was annoyed.

"No, he's not here." I started to cry. I'd looked under the car seat and in my bag with the magazines and activity books. Bunny was gone. *He's never going to see Florida,* I thought.

"I'm so sorry, honey," my father said, glancing at me from the driver's seat with a concerned look on his face. "We should go back to the hotel to look for Bunny, don't you think?"

"Are you crazy?" my mother said. "We left over two hours ago." She turned to look at me. "Kristin," she pleaded, "we'll get you any kind of stuffed animal you want." Then she turned back to my father. "We've driven over a hundred miles. We can't go back now."

"I don't want another animal!" I wailed, "I want Bunny!"

Without further discussion, my father pulled off at the next exit and turned around to drive back to the hotel.

"We'll find Bunny," he said calmly, his eyes focused on the road. "Don't worry."

My mother sulked and I remember feeling guilty that she was mad. But I also didn't care. I was relieved to be rescuing Bunny. We made it back to the hotel. Luckily the housekeeping staff hadn't cleaned the room yet and I found Bunny tangled in the sheets of the bed I had slept in the night before. I hugged Bunny tightly, near tears, exuberant to have him back.

"I hope you're happy now," my mother said to my father, half-annoyed, half-relieved.

Bunny would make the move to Florida much easier for me, as my father knew that he would.

~ೊ~

After two days of driving, we finally arrived at our new ranch style house in Plantation, a suburb of Fort Lauderdale. The neighborhood was packed with newly constructed homes, most of which had swimming pools as well as tropical plants sturdy enough to survive the intense Florida sun.

My mother climbed out of the car and smoothed her hand over her hair to push it into place. The humidity was making it frizzy. She straightened out her clothes, then walked slowly into the house. My father and I followed behind her, eager to see our new home.

"I love it, Anthony!" my mother finally said as she walked over the new shiny linoleum floors in the kitchen.

"I think we'll be happy here," my father said. He sounded relieved and he flashed her a grin.

We examined every room of the house, which was sunny, and we turned on every faucet and opened every closet door. My room had a bright yellow carpet, which I loved. Later, we gathered on the patio to stare at the crystal blue pool encased by a screen dome that had a view of the canal behind our house. I felt like we were rich. No one we knew in Philadelphia had a pool.

"Kristin doesn't know how to swim," my mother said, glancing at my father nervously. "She'll have to take lessons."

"Of course," he replied. "You know, I heard there are alligators in that canal."

"What? I don't like the sound of that," Mom said.

"If we leave them alone, hopefully they'll leave us alone, too."

It seemed like we had moved into the jungle. But of course we would quickly learn how to cohabitate with all the insects, gators, snakes, lizards, and other Florida critters, and our house on West Plantation Circle would very soon feel like home.

The next day we visited the Arnone family, who lived about five minutes away.

"Welcome to Florida!" said Pat Arnone, Tony's wife. She looked like a happy Floridian—she was slightly tanned, wore bright clothing, and her brown hair was cut short with bangs that swept across her forehead.

"Hi, Pat," my mother said, giving her a big hug. In the last few months, Pat and my mother had spoken frequently over the phone about living in Florida and they had become good friends.

"You finally made it!" Tony Arnone said, appearing in the doorway beside his wife. He shook my father's hand and laughed heartily.

The Arnone family had moved from Red Bank, New Jersey, to Fort Lauderdale several years before. Theirs was a large Italian family with six children, the youngest of whom was Linda. That afternoon, Linda came whirling around the corner, her blue eyes wide and twinkly, and her thick blond hair bouncing in all directions on the top of her head. She quickly pulled me inside the house. We were both six years old.

"Come on, let's go!" she said in a stage whisper. "I want to show you my room!"

This pretty girl who would become my new best friend quickly yanked me inside the house and began pulling me down a long hallway. I was barely able to keep up with her.

"Linda, don't yank on Kristin like that!" Pat said. "Slow down!"

"Okay, Mom," Linda yelled back, but we were gone in a flash.

Linda showed me her room, the playroom, the pool, and the backyard. "Here's a little duck," she said as she picked up a baby duckling near the canal in her backyard. A moment later, the mother duck was in an absolute frenzy, honking at us like we were predators.

"Oh, how cute!" I said, flabbergasted by Linda's boldness.

"Put that duck down, Linda!"

It was Pat again, screaming from the patio.

"Okay, Mom!" Linda called back. Then she whispered to me, "Come on, let's go."

I happily followed along to continue our adventure.

Linda and I quickly became inseparable. There were sleepovers, birthday parties, play dates, and much, much more. From that moment on, Pat and Tony Arnone became "Aunt Pat" and "Uncle Tony" to me and I considered all the Arnone children to be my cousins. I spent lots of time at their house, and for the only time in my life, I felt—just a little—what it was like to have sisters and brothers. When they fought with each other, I was glad to be an only child, but the fun times the Arnone kids shared made me wish I had siblings.

&c⁀͜͡2⁀

There were lots of other young children who lived on our street and everyone in our neighborhood seemed to be transplants from the Northeast. That summer, my evenings were spent playing tag, riding bikes, or swimming until dark. Our next-door neighbors, Hans and Aggie Mueller, were an older German couple. They were excellent neighbors and they frequently offered my mother advice as we settled into our new home.

"Hans and I noticed how nice it was that your friends pick up your garbage," Aggie said one day on the phone with my mother.

"I'm sorry?" my mother said, her voice puzzled.

"But don't buy the City of Plantation garbage bags if you've got someone else picking up your trash. That's a waste of money."

"Oh yeah . . . that's a good point, Aggie. Thanks."

"Are you okay?" Aggie said.

"I'm fine. I think it's too hot . . . I need some water. Thanks for calling."

"Have a dip in the pool, love! You'll feel better!"

My mother hung up and immediately called Pat.

"So my neighbor just called to tell me that someone is picking up our garbage."

"What?" Pat said. "You sure it wasn't the lawn service?"

"I'm sure. Aggie mentioned something specifically about the Plantation garbage bags."

"Gosh, Frannie. That sounds strange."

"Really strange," my mother said, unable to keep the fear and confusion out of her voice.

"Well, don't panic," Pat said. "I'll come over on the next garbage day and we'll watch to see who picks it up."

"Have you noticed anything like this going on at your house?"

"No. Not at all."

On the next garbage day, Pat and my mother hid behind the drapes of our living room window and watched the curb. In the early afternoon, just before the normal city pick-up time, they watched a dark sedan pull up. A man in a black suit and sunglasses jumped out and quickly tossed our trash bags into the trunk of the car.

My mother gasped. The man glanced back at the house. Pat and my mother both hit the carpet.

"Oh . . . my . . . God," Pat said slowly. "Frannie, maybe it's the FBI."

"But why? What do they want with my trash?"

"I don't know."

"If we're being watched, they must be watching your family, too," my mother said.

Pat's eyes widened.

After a few minutes, they'd recovered from what they had witnessed and they talked at the kitchen table over coffee.

"What are we going to do?" my mother asked.

"We just need to tell Anthony and Tony what we saw."

"You know, I've heard clicking sounds on the phone. I bet they tapped the line, too."

"What?" said Pat, shaking her head and frowning. "Now I am going to be paranoid on the phone, too!"

"I heard the same type of clicking on our phone line in Philly," my mother reported to Pat.

"So this must have been going on for a while."

"Yes," my mother said. Then, completely out of nowhere, but unable to resist, she asked, "What do you think happened to Bobby DeSalvo?"

Pat stared at her blankly. "I don't know, Fran. But his disappearance was strange."

"What do you mean?"

"Well, I talked to his wife, Janice, about it. She said he went to England on business and they spoke once when he arrived there. Everything seemed fine. And then she never heard from him again."

My mother buried her face in her hands. "That's awful," she muttered.

"Janice was so distraught," Pat said. "It was tragic."

"Do you think . . . uh . . . maybe he left her?"

"I don't know."

"Or was kidnapped? Murdered?" My mother's voice was growing unsteady.

"I don't know. I don't want to think about it."

"So maybe he was whacked?"

Pat winced. "Please don't, Fran. No one knows for sure."

My mother sat in silence, covering her mouth with her hand. She didn't know what to say.

"Tony used to be really involved with the Perainos," Pat said. "It was only for a short time and nothing like Bobby. But it's still scary. Those short Italian men all look like the mob to me."

"The mob? I can believe it. Once, at this event I went to at the Plaza Hotel when the Perainos were promoting some other film, they all looked like they could be in *The Godfather*."

Pat shook her head in disgust.

"I liked Bobby," my mother went on. "He was a funny guy. Anthony liked him, too. I don't know why anyone would want to . . . ." but her voice trailed off.

"He was a nice man," Pat agreed, but her voice was cold and empty.

Later that afternoon, my father arrived home from his trip to visit the Premier Theater in Orlando. He traveled frequently to Orlando,

Tampa, and Lakeland to oversee the operations of the theaters and meet with other business partners.

"Anthony!" my mother said impatiently. "You're never going to believe what I saw today!"

She told him quickly about the man in the dark suit who had stolen the garbage.

"Our garbage? Who would take our garbage?"

"Maybe . . . the CIA? FBI? I don't know. The guy just looked really serious and he was in a hurry."

My father listened attentively as Mom recounted what she and Pat had witnessed and slowly the gravity of what she was saying began to sink in. When she was finished, he looked her in the eyes and said calmly, "Frannie, the FBI might be watching us."

She nodded slowly.

"Be careful what you say on the phone. And the trash can in my office? Don't ever empty it."

"Oh, gosh," my mother said—she was starting to feel nauseated. "Are they following us?"

"I don't know. But don't worry."

"How long do you think this has been going on?"

My father broke eye contact with her and looked down at his hands. "Maybe a few months? Maybe a few years?"

"Years?!" my mother muttered, her mind racing. "So I guess the FBI knows I have a very boring life."

That evening my father then called Tony Arnone. "I think we have a problem," he said.

⚭⚮⚯

For a time, we were much happier in Florida—but our boxes were barely unpacked when on August 31, 1977, my father was indicted by a grand jury in Fort Lauderdale, Florida, by a special taskforce on obscenity. The local taskforce, in coordination with the FBI, had linked my father to the Spectrum Design Company, which was a film warehouse in Fort Lauderdale where the films for the Florida theaters were stored and where 245 porn films were seized. Evidence from our trash had connected my father to Spectrum and local law enforcement officers claimed that Dad was setting up accounts to distribute the films in Philadelphia.

A warrant was issued for my father's arrest in Broward County. He turned himself in that day and he was quickly released on $10,050 bond. Larry Parrish—from his office in Memphis—attempted to have my father's bond revoked, but Judge Wellford denied Parrish's motion in September 1977.

"Anthony Battista was in violation of his probation," Parrish said to a *Press-Scimitar* reporter in reaction to Wellford's decision. "The obscenity charges in Broward County indicated he willfully committed a repeat felony and was a danger to the community."

My mother was taken by surprise by these new charges and felt responsible since she later learned the evidence was collected from our trash. Her compulsive neat-freak tendencies had made things worse, she thought. They had enough to deal with and she was frustrated by this new challenge. My father didn't hold my mother responsible. He was angrier at the police for wasting their time indicting him.

⤞⤝

"Kristin is *not* going to the trial," my mother said defiantly one evening on the patio where she was sitting with my father.

"Frannie, please. Bob thinks that if the jury sees that I'm a father, it might help sway their opinion."

"I don't care, the courtroom is no place for a child."

"She'll be fine."

"No, Anthony. She's getting a cold and sitting in a chilly courtroom isn't going to help."

"Look, I wish we didn't have to consider it, but Bob thinks it's my best chance."

"No," my mother said in a quiet voice. "This is going too far."

"I know, Frannie. But we don't have a choice."

A few days later, I sat in a courtroom by my mother's side, watching my father, who sat directly in front of us. Bob Smith, who was Tony Arnone's attorney during the Memphis trial, acted as my father's attorney for the Broward County trial, which started in March 1978, and lasted for three weeks. My mother had attended every day of the trial and was even a witness for the defense.

She was called upon to confirm my father's whereabouts on certain dates the prosecution claimed he was elsewhere distributing adult material. Bob had prepped her extensively before her testimony but she'd still been very nervous even though she portrayed a façade of calm in her khaki safari suit. This local trial was turning out to be much more intense than the *Deep Throat* proceedings in Memphis, both for my father and for her.

My attendance came near the end of the trial. It was hoped that the jury's opinion might be softened if the "smut dealer" they were trying to convict had a cute seven-year-old daughter. So, for the first time in my life, I played the part of the innocent pornographer's daughter. I was dressed in a bright yellow sundress and cardigan sweater. And I did my best to behave, smile at the jurors, and occupy myself with a pile of books.

Before that day's proceedings, my father turned around and gave me a wink. I waved back at him. After that, I had no idea what was going on for the rest of the day. To me, all the lawyers sounded very mad, and my mother seemed tense as she simply stared straight ahead. Eventually, the hard wooden bench became so uncomfortable that I ended up lying across my mother's lap and fought being bored.

At some point, there was a break for a few hours and everyone milled about the lobby outside of the courtroom and made friendly conversation. I took the opportunity to stretch my legs.

"Bill, I want you to meet my wife. This is Frannie," my father said as he introduced my mother to Bill Kelly, who was an FBI agent from the Miami office.

Despite the fact that many people were on opposite sides of this case, some—like Bill Kelly and my father—were actually friendly with each other.

"Hello, there," Bill said, politely gripping my mother's hand. "The agents mentioned that your wife was very pretty," he added, glancing at my father. "Nice meeting you, Mrs. Battista," he said, and then he walked away.

"Uh . . . nice meeting you too?" my mother said. She looked at my father with wide eyes. How did the agents know what she looked like? Bill was insinuating that other FBI agents had seen her, though she had never met any of them before.

When we returned to the courtroom, I promptly fell asleep. My mother hoped it would lessen my memory of the event. Ultimately, my presence didn't help; a few days after I attended the trail, the jury found my father guilty.

~•~

"Excuse me," said a woman who had approached my mother in the supermarket one afternoon. The woman was short, with a round figure, and her visor and white outfit looked like she had just come off the tennis courts. Her cart happened to be right next to my mother's in the cereal aisle.

"Oh," Mom said, startled. "I'm sorry, do I know you?"

"No, but I know you."

"You do?"

"I was an alternate juror in your husband's case. And I just have to tell you, I wouldn't have found your husband guilty."

"Oh, thanks," Mom said, dumbstruck. The woman smiled and walked away. A moment later, my mother abandoned her cart and quickly left the store. She was shaken that a complete stranger had approached her with such a statement.

~•~

The sentencing and possible appeal in the Broward County case was delayed for four more years since the *Deep Throat* convictions were still under consideration to be overturned. The final rulings in the *Deep Throat* case would affect the Broward County convictions. On July 13, 1978, the US Sixth Circuit Court of Appeals reversed the 1976 *Deep Throat* convictions and ordered a new trial for all eleven defendants, including my father and Tony Arnone. An error in the instruction to the federal grand jury to include children, when it should only be applied to adults, in their application of the community standard law was cited as the reason for the reversal. This also nullified any attempts by the prosecution to force the defendants to pay the costs, finally assessed at $50,000, of the first trial. While this all seemed like good news at first, attempts to change the venue of the trial to federal court in the Eastern District of New York had failed. My father knew the new trial would be an uphill battle.

Then, in August 1978, his mother passed away from lung and asthma complications. Grandma Emma had been in and out of the hospital for the past year with various breathing issues. It was a shock and a stressful time for everyone, and as we laid Grandma Emma to rest, my father felt pulled in so many directions, with many things weighing on his mind. He still had to contend with the next impending Memphis trial, let alone his conviction in Florida. My mother tried to remain calm, like my father, and became used to the duration of these indictments. She was almost numb to the latest legal wrangling and tired of worrying about the future. To support the household expenses, since the legal bills were mounting, and to focus on something positive, she had taken a full-time job as a receptionist at the Fenster and Farber law firm in September 1978. I went to the Wee-Care daycare center after school and later that year begged my mother to let me become a latchkey kid. After a year, she allowed me to come home alone. I was mature for my age and desperately wanted the independence and to come home to a peaceful and empty house. I never felt scared or lonely during my after-school hours.

The second *Deep Throat* trial began on November 11, 1978, and again my father and Tony Arnone moved to Memphis for five weeks. This time, Bob Smith was my father's attorney. Philip Kuhn represented Lou, Anthony, and Joe Peraino, and he and my father parted ways amicably. Tony Arnone, on the other hand, represented himself, which was a clever tactic that he and my father had thought up to save on attorney's fees. Bob was perfectly fine with the plan and would use it to his advantage in court.

"Is this a ploy to create more problems for the court?" Judge Wellford asked Tony Arnone angrily in regards to the drama he was creating by representing himself.

"No, your honor," Tony said, standing before the judge. "I simply don't believe an attorney can present my case as well as I can to the jury. The Supreme Court gives me the right to act as my own counsel."

In the end, Judge Wellford ruled that Bob Smith should act as Tony's adviser throughout the proceedings. But this, unfortunately, was the last victory my father and Tony would enjoy in Memphis.

～∽∾

On December 28, 1978, my father was convicted yet again by a Memphis jury. Then, on March 3 of the following year, he was fined $2,000 and sentenced to two years in prison, with all but four months suspended. My father and Tony Arnone would appeal the decision to the Supreme Court (in Battista and Arnone versus the United States), but on November 9, 1981, the court, in a 7-2 vote, refused to review the case, thus upholding the convictions. The Supreme Court felt they had already debated and decided upon the obscenity issue. Justices William J. Brennan, Jr. and Thurgood Marshall dissented, saying that if the case had come to trial, they would have reversed the convictions.

In January 1982, a mitigation hearing on the Memphis and Broward County convictions for my father was held in Fort Lauderdale. His original sentence for the local convictions—which had been whittled down to one year in county jail—combined with the Memphis convictions was changed to probation and two months in a halfway house. By June 1984, my father's probation had ended.

The *Deep Throat* and Broward County trials were finally over but they had left a lasting legacy for our family. It had been nearly ten years since my father was arrested for distributing *Deep Throat* and I was fourteen years old when his probation ended. This saga had dragged on most of my childhood and for the majority of my parent's marriage.

# 12

# *Pornographer's Daughter*

I stood in front of my bathroom mirror and stared at the awful Catholic school uniform I was wearing: an unflattering green-plaid polyester skirt and a white oxford button-down shirt. The outfit made me look too skinny and my brown-framed glasses made me look like a geek.

It was August 1984, and I was now fourteen years old, getting ready for my first day at St. Thomas Aquinas High School in Fort Lauderdale. So I did everything I could think of to improve my looks. I attacked my hair with a curling iron. I blasted myself with hairspray to make my bangs stand up high on my head. I tried to select the right dangling earrings. Then I put on gray eye shadow, pink lip gloss, and powdered my face with corn silk.

I shouldn't have been nervous. Kelley Wyatt, my best friend from middle school, and Linda Arnone would both be attending St. Thomas, and it was comforting to know I would have a few friends. But still I worried about fitting in.

*Will people think I'm a dork?*

*Will the popular girls be mean?*

*What will people think if they knew my father was in the pornography business?*

Thankfully, this last question was not always at the forefront of my mind, but it did pose an interesting dilemma. The dilemma was this: Students at St. Thomas Aquinas were either from wealthy families—lawyers, doctors, or local business owners—or from middle-class Catholic families. And as my family had experienced firsthand, people from both groups thought what my father did for a living was wrong, sinful, and disgusting. My father was still involved in the adult industry. He owned interests in five theaters that had recently been converted to video rental stores. VCRs had changed the business and my father and his partners were keeping up with the times.

But here's the thing: even back then, I never believed that my father's profession was wrong. I'd never watched pornography, but I understood that consenting adults had the right to decide if they wanted to view these types of movies. Still, I knew that I'd never be able to change people's minds about pornography. So I'd decided that if anyone asked me about my father's job, I would forgo the possible stigma and give them a generic answer—I would tell them that he invested in real estate (which was true), or that he was in the movie theater business (also true). I didn't want people to judge me or my family, and I hoped, naively perhaps, that they would simply assume I could get into the movies for free, and then leave me alone.

⚘

As it turned out, I loved my new school, and I did fit in, at least with my own small group of friends. I joined clubs, studied with my friends, and on the weekends, I went to school dances, football games, or the movies. All my worrying had been for nothing. I wasn't the most popular girl in school, but I wasn't a social pariah either.

Because Friday night football was the social highlight of each week at St. Thomas, Kelley and I fell into a routine of attending every game. At the games, students would congregate in an open area that faced one end zone and the home team side line. The field glowed from the bright stadium lights and you could hear the cheerleaders chanting constantly in the background. I loved it. While I was a student there, St. Thomas won most of their football games, one of the reasons was because they recruited the best players from public schools across the county. With a winning team, school spirit was infectious.

Despite the fun I was having, St. Thomas Aquinas did have its hard edges and a strict adherence to the traditional Catholic doctrine that my father was vehemently opposed to. One day, my freshmen class was herded into the library to watch an educational film about abortion. We were shown graphic pictures of aborted fetuses and footage of the actual surgical procedure, which sent some students into the hallway to vomit into garbage cans. The film also featured tearful testimonials by women who had had abortions saying that they had made a terrible mistake. That afternoon, we were sent home with glossy literature with pictures of bloody aborted fetus and with "Choose Life" messages on every page. We were told to discuss the issue with our parents.

"I guess it's a private school, so they can teach what they want," my mother said, shaking her head in disbelief as I showed her the brochures.

I was very confused. The pictures looked so bad and I thought abortion must be horrible. It would take me years to realize that the issue was much, much more complicated, and that this reading material, as well as the program that day, had been propaganda of the highest (or lowest) form.

"I can't believe they show this stuff to kids!" my father said when he saw the brochures. His face was redder than I'd ever seen it. He was fuming, but he calmly asked me what I thought about abortion.

"I guess it seems wrong," I said hesitantly. "They say life starts at conception. And the women they showed in the film who had abortions seemed so sad."

My father nodded. Then he said, "There are a lot of conflicting views on abortion, Kristin. St. Thomas really didn't tell you the whole story. Many believe women have the right to choose what happens to their own bodies. Did they even mention Roe versus Wade?"

"What's that?"

He shook his head. "It's a very famous Supreme Court case. I'll explain it to you, I promise."

"But what about them saying it's a baby from the beginning?"

"There are different schools of thought about that, too," he said reasonably. "People aren't really sure when life begins. It's debatable."

"Really?"

"Kristin, when forming an opinion about something serious, it's very important to weigh all the available information. St. Thomas didn't do that for you. They just shared one side of this debate. Always try to remember that."

After this incident, my parents considered removing me from St. Thomas, but in the end they decided that I would stay and they didn't push the discussion with me any further. But the next day, I listened more carefully in theology class as my teachers discussed the film. There was no mention of the Supreme Court, nor of the heated debates in the 1960s, nor of the terrible consequences of underground abortions. All I heard was Bible verses that supported why abortion is wrong. I was too shy to speak up in class, but I began to feel that blind faith in any doctrine didn't really address the complexities and realities of abortion or, for that matter, any complex issue. The credit goes to my parents for urging me to always think about every side of an issue.

❧

During my freshman year at St. Thomas, I was coming to realize that my parents' marriage was finally falling apart. In fact, many of my friends' parents were going through the same thing. Divorce seemed to be in the air, so at least I was in good company. My friends and I would talk about how each divorce was unfolding. Our conversations would revolve around a mother's new boyfriend, or a new wicked stepmother, or how to effectively divide our time between our moms and dads while still maintaining a social life, or how to extract the most money and freedom from our guilt-ridden parents.

My friend Kelley had it particularly rough, and during freshman year I was witness to the unfolding chapters of her parents' bitter divorce. My mother dropped me off every day at Kelley's house so that Jim, Kelley's father, could drive us to school, and there were several weeks when her mother Nancy—who was an angry alcoholic—was in the midst of moving out. Every day, more boxes were piled in the living room, and it was clear that Nancy was trying to take everything. On top of this, Kelley had rightfully chosen to live with her father, so there was added tension between her and her mother.

Jim was a charming, jovial man who always made us laugh during our rides to school. He often poked fun at my tall, skinny frame by saying, "Hey Bones, you ready to go to school?" Despite his outgoing personality, he had struggled to hold down a job as a salesman at various companies, or even to drop of us off at school on time. Routinely, Kelley and I would barely arrive before the last bell.

"I'm sorry we're always late," Kelley said to me one day, as we rushed from her father's car toward the school. "Why don't you get another ride?"

"No way. My only option is the bus, and I hate the bus. Besides, at least we're together."

"I'll do my best to get Jim off on time."

"Don't worry about it. Are you coming over after school today?"

"Sure, I'll meet you by the buses."

"Bye, ho," I said playfully.

"Bye, slut."

We laughed at each other, ever the best of friends, then went our separate ways.

That afternoon at my house, while we stood in the kitchen over a pan of rice crispy treats, we talked endlessly about our part-time jobs at Carvel Ice Cream and how to accessorize our uniforms with earrings, shoes, and different kinds of EG socks. My mother was at work and my father out of town so, as usual, we were alone.

"Have I ever told what my dad does?" I asked.

Kelley shrugged. "He has movie theaters or something like that, right?"

"Yeah, he has stores now, which used to be theaters. And the stores . . . they sell and rent porn tapes."

Kelley set down the rice crispy treat she was about to put in her mouth and she stared at me like my head was on fire. "What?" she finally managed.

"It's true."

"Does he make the movies, too?"

"No, nothing like that," I said laughing.

"But your dad looks so businesslike."

"I know."

"I never would have thought."

"I know."

"Does he have any videos or stuff here? In your house?"

"Umm . . . I don't think so. But I'm not sure."

We snooped around my father's office, in closets, and under beds in search of porn. In the end, it turned out to be a boring, futile mission, because there didn't seem to be much to find. All we uncovered (in the back of a closet) was a stack of *Forum* magazines that had a few nude pictures but mostly they were just a bunch of articles. The only other thing we found was a Ping-Pong ball in my father's top desk drawer with a small drawing of a penis on it, and GREAT BALLS TONY written in black ink.

"What the heck is this?" Kelley asked, smirking.

"I have no idea."

Many years later, I learned this was a souvenir from Honeysuckle Divine.

After this discovery, I turned to Kelley and said, "I'm tired of this. You want to do something else?"

"Yeah. Let's go watch *Guiding Light.*"

Thus our search for the pornographic material ended and we happily went into the living room to watch our favorite afternoon soap opera. My father, apparently, was as boring as everyone else's.

⁓⁓

One morning, my mother was making breakfast in the kitchen. When I walked in, my parents abruptly stopped talking. They had guilty expressions plastered on their faces.

"Breakfast is ready," my mother said in a hoarse voice. "Can you take your plate out to the patio?"

"Sure, Mom."

I picked up my scrambled eggs and bacon and carried it to the patio table near the pool. My parents joined me, and as we began to eat, I had an uneasy feeling in the pit of my stomach.

"Kristin, we wanted to tell you . . ." my father began weakly. "Your mother and I have decided to separate for a little while."

"Separate?"

"Yes."

I choked up immediately. Tears burned my eyes. "Does that mean you're getting a divorce?" I asked.

"No, it doesn't," my mother said quickly. "We just need some time apart."

"We don't want to get a divorce," my father said, who was also near tears. "We really don't."

But I barely heard what they were saying; I just cried at the table. Though I'd been expecting the news—because everyone's parents were getting divorced—I still felt blindsided. "Okay," I said a few minutes later, and I took my napkin and began wiping tears.

I glanced at my mother. She seemed stoic—she hadn't cried or expressed even a hint of sadness. We ate the rest of our breakfast in silence. I couldn't wait to escape to my room.

Later, I stared out my bedroom window into the frontyard and remembered the many times my parents had argued and the awful knot I would always feel in my stomach whenever they did. As a child, I'd felt helpless listening to the screaming and the sound of doors slamming. During their arguments, I would hide in my room and act out elaborate stories with my Barbie dolls.

But I was a teenager now—and Barbie wasn't going to be of any help.

In the few years since my father's probation had ended, my parents' relationship had only gotten worse. They fought constantly. My mother seemed to hate my father. She would become angry if he left his shoes in the living room, a mess in the kitchen, or bought something at the grocery store she didn't like. She was always nitpicking at him and the smallest thing would set her off. In response, my father would become angry and start cursing and yelling. Being around them was intolerable.

She also seemed to hate her life, and at times, that seemed to include me. In recent years, she had begun berating me about the silliest things, from leaving the bathroom untidy, to my requests for rides to the mall, to hanging out too much with friends. And she accused me of weird things, like stealing her clothing and jewelry, which never happened, and of being selfish and inconsiderate. Once she just screamed at me to get out of the house for no reason at all. I didn't understand her anger and I'd basically decided to avoid her as much as possible.

"My parents are finally splitting up," I said to Kelley on the phone that night.

"Oh, my God," she said. "But it's not a big surprise, right?"

"No. But it still sucks. A lot."

"Yeah. So how are you?" Kelley asked.

"I cried at first. But I think I'm doing good."

"Of course, you'll be fine."

"They say it's only a separation, but I think it's permanent."

"Most likely."

"My parents are so stupid," I said.

"Mine, too," Kelley said. "Why is it parents today can't get their shit together?"

"It's like an epidemic."

"A divorce plague."

I forced a laugh. "So, what's the latest at your house?"

"My mother is fighting with my father over money. It looks like I might not be able to go back to St. Thomas next year."

"What!"

"I know. Sucks. My mother refuses to help pay my tuition since I chose to live with my father."

Weirdly, at that moment, I felt more upset about Kelley and I not attending the same school than about my parents' separation. Kelley and I had become each other's support system . . . fellow soldiers against the forces of domestic strife. It just seemed like our parents were being so damn selfish.

⁓ఁ∾⁓

After that breakfast on the patio, I never cried again about my parents' impending divorce. Instead, I threw myself into working at my part-time job at Carvel on the weekends, filled my days with after-school activities until late into the evening, and I spent as little time as possible at home.

Things between my parents just got weirder and weirder. My father finally moved out in 1985. He rented an apartment on the east side of Fort Lauderdale and I only saw him maybe once every two weeks. He seemed to be very depressed. My mother began going out like crazy on the weekends, sometimes not coming home until 2 or 3 a.m. She performed all the basic parenting tasks, like cooking meals, grocery shopping, and cleaning, and she was always home on weekday nights, but after my father moved out, their separation moved quickly to divorce with no chance of reconciliation. My father filed the divorce papers in 1985, when I was a sophomore in high school, but my mother was the one who most wanted out of the marriage. The divorce was eventually final by the end of my junior year in 1987.

My parents sold our home with the pool and my large room and I was so sad to move from the place where I had spent most of my childhood. My mother and I moved to a small townhouse only a short distance away. She quickly created her own new world with a large circle of friends. And her late-night weekends essentially left me without a curfew. (All my friends had curfews, so I rarely put my freedom to mischievous use.) Altogether, her behavior started to take its toll on our relationship and I began to lash out against her.

"Kristin, get off the phone," my mother said one night, leaning into my room and glaring at me with frustration.

I just kept talking, not even acknowledging that she had spoken to me. She had given me my own line since she was tired of fighting me to use the phone, so I didn't understand why this was suddenly a big deal.

"Kristin, get off the phone!" she said again.

"Let me call you back," I muttered into the phone receiver.

I rolled my eyes and hung up. Finally I looked in her direction. She stood in the doorway, arms crossed, and stared at me.

"When I tell you to get off the phone, that means get off, *now*."

"Why should I?" I responded.

"Don't talk back to me! It's late! And you have school tomorrow!"

"You talk on the phone constantly," I said, raising my voice to meet hers. "I don't need you telling me when I can talk on the phone or set my schedule."

"Look . . . I think you're very angry with me . . ."

"What, is that some psychobabble from your therapist?" I shot her daggers with my eyes again. "Did you tell your therapist how you're never here? That you practically ignore me? How you're always on the phone with your friends or whatever guy you're dating?"

My mother's voice rose to a scream. "Do you want me to sit around and bake cookies all day?!"

"It would be nice if you were around," I said, and then I slammed my bedroom door in her face.

My father's company wasn't any better. He'd moped around for a while and slowly recovered from the divorce. I spent a weekend evening with him once every few weeks but these visits were always taxing for me.

"I wish things could have been different between me and your mother," my father once said.

"Well, at least you're not fighting anymore," I replied, pushing spaghetti around my bowl, not hungry at all.

"So . . . how's school?"

"Fine."

"How do you think your grades will be this quarter?"

"Okay."

In many ways, I was just acting the role of the typical teenager, but still, these forced conversations were torture for me, as was the fact that I just couldn't help my father with his own personal problems with my mother. Everything had fallen apart. And there was nothing anyone could do, least of all me.

One evening, my father came to visit me at my part-time job. In between making ice cream cones for customers, he took me aside and shared his new plan with me.

"Now that your mother and I are getting divorced, I think I need a new start. I want to move back to Philadelphia, but I wanted to see what you thought about that."

"Just go," I said, pretending to be distracted by scraping the sides of the ice cream buckets.

"I was also thinking about getting my stockbroker's license again."

I shrugged. "Sounds like a good idea."

"Are you angry?" he asked.

"Why should I be angry?"

"I don't know. I just wondered."

"I guess if you need to do this, then go to Philadelphia."

"Thanks for understanding," he said.

Customers were starting to pile into the store. "I see you're getting busy," he said. "I guess I'll talk to you later."

As I scooped more ice cream and made sundaes, I thought about my father moving back to Philadelphia. I couldn't tell him not to go, especially since he seemed so unhappy. But it would have been nice to have him around if he was happy and in a better place.

Later that year, he did get his stockbroker's license reinstated and he moved back to Philadelphia. But that lasted only for a short period of time—a few months later he returned to Florida. He told me that he just hadn't liked the cold weather. I nodded in agreement, unsure how to respond, and resolving, at that moment, that I didn't want any part of my parents' drama.

# 13

# *College Bound*

When I graduated from high school, I didn't have many college opportunities waiting for me. Grade-wise, my high school career had been pretty mediocre. I had tried my best but I was unfocused and distracted by various problems at home. I applied and was accepted to a few small, not-so-great universities in rural North Carolina, but I decided those schools weren't great options for me. Instead, I begrudgingly opted to attend local community college in the hopes of applying to a few state universities in Florida and Pennsylvania for my sophomore year.

So, in the fall of 1988, I enrolled at Broward Community College, which I soon came to think of as "college purgatory." No one I knew had aspired to go to community college—and I understood why. Really, community college was just an odd, in-between place filled with people trying to figure out their lives. Either they had flunked out of college, or they dreamed of going to a four-year university but couldn't afford it, or they hadn't been accepted anywhere else, or worse. I hated that I'd been left behind as my friends moved away to have great college adventures. To top it all off, I was stuck living at home with my mother, while working part-time at Sears in the housewares department while going to school.

Luckily, my college prospects improved sooner than I thought. The summer after high school graduation, I traveled with my friend Kristine to visit Florida State University. Kristine was making the trip to attend her student orientation and she invited me to tag along. It was a long bus ride, but it turned out to be well worth the trip. After a night of parties at dorms, friends' houses, and various fraternities, Kristine encouraged me to stop by the admissions office.

So the next day, I walked across campus, excited about the prospect of possibly attending FSU. I felt like anything was possible.

"Well, with your GPA, SAT, and ACT scores, you might get admitted to the winter semester starting in January," said an enthusiastic admissions counselor, a guy with curly brown hair and round glasses.

"Really?" I said, surprised. "I think I could really love this school."

"But you'll have to perform well in your community college courses," he warned. "Any admittance would be contingent upon those grades."

I took his warning seriously. As soon as I got home from Tallahassee, I applied to FSU and worked hard at Broward, and within two months, I had been conditionally accepted to FSU.

※

In January 1989, my father helped me move to Tallahassee. The night after I moved into my new apartment, he and I had dinner and saw a movie together. I could tell that he was excited about my college experience. He knew how hard I'd worked to get here.

"I'm really proud of you, Kristin," he said before leaving me at my apartment for the last time.

"Aw, thanks Dad," I said, a shy grin spreading over my face. "And thanks for helping me move in."

"You went after exactly what you wanted and you got it. I'm sure you'll have a wonderful time here."

"I can't wait to get started."

"Oh, and also, don't get stoned and drive."

I stared at him blankly. Then I burst out laughing. "Okay, Dad. Thanks for the advice." I gave him a final hug goodbye.

At this time, my father's businesses were doing well and I was lucky; he was paying all my tuition and living expenses so I would never have to worry about student loans or working while going to school.

The divorce had been final for about three years, but there was still tension and hurt feelings between my parents; feelings that I wasn't sure would ever heal. But my father had started dating again and he seemed to be in at a better place in his life, which I was happy about. I was very ready to move out of my mother's house and thought she was ready for me to go, too. So I was surprised when she said, "The house is going to be so empty when you leave."

⊰∾∾⊱

During freshman year, I shared a furnished apartment with Kristine and two other high school friends at a complex called The Plaza, which was right across the street from campus and behind the Burger King on Tennessee Street. The apartment was a dump, but I felt like it was a step above dorm life—no group bathrooms or shower shoes. Standing outside our front door, if the wind was blowing just right, you could smell French fries and hear a nearby garage band practice the Guns and Roses' song "Sweet Child of Mine" over and over. I thought it was just perfect.

My first semester at FSU was the happiest time of my life. I was relieved that everything had fallen into place and I wasn't homesick at all. I was excited by everything about college life, like owning a miniature coffee pot, Corelle dinnerware, and a new comforter set with matching sheets. I was finally on my own.

And, of course, there was the partying. There were festivities or happy hours at all the local bars, like the Phyrst, at least five days a week. Friends with fake IDs kept me and my roommates in a steady supply of Captain Morgan and cheap beer, and it was fun going out and laughing with friends and getting drunk enough to work up the courage to meet cute boys. We partied more nights a week than not, and we tried, rather consciously, to replicate the college experience as portrayed in *Animal House*, a film that was burned into our consciousness. Like many people in my generation, we only recalled the hilarity of John Belushi's character as the always-drunk, always-crazy frat brother, and we ignored Belushi's real-life tragic end of a drug overdose. The toga party temporarily won out over intellectual pursuits, and very often the most intellectual thing we considered on a given night was which party or bar to go to.

Drinking was one aspect of college life and casual sex was another. Though my father was a pornographer, I was a child of the eighties and the AIDS era, and I was still a virgin when I started college. I feared that if I engaged in casual sex, I would almost certainly die of AIDS or contract some other sexually transmitted disease. I also wasn't a flirt or overtly sexual at all. I avoided wearing tight clothing, and my wardrobe consisted of mostly baggy T-shirts, jeans, and shorts. I had a voluptuous figure, but I felt very self-conscious about it. My breasts felt out of place on my skinny frame and I did everything I could to hide them.

But things changed in my first semester at FSU when I started seeing Sean, a former athlete from my hometown high school. He was two years older, he had blond, spiky, Billy Idol hair, and I thought was gorgeous.

I was smitten. I thought my virginity might soon be a distant memory. But as much as I liked Sean , maybe even loved him, he insisted that he didn't want to date exclusively, despite the daily phone calls, frequent time spent together, and sleep overs. He told me things would be less complicated if we weren't having sex. So we didn't have sex, and for months, I settled on this sort of relationship and it was so stressful that I began to realize why people get divorced and why some women just don't bother with boyfriends at all.

⤜∽⥈⤝

"I don't want to go home for spring break," I complained to Sean one morning while we were lying in his bed (after another night of *not* having sex).

"What's the big deal?" he asked.

"It's depressing. My parents are divorced, and my mother acts like a teenager, and it all drives me crazy."

"It can't be that bad," Sean said, his voice a little dismissive.

"You have no idea what it's like, Sean. Your parents have been married forever."

"No, I get it. But they're still your parents," Sean said, almost chastising me.

I sat up in the bed. "You really *don't* get it. My parents had a very rocky relationship. So much craziness." I shook my head, then continued, "You know, I don't tell many people this, but . . . my dad has been in the pornography business for years. He doesn't make the movies, he just sells them. And he owns a bunch of porn stores in Florida. In fact, he used to sell that movie, *Deep Throat.* So my parents are complicated, Sean. And I just don't like to get in the middle of all that."

I couldn't believe I'd just spilled my guts. I lay back down, turned over, and buried my head in the pillow. He tugged at my shoulder to make me face him. I cautiously looked him in the eyes.

"Well isn't that something," he said with a wry grin. "A virgin with a dad in the porn biz. I'd never have guessed."

Suddenly, I was laughing. Sean didn't seem to care at all what my father did for a living. To him it was joke, nothing more.

✦

Before heading home that break, my girlfriends and I drove to Daytona Beach for the weekend. It had been nice to delay going home. I loved my parents, of course. But I also knew that a predictable pattern would emerge as soon as I arrived. It would be great to see them for about an hour but after the glow of "being home" wore off, I would have to deal with them fighting about where I spent every second of my time.

I hadn't even been home for a full day when the tug of war began.

"I want to have breakfast with you on Saturday *after* I go to the gym," my mother said with an edge to her voice, her big brown eyes widening. "You're just going to have to wait to shop for a new car with your dad."

My mother knew this was the last thing I wanted to hear. My ancient Toyota Camry had just died and I was desperate for a new car. So I begrudgingly I picked up the phone to negotiate the schedule with my father. They didn't want to talk to each other, of course, so I agreed, with great reluctance, to act as go-between.

"Unbelievable," he said, a little pissed off but trying to restrain himself. "What's the difference when she goes to the gym? We'll just have to go car shopping later. Tell her it's fine."

After I relayed the news, my mother smiled, and I could tell that she enjoyed this small victory. But I also knew that he had only given in to make it easier for me. Besides, he probably thought he owed her a win for the years she supported him through the *Deep Throat* trials.

⁓⊙⁓

Since the divorce, my mother seemed much happier. But I still didn't understand her at all. She would bounce around the kitchen, making fresh-squeezed orange juice while wearing white sneakers and a tight green leotard. The tight workout gear was attention-grabbing and showed off her breast implants, which she had gotten just before my parents separated. The gym had become very important to her and her devotion to exercise had paid off; she looked younger than her years, which proved she wasn't past her prime.

She also idolized the reinvented Cher who sang "If I Could Turn Back Time" and danced around in a G-string in her provocative MTV video.

"It's soooo great that Cher dates younger guys," my mother said, referring to Cher's twenty-six-year-old boyfriend, the bagel maker Rob Camilletti.

"I guess so?" I said, looking at my mother strangely. "I liked her in *Moonstruck*."

"If Cher can date a younger guy, then why can't I?"

"Mom, you say that like you're not *already* dating younger guys. I mean, you dated the older brother of one of my high school boyfriends! That's just creepy!"

⁓⊙⁓

It wasn't unreasonable for my parents to want to spend time with their only daughter during her first college spring break. The problem was that I didn't recall them at any other point in my childhood being so eager for my attention. The push and pull I experienced that week gnawed at me. Their behavior was irrational. When I was younger, my grandparents had explained their arguments as "adult problems," but as I became an adult myself, this excuse didn't hold water.

They weren't adults. They were acting like teenagers.

Unable to sleep one night at my mother's house, I climbed out of bed, sat cross-legged on the mauve-carpeted floor, and leaned against the padded edge of the waterbed I had begged for when I was ten years old. There, I leafed through the photographs I'd just had developed from my trip to Daytona Beach and I smiled as the memories from that great weekend flooded back to me.

Then—though I'm not exactly sure why—I surrounded myself with a collection of yellowing, crinkly newspaper articles from the 1970s about my father and the *Deep Throat* trial. For years, my mother had kept the clippings in a big shopping bag. I had asked for them recently and she put them in my room. The bag was heavy, so I figured that people had lots to say about *Deep Throat*. I had known about these clippings for a while, but I had never wanted to read them until then.

That night was rather an off juxtaposition of the past and present. I gently spread the old articles over the floor, trying to preserve these historical family documents, and I moved between reading news articles that chronicled the most tumultuous time in my childhood, while reminiscing about my carefree spring break trip.

Some of the clips merely described the daily accounts of the Memphis trial. In one short article, there was only a brief mention of my father at the end that proved he had even been there at all. "Also on trial Philadelphia stockbroker, Anthony Battista," the article read, like he was a side show to the main attraction of Harry Reems and the Peraino brothers.

But some of the articles featured my father more prominently, also more menacingly, and depicted him as a Philadelphia stockbroker-turned-notorious-pornbroker at the helm of a successful strip club and the target of a major federal indictment. I even found an old photograph my grandfather had taken of my dad straight off the TV screen, when he was being interviewed for running porn films at the Lane Theater and was picketed by neighborhood residents. I remembered that interview. In the picture, Dad's thick glasses looked like chemistry goggles. I shook my head. He simply didn't fit the pimp-persona described in these articles. To me, he looked like an accountant.

The highest profile piece I found, STOCKBROKER TO PORNBROKER, was published in May 1977 in the Sunday magazine insert of the *Philadelphia Inquirer.* The cover photo showed a female executive with her feet propped up on a desk, under the headline PROBLEMS FOR THE FEMALE EXECUTIVE—all very cliché 1970s feminism. I remember thinking that the same female executive featured on the cover would have been the first to malign the Golden 33 and my father "the pornbroker." I laughed out loud when I read, "The big difference between selling stock and selling smut, according to Tony Battista, is the hours. Also, he doesn't wear a tie anymore." There was that word—*smut*—used so often by my grandmother.

But when I read about my father saying, "I never seem to get enough time with my family," I winced. I remembered how deeply separated my family had been during that time and that, really, those events had been the beginning of the end of my parents' marriage. I pictured our old row house in Upper Darby, and my old room with the pink gingham bedspread and matching curtains, and my father being there only sometimes. It seemed like the reporter had tried to pry more information about us but my father had obviously been reluctant to elaborate. I know why. He always wanted to protect us and being away from home was, he had told me, his greatest disappointment.

After reading the article, I stuffed everything back into the bag. I didn't understand a lot of what I had read, but it was incomprehensible to me that this successful stockbroker had become involved with something that so many people hated. How my father was portrayed didn't square with my reality at all and I didn't want to acknowledge they were in fact one and the same person. The depictions of the strippers, the hysteria over the trial—all of it seemed so much bigger than my small family. I was just beginning to understand how these events had impacted and overwhelmed my family, and I just wanted to give these articles back to my father, reasoning that this was *his* story, that this was his burden to bear. Why should my mother keep these clippings in the back of her closet?

The next morning, my mother and I went out for breakfast at a local bagel shop on University Drive, which had been a ritual even when my parents were still together. The bagels and the coffee helped me tolerate the boring conversations about my mother's latest boyfriends and the inane gossip about her fitness club pals.

"So," I said, looking at her seriously. "I looked through those articles. The trial was a bigger deal than I thought."

"Well, it did make national news. There were so many newspaper articles that I just got tired of cutting them out."

"That one article, 'Stockbroker to Pornbroker,' was a pretty big spread on Dad. Were you interviewed for that?"

"No. But that article was a huge deal at the time. I remember when it was published. We moved a month later." She sighed.

"Were you harassed by reporters?" I asked.

She shook her head, no. "One day, I was sitting out on our front step, and a reporter approached me and tried to interview me. I just said, 'No comment,' and then went in the house. Other than that, your father got most of their attention. He was kind of famous in those days."

"Oh really?"

"Well, yes, it was a big trial and he was a part of it."

"What else do you remember?"

"The girls at the club just loved your father. They thought he was a big deal," my mother said with a bitterness in her tone.

"What do you mean exactly?" I asked realizing there was something just below the surface of her comment.

"Well, there were girls at the club he fooled around with."

"How do you know?" I asked a bit surprised.

"He admitted it years later when we were in counseling. By then it was too late."

"That doesn't sound good," I said. Relationships are complicated and I didn't know how judgmental I should be about it.

"Your dad was a good father, just other things were not so good," my mother tried to explain.

We sat quietly for a moment and both nodded in acknowledgment of her comment.

"Mom?"

"Yes?"

"I want to give the articles back to Dad."

She frowned. "Why?"

"I feel like he needs to keep his own story."

She shook her head. "I want to keep these."

"I know, but . . ."

"Beside, your father's just going to lose them."

"No, he isn't," I said defensively. "They chronicle the whole trial that he lived through. It seems like he should have them."

"But you might want them someday, Kristin. You should let me hang on to them."

We argued for several minutes and my mother finally relented. "I think this is a mistake, but okay," she said. "If you think he should have them, fine. But he won't be careful with them. I guarantee it."

❦

When my father came to pick me up a few days later, I hauled the big bag with me while walking awkwardly through the foyer of my mother's townhouse.

"What's in the bag?" he asked.

"Articles from the *Deep Throat* trials. Mom kept them all these years, but I thought you should have them since they're all about you."

"Thanks," my father muttered, and without much gratitude, he accepted the bag I thrust into his hands.

He wasn't excited to have the articles and now I realize that he just probably didn't want to relive the painful memories. But he knew he should take the bag, since I had asked him to. I felt relieved.

In the end, my mother was right. Years later, as I became more and more interested in my parents' past, I wanted those articles back but my father had lost them during a move after his second divorce. I should have trusted my mother. I should have realized this was as much her story as it was my father's.

# 14

# *New York State of Mind*

The summer before I moved to New York City, I sang along to Billy Joel's *New York State of Mind* every single day as I drove to my waitressing job while still living in Tallahassee.

I was trying to reverse my dread about moving to Manhattan. In the fall of 1992, I would be starting in the Master of Social Work program at Columbia University and I was overwhelmed by the prospect of living in a big city and leaving all my friends behind.

My Aunt Dolores had helped me select and apply to a number of reputable programs, and while my father and my mother had been supportive, they didn't really understand why I wanted to be a social worker. I barely understood it myself. Nonetheless, I felt compelled.

"Can you make any money at this?" my father had asked me on the phone.

"Sure," I said. "I could be a therapist or pursue public policy work."

"Like a private practice? You could put out your own shingle," he concluded, thinking, I suppose, that a counseling practice would be like running a small business.

"Something like that," I said, nodding and going along with it.

"What schools are you applying to?"

"Florida State, Catholic University, UNC Chapel Hill. Aunt Dolores even suggested Columbia University."

"Columbia!" he said enthusiastically. "Now *that's* the school you want to go to."

"I doubt I'll even get in," I said, managing my father's expectations.

"If you get the chance, you need to live in a real city like New York or Washington, DC."

"Fort Lauderdale is a real city."

"No, it's not. And the South is *not* like the rest of the world."

"I like the South, Dad."

"But in the Northeast, you'll have access to the theater and museums, which you don't in Florida. If things were different, we never would have left Philadelphia."

"I'm glad we moved to Florida," I said. "I've loved living here."

"I guess, but even if you get into Florida State, I don't think you should go. You've already had that experience."

I agreed. I'd been thinking the exact same thing. Fortunately, I made it into Columbia, so my decision seemed simple. Except that it didn't turn out to be simple at all.

～૭ܢ৽～

So, with great reluctance, I shipped everything I owned by UPS to my new student apartment and my father and I made the long trip to New York by car. We stopped along the way in Washington, DC to visit my Uncle Gabe and Aunt Rose, who had moved there from Philadelphia several years before. Then we went to Philadelphia to see our extended family before finally making our way to New York City.

It was a warm summer day and my stomach was in knots. As we approached the George Washington Bridge, Manhattan appeared on the horizon. It looked so huge and intimidating. We crossed the bridge, drove up 122nd Street, and parked between Broadway and Amsterdam. I had finally arrived at my new home.

We rang the buzzer and within a few moments, Mr. Maldanato, the building superintendent—a short, friendly Latino man with glasses and a wide smile—greeted us in the lobby. Mr. Maldanato handed me the keys and reviewed some important facts about living in the building, like how to buzz in visitors and where to do laundry. I bobbed my head up and down and said quick thank-yous, but I wasn't retaining the information. I was brimming with anxiety and my father knew it—his presence was reassuring.

My apartment was located on the building's first floor, and the first thing I noticed when I opened the front door was the space's musty smell and dorm-like furnishings. I went into my bedroom—which was fewer than three steps from the front door—and I peeked into the tiny closet. Then I sat on the bare twin bed and I looked out my window at a view of a dirty brick wall.

My father entered the room and leaned against the doorway. He smiled at me.

"How am I actually going to live here?" I asked weakly.

"This isn't so bad," he said.

"I miss Florida already."

"Come on. Let's get out of here," he said, "We can go to campus and get some lunch."

I had visited Columbia a few months earlier, and as we strolled, I tried to remember where things were in relation to the apartment to get my bearings. I looked over at my father and I doubted he would mind if we got lost. He was beaming. He truly seemed to love all the traffic and noise and human bustling of the city, the same things that were driving me crazy.

"Hey, let's go to the Columbia bookstore!" he said, stopping all of a sudden.

"Sure . . . I guess so," I said unenthusiastically.

"You want a sweatshirt?"

"No, thanks."

After that, we walked around the campus, stopping in front of Low Memorial Library, which was the most beautiful library I had ever seen. Staring up in awe at the stately marble columns, I realized I needed to embrace this enviable opportunity even though I felt strange and out of place.

At the registrar's office, my father wrote a check for the first semester's tuition and we left with a Paid in Full receipt. Then, as we headed out to have lunch, I started to cry.

"What's wrong?" my father asked.

"This is great," I said, gesturing to the beautiful scenery of campus, "but I miss Florida . . . I miss my friends."

He gave my shoulder a sympathetic squeeze. "Before you know it, you'll fit right in. You'll have lots of friends."

"I guess so," I said, dabbing my tears with a tissue I'd found in my purse. I felt like an idiot. Why was I crying? I should have been thrilled to be living in New York City.

"It's okay to be upset," said Dad.

"No, it's not."

"This is a strange place. It's overwhelming. But I promise you'll adjust. Just take advantage of everything the city has to offer and you'll be fine."

❧

After lunch at a small student bar, Dad and I walked back to my apartment. He would be leaving soon for Philadelphia and our time together was quickly slipping away.

"This isn't jail, you know," he said. "You don't have to stay."

"I know, Dad. But I won't quit. I'll be fine."

"I know."

Then I gave him a hug goodbye. "Thanks for everything, Dad."

Ten minutes after he left, the phone in my apartment rang. "I just passed the block where your internship will be," Dad said with the city noise muffling his voice. "Down at the drug rehab center."

"Where are you?"

"Ninety-fifth and Broadway. Phone booth."

"So how is it?" All I knew about my internship was that it was at 106th Street and Columbus Avenue, in Morningside Heights, just west of Harlem.

"Well, it's not too bad, but it's not good either."

"Oh, God, Dad. Are you trying to make me feel better or worse?"

He laughed. "I'm sorry, I'm just surprised about where you'll be spending your time. Look honey, I just wanted to tell you, I'm so proud of you. I think what you're doing is great. Call me later if you need to."

"Okay, Dad. I will."

During my time there, my father made regular trips to conduct business with adult toy and movie distributors, and whenever he was in town, we always went to dinner and a Broadway show. I looked forward to his visits, when we'd catch up about school and about all the new places I had discovered in New York.

❧

My father was right: I made friends at Columbia. And I believed that I was in the best social work program in the country, learning from professors who were the best in their fields.

But despite all this, during my first year living in New York City, I became depressed. Adjusting to city life was hard for me and the program was difficult. I hated how it became dark so early in the evenings, and as winter approached and the temperature dropped, putting away my sandals was truly traumatic. Getting out of bed in the morning became a struggle. I would immediately experience waves of anxiety that would then be accompanied by nausea and crying. I was always able to pull myself together to attend class or my internship, but deep inside, I hoped and prayed that these crippling feelings would pass.

At my internship, I had been placed with three other Columbia students and we had all become great friends. I had a caseload of five clients with whom I met weekly, but I was having trouble establishing trust and rapport with any of them.

"I understand how you feel," I once said in a session with a young Latino man in his twenties.

"How could a white girl like you, from an Ivy League school, *ever* understand a drug addict from Harlem?" he snapped back.

"God . . . you're right," I said, stunned. "I guess I don't understand."

Terrible moments like this were frequent during my first semester and I wondered if I would ever become a good, or even capable, social worker.

In regular meetings with my supervisor, Sue, we discussed my struggles. Sue was a tough redhead in her late thirties and she was quick to tell me the truth, even if it hurt. She was also kind and nurturing, like a mother.

"It's okay to acknowledge that you don't have all the answers with a client," Sue said to me one day in her office. "No one expects you to be perfect."

I was holding back tears. "I just felt so stupid," I managed. "I'm supposed to be the expert, right?"

"Oh, honey," she said soothingly. "You're really beating yourself up, aren't you?"

I nodded my head, unable to respond.

After a series of long conversations between the two of us, Sue finally said she thought I was depressed and recommended that I see a therapist. "I think it could be helpful," she said. "Things seem to be very hard for you right now."

"Oh, God. Am I that bad off?"

"No," Sue said calmly. "Going to counseling is nothing to be ashamed of. This program taxes everyone's emotional limits. You have to deal with clients' overwhelming problems, plus your schoolwork, plus your own issues."

"That makes sense . . ." I said through sniffles.

"To best help your clients, you have to become keenly aware of your own weaknesses, then appropriately integrate them in how you react to the world. And to make things more difficult, you have to do this all without being judgmental."

I nodded, then agreed that seeing a therapist would be best.

"I know the perfect person. Her name is Libby Miller." Sue scribbled down Libby's phone number and handed it to me. "Make an appointment as soon as you can."

I trusted Sue. She was an excellent teacher and clinician. I had shed many tears in our supervision sessions and she had noticed all the hallmark symptoms of depression. And though I hadn't yet told Sue, the thing I really feared was that, given the right circumstances, I might become as depressed as my mother. The thought was terrifying.

⤜◦❧◦⤛

During that time, a scene from my youth kept replaying itself through my mind. It was the day I learned the truth about my mother's attempted suicide.

I was fifteen years old, and I was sitting at Grandma Maria's kitchen table, as I had so many times before, to learn more about the *Deep Throat* days. As I listened to Grandma Maria tell her version of the story, I swung my body back and forth on a swivel bar stool, totally engrossed.

"It was a terrible time, Mommy," Grandma Maria said, using her funny nickname for me. "But I think you're finally old enough to know more."

"What do you mean?" I asked.

"There are some things that happened we haven't told you."

"I know it was bad time."

"You have no idea how bad."

Just then, my mother joined us at the table. "Mom, you don't need to tell this story," she said.

"She's old enough, Frannie. When I was fifteen, I married your father. It's okay for her to know."

My grandmother's face grew intense. I looked at my mother, who was staring at her feet. Then I listened as Grandma Maria described my mother's attempted suicide. After the story was finished, my mother didn't say much to me except, "Now you know" and "It was a longtime ago," trying to make it seem like this event in her life wasn't relevant in the present day. We never talked about it again, like it was a secret meant to stay buried. But now I knew, as I was working toward my degree in social work, that this was nothing to be ashamed of and I empathized with her.

I struggled to understand just how badly she must have felt, so desperate to end her pain. Grandma Maria had said that my mother was depressed—the same word Sue had used to describe my state of mind. I had to get things under control or I might wind up with the same fate.

⤳⤳⤳

I didn't tell my parents I was going to see a therapist or how badly I was feeling. It was something I wanted to handle on my own and nothing I thought they could help me with. It was an instinct to be independent that mirrored the times as a small child when I was always on my best behavior. I never wanted to burden them with my problems when I knew they had problems of their own to deal with. My first visit to see Libby was on a cold and rainy Friday afternoon. Libby's office was in a pre-war apartment building on Fourteenth Street in the West Village. I was buzzed in, and an old elevator slowly delivered me to the eleventh floor.

Before I could knock, Libby opened the door and invited me in. She was a tall woman with a salt-and-pepper pageboy hairstyle, and her narrow face and pale skin were offset by a friendly demeanor. She also had a charming British accent.

"Oh, a little dog!" I said, noticing a terrier with shaggy, beige fur sitting in an open crate near the door. "How nice you can bring your pet to work." I was straining to be polite. I didn't like dogs at the time (but would later on) and was worried that Libby's dog would try to jump on me.

Libby smiled and escorted me to her office, then asked me to sit in a comfortable, high-backed chair. She sat across from me, and we began our forty-five-minute session.

"So, what brings you here today?" Libby asked, her hands and legs folded primly in front of her.

"My work supervisor, Sue, thought this would be a good idea," I said quietly. "And, um, I'm just very sad."

Libby nodded.

"I've been in New York City about three months. I don't think I'm adjusting well."

She nodded again. "New York can be a very hard place," she said. "Tell me a little bit about yourself."

"Well, I'm from Florida," I said hesitantly, dreading this open-ended question. "I'm a social work student at Columbia University, and as you can tell, I don't like New York City."

Libby waited for me to continue and I realized that my clients probably felt the same discomfort I was now feeling whenever I asked them such basic, pointed questions.

"And how do you like the social work program at Columbia?" Libby asked, finally breaking the silence. "I've heard good things about it."

"It's challenging. But I'm learning a lot."

"I got my master's degree at Hunter College. All the New York City programs are very good."

I responded that I'd heard good things about Hunter.

"Now," Libby said, "tell me about your family. Do you have brothers and sisters?"

"I'm an only child."

"How do you get along with your parents?"

"Okay."

"What do your parents do?"

I took a deep breath. "My father owns pornography stores in Florida. He sells videos, magazines, adult toys . . . you know, stuff like that. My mother is an office manager in an eye doctor's office."

As I was speaking, I'd noticed that Libby hadn't reacted at all about my father's career.

"Are they still married?" Libby asked.

"No, they split in 1985, when I was fifteen years old."

"Oh, I'm sorry," Libby said empathetically. "Divorce can be tough."

I looked down at the floor and I felt tears beginning to dampen my cheeks. "I guess it was tough," I said. "They tried to be civil about it. But they were so unhappy. I know it was for the best."

"Well, they may have been better off apart. But your family still *fell apart*. You obviously have some grief about that."

"I guess so."

"Does depression run in your family?"

I told Libby about my mother's depression and suicide attempt. I also admitted that my father was a rather melancholic person.

"I see," Libby said slowly.

"I'm not that bad, though," I said, suddenly feeling defensive. "I can still get out of bed and function day-to-day. My mother completely fell apart."

"Then why are you here?"

I looked at Libby closely. My crying had stopped. "That's a very good question," I said with more attitude than I would have preferred. "Maybe you can help me answer that."

Libby laughed slightly, but not rudely, at my off-putting comment. I was irritated. Starting therapy was like learning to dance. It was awkward and tense as we tested each other's limits.

Undeterred, Libby asked, "Tell me more about what happened during the time when your mother was hospitalized."

"I was so young. I don't remember much. But it was a very bleak time."

"How did your mother try to commit suicide?"

"She took a bunch of pills with alcohol while my father was at work. When I woke up the next morning, my aunt was at our house, and my father just told me that my mother was in the hospital. Nothing was mentioned about suicide, just that she was sick. I didn't learn the whole truth until years later."

"Still, that all must have been unsettling for you."

I shrugged my shoulders.

Then there was another awkward pause.

"Depression can be hereditary," Libby offered. "You might be predisposed to it, but talk therapy can be an effective treatment."

"Will I always feel like this?" I asked, my voice cracking slightly.

"I'm sure you'll feel better," Libby said. "We'll work hard and try to get to the root of your feelings. Let's say we meet once a week and see how it goes?"

After our session was over, I left the office that day feeling drained, and on the subway ride home, my thoughts were heavy. I didn't know if I wanted to do this every week, and I tried to think of a convincing excuse *not* to return to therapy. Both the divorce and my mother's suicide attempt were so long ago and I just didn't want to dissect them in detail. Also, I wasn't comfortable with Libby's dog. It was probably just a classic case of transference; I was projecting my ambivalent feelings about therapy onto the poor dog.

Did my father's profession matter to Libby, I wondered. When she asked if my parents were still married right after I mentioned his career, what was she insinuating? Could I really trust Libby?

Over the next few months, I saw Libby once a week. When she asked me to call her after dates with guys, I thought it was weird and stopped seeing her. In addition to this weird counseling tactic of Libby's, I was also in denial about how sad I really was and reluctant to deal with my family's past.

# 15

# *Family Secrets*

In the summer of 1993, between my first and second year of graduate school, I interned at the AFL-CIO in Washington, DC. It was a respite from New York and, more importantly, seemed like the perfect place to start *really* making a difference in the world. By this point, I'd definitely "drunk the Kool-Aid," wholeheartedly believing what my professors at Columbia University taught us: that social workers were the champions for those who were forgotten, pushed aside, and less fortunate.

I also believed working at the AFL-CIO would offer me valuable lessons about advocacy. In reality, a lot of the work I ended up doing that summer wasn't very exciting. There were hours of boring research, hearings on Capitol Hill on myriad obscure issues, and the revision of a safety manual for the bakery, confectionery, and tobacco workers union. Not the most exhilarating stuff. But at least I got to work in Washington, DC, inside the beltway, which gave me the chance to indulge my growing fascination with politics. I had Democratic leanings and Bill Clinton had just been elected president, so seeing his administration's triumphs and stumbles up close was incredibly interesting.

That summer I was also more reflective about how my family's interests had influenced my choice to become a social worker. My father was always interested and engaged in politics, mainly because his arrest seemed politically and culturally motivated. I also realized the term *arrested* could mean many different things.

Most people who are arrested are petty criminals. Others are truly nefarious characters—murderers, child molesters, rapists— who commit violent unforgivable crimes. And then there are the businessmen who embezzle millions of dollars through elaborate Ponzi schemes that destroy many people's life savings. When any of these people get arrested, we feel no sympathy.

But there are also the noble crusaders, who choose to be arrested for a great cause. Such criminals only break laws they believe to be unjust. Whenever I see Rosa Parks's famous mug shot, it alters for me the concept of being "arrested." I've imagined being arrested someday for something I feel so passionately about that I would even welcome the hard restraint of handcuffs if my arrest helped send a transformative message to the world.

As a young adult navigating my first real-life experiences, I had decided that my father was, in some ways, more of a crusader than a criminal, since he had committed no violent or white-collar crime. His crimes hadn't hurt anyone, and the *Deep Throat* case had important first amendment implications. I also didn't understand why distributing pornography broke the law in the 1970s, since people watched pornography all the time.

While on a research assignment for the AFL-CIO at the periodical room of the Library of Congress, I tried, for the first time, to do some research about the *Deep Throat* case. I wrapped myself tightly in a sweater to fight the chill in the overly air-conditioned room, and I set out to discover my family's past.

"How would I find information about a specific court case?" I asked a friendly looking librarian behind the counter.

"You're not in the right place for that," she said, peering over her glasses. "You need to go to the law library."

"Oh."

Sensing my disappointment, she added, "But you could find news articles here about major court decisions. What case are you trying to research?"

"*Deep Throat*," I said, and I looked over my shoulder to see if I'd been overheard.

"You mean Watergate?"

"No, I mean the pornographic movie."

"Oh," she said in surprise. "Well, let's see. What date was the case decision?"

"The date, um . . . I'm not sure. A final decision was maybe in the early '80s?"

The librarian smiled at me sympathetically. Finally, she said, "You'll need an exact date to search the periodicals."

"Um . . . right."

"But you could go to the stacks and look through newspapers during a particular year to see if you stumble onto something about the exact dates regarding the case."

"That sounds like it might be tough."

"It's not ideal, since we have microfilm of major newspapers dating back to the turn of the century."

I sighed. "Do you have the *Philadelphia Inquirer*?" I asked hopefully, thinking that something must have been written about the case in my family's hometown paper.

"Yes, of course. Let me take you over there."

I followed the librarian to the large metal cabinets with endless drawers that cataloged the microfilms of the *Philadelphia Inquirer* by month and by year.

"What year do you need?"

"I'll start with 1975."

"Here you go," she said in a quick whisper, showing me the correct drawer. "And good luck."

I grabbed a roll of film, threaded it into the reader machine, and began painstakingly looking at every single ad and miscellaneous article from 1975. I looked for any mention of my father or *Deep Throat*, but I found nothing. The sea of information was overwhelming and I gave up after a few hours. The stories Grandma Maria and my parents told me weren't enough. I needed dates and details.

I left the library that afternoon grateful to be in the warm sun, and I walked to the Capitol South metro stop to head back to the AFL-CIO's downtown offices. As I walked past the Capitol Building, I thought about finding out more about my family, and I fantasized about finding a cause of my own that would be worth getting arrested for.

⤝⥲⤞

That summer, I lived with my Uncle Gabe and his family in the DC suburb of Potomac, Maryland. After my family had moved to Florida, I had only seen them about once a year and living with them gave us a chance to reconnect.

"I'm so glad we're getting you back!" Aunt Rose had gushed. Although she and my mother didn't get along (as evident from the infamous food fight), Aunt Rose still treated me like a daughter. She was much the way I remembered her—friendly, open, and opinionated—but I found out that summer that she also had an adventurous side and was taking both motorcycle riding and flying lessons.

I also got to know my Uncle Gabe better. As a child, I remember him having a stern presence—he was the cool and distant executive focused entirely on climbing the corporate ladder. But now I saw that he could also be kind and generous when he expressed a genuine, almost warm concern for my well-being and professional development. In conversations, he had made it a point that if there was anything he could do to help me find an internship, he would do so. I was, after all, his only blood-related niece.

Yet despite seeing glimmers of his softer side, Uncle Gabe could still be intimidating. In his years in DC, he had carved out a high-power career in the telecommunications industry, and he had held senior management jobs at General Electric, GTE, and US Sprint's Eastern Group. His impressive education—which included master's degrees in both business and electrical engineering—granted him a commanding authority in media interviews, thus inspiring stockholder confidence. His light green eyes, olive skin, and tall, trim frame were complimented by custom-made suits, pressed white shirts worn with cufflinks, and tightly knotted ties.

I was one of the few people able to see Uncle Gabe's flaws despite all of his accomplishments. Like most successful businessman, he had difficulty connecting with his family. I also struggled to find something in common with him. Uncle Gabe was a Republican, and an avowed Reaganite. He also believed in the pull-yourself-up-by-your-bootstraps mentality and that trickledown economics had been a sound economic philosophy. I, on the other hand, was a liberal-minded idealist who believed that Reagan had failed miserably, especially in protecting the most vulnerable citizens of our country. I believed that Reagan's effort to deinstitutionalize people from psychiatric hospitals without properly funding community-based services, as well as his demonization of the welfare mom and turning a blind eye to the AIDS epidemic, had made him one of our worst presidents.

In addition to our political differences, Uncle Gabe could have a controlling and prickly temperament. He was uncomfortable with me inviting friends over. He needed everything in the house in a particular order and if you went against his specific requests or instructions, he got mad. This demeanor was something I wasn't used to because my father was just the opposite—always warm and laid back.

Uncle Coke had once said to me, "Your uncle's got ice water running through his veins."

～ৎ৴৹～

As I developed my clinical skills in school, I learned that many of my clients kept secrets—secrets about sexual abuse, domestic violence, drug use, or other personal failures. And I learned that what people kept secret was often more important than what they shared.

My family was no different. That summer I came to understand that my father's career, as well as his legal difficulties surrounding *Deep Throat*, was something that my aunt and uncle didn't talk about, not even with their own children.

While I was living with them, my cousin Christopher—who was three years younger than me—was also living at home while preparing for his junior year at Drew University in Madison, New Jersey. Christopher and I had grown apart over the years, and I imagined his most vivid memories of me were of my collusions with his brother, Stephen, to torture him as a child. He and I came to realize that we had many preconceived notions about each other. He thought of me as an empty-headed sorority girl, who was nice enough (maybe too nice), and who had graduated from unimpressive party school. I thought he was stubborn and that he had a general disdain for all people, not just me.

And there were more differences:

I was a Democrat. He was a Republican.

I embraced Greek life in college. He detested it.

I was a college football fan. He thought college football defined second-rate universities and was a lesser version of the NFL.

These differences were minor, but together, they made it seem like we had nothing in common. But I learned there was so much about him that I did like. He was a stocky guy with a gruff and unpolished exterior, who wore combat boots and reminded me so much of our Uncle Coke. He was tenacious, loved rap music, smoked too many cigarettes (although he was trying to quit), and never minced words. He drove his parents crazy because he spoke his mind and defended himself, and I loved that about him.

Christopher and I were slowly able to bridge gaps and we came to appreciate one another's unique outlook on life. We would debate and contemplate life on our commutes each morning into the city and while playing pool in his parents' basement. I discovered that, despite our differences, Christopher was a smart and interesting guy, and not at all what you would expect from the son of a corporate executive.

One night, when Uncle Gabe and Aunt Rose were away for the weekend, Christopher and I settled on the back porch to drink and talk. It was a warm, cloudless summer evening, and the light from the kitchen window illuminated the deck and reached out into the seemingly endless and dark backyard.

"Remember how we played hide and seek in Grandma's backyard," I said, "and Stephen and I would never go look for you?"

"Fun times," Christopher said sarcastically, then shot me a crinkled frown. "You guys were hilarious."

"I really missed you guys when we moved away," I said matter-of-factly. "But because of the *Deep Throat* trials and Dad's adult theater business, there just wasn't much of a choice..."

Christopher interrupted me, choking on his Jack and Coke. "Huh?" he said, gathering himself. He stared at me intensely. "Say that again?"

"Say what again?"

"The part about *Deep Throat* and the adult theaters."

I frowned. "You know, my Dad's pornography business."

Christopher stared at me, wide-eyed.

"Wait a minute," I said, sitting up straight in my chair. "You don't know about my dad's arrest for distributing *Deep Throat*?"

"No."

"Or that he owns adult video stores in Florida?"

"No!"

There was a long pause.

"Wow," I finally said, unable to come up with anything more profound. "I just can't believe you didn't know. I assumed you did."

Christopher was shaking his head, and looking angrily down at his drink.

"What?" I asked.

"My parents lied to me!"

"Oh, come on. They didn't lie. I'm sure they just didn't know how to tell you."

"Stop trying to sugarcoat this, Kristin. They withheld vital information about my family. About you. That's the same as lying."

"Withheld vital information..." I repeated in a gruff lawyerly tone, trying to get him to lighten up.

"Stop that," Christopher said. "I remember asking my parents what Uncle Anthony did for a living. They told me he owned real estate."

"Not exactly a lie," I pointed out. "That was actually a line I used sometimes."

Christopher was still fuming.

"Well, so, now you know," I said hesitantly. "What do you think about it?"

He glanced at me. "It's pretty interesting," he said with a shrug. "I'd like to know more about it."

"I'll tell you what I know, but some things I'm not totally clear on. I tried to do some research at the Library of Congress but didn't get very far," I said. The story I was trying to tell came out disjointed and incomplete and we realized that there were many, many questions to be answered. Thankfully, Christopher seemed to have no misgivings about my father's profession—perhaps he thought my father could score him some discounted porn.

"Maybe your parents thought that if they told you, you'd end up working in the pornography business?" I giggled. The alcohol was going to my head.

"Why not?" Christopher joked. "It's not a bad job, right?"

"You could be a lawyer for the porn industry?"

"People gotta have their porn!"

That night Christopher and I made a promise to each other: one day, we would go to Florida to visit my father's stores. We both wanted to know more about this family secret. I had never been invited to visit my father's stores, even though I had fleeting thoughts about seeing them. There was an unspoken understanding that there was this dividing line between me and my father's business. But now that Christopher wanted to learn more, it was an extra incentive to make the trip.

As I lay in bed that night, I felt a bit woozy and sad. My aunt and uncle must have been so embarrassed by what my father did for a living that they had opted to not share the details with their own son. I knew they were conservative, and I tried to imagine how hard it must have been for them to see their last name broadcast on the news in association with a pornographic movie and a major federal case. They had welcomed me into their home with open arms—especially Aunt Rose—but I wondered if maybe they just felt sorry for me.

Years later, Aunt Rose would confess, "I can't believe you turned out normal!" And I realized that any pity they might have felt for me was actually motivated by a deep concern for my well-being. After all, the *Deep Throat* trials, my mother's suicide attempt, and our move to Florida had been a very chaotic time in all of our lives.

# 16

# *Good Girl in a Dirty World*

Even though it was early spring, I still was wearing a hat, scarf, gloves, and a heavy coat. A horrible winter in 1996 was lingering in New York City, and I was miserable, so I couldn't wait to leave for Florida later that week. It had taken Christopher and me three years, but we had finally made plans to visit my father's stores.

Just days before my trip to Central Florida, I slowly climbed the stairs to my third-floor office at the Burden Center for the Aging in Manhattan. With each step, hot coffee spilled out of the cup I held, slightly scalding my freezing hand. And the weight of my winter clothing was giving me a slight aerobic workout.

I had now been a full-fledged social worker for two years, and at the Burden Center for the Aging, my job was to help homebound clients live independently in their homes. Most of them lived in rent-controlled apartments nestled among the fancy residences and boutiques on Fifth and Park Avenues. Many were former maids, seamstresses, or bus drivers who had come to America to escape World War II. For the most part, my clients had outlived their savings and had no family. In many cases, I was the only person who ever visited them.

The office door let out a low, mournful sound as I opened it. Edie, my boss, immediately poked her head out of her office to get my attention. The entire office space itself was really just two small apartments combined into one, with a wall knocked out and cubicles created from movable panels.

"Love, come quickly before you get settled in," Edie said in her thick German accent. With a cigarette in one hand, she waved me in her direction. Smoke spilled from her office doorway.

"Just let me put my bag down," I said, sighing. I'd heard that urgency in Edie's voice before; it probably meant something had happened overnight to one of my clients.

Edie had been the director of the Homebound Unit for more than twenty years. She was a large, intimidating woman, with blonde hair cut in a sleek bob that neatly framed her square jaw line. As a teenager, she had moved to America from post-Nazi Germany because she was disgusted with her country's role in the Holocaust, and this disgust had then morphed into a strong sense of social justice. By the 1990s, Edie had the Upper East Side wired. She knew virtually everyone at all the nearby hospitals and senior centers. She didn't have master's degree in social work, but she was an expert on case management for older adults and her assistance was often sought out for the most difficult cases throughout the city.

I hurried into Edie's office, taking my last breath of fresh air before being enveloped by her smoke-filled bubble. I hated the smell of cigarettes, but I tolerated it because I liked Edie so much.

"Look," she said as we sat down, "I know you are running off to Florida, love, but before you go, I need to know who your most critical clients zat might need friendly visitor calls."

"Okay," I said. I gave her my list of clients from memory, all the time thinking, *That can't be all.*

"Also, let's talk about what's going on with your cases at the end of the day," Edie went on, pausing to take a drag on her cigarette.

"Is that it?" I asked, waiting to be dismissed.

"No, I'm not done yet. There's more. It's Mr. Murphy."

"Oh, no. What?" My heart sank—James Murphy was one of my favorite clients.

"He was found in the hallway of his apartment building, muttering to himself and having all kinds of hallucinations. The neighbors called the paramedics, but zey didn't take him to the hospital. He didn't seem to vant to harm himself or anyone else."

I nodded, taking a deep breath. "This is odd behavior for him," I said.

"It seems serious, love. He is only sixty-five. Something else must be going on, and I vant you to get to the bottom of it. The mobile geriatric team from Mt. Sinai is going to Mr. Murphy's today to do an evaluation. I vant you to sit in on zat meeting."

I was truly alarmed. I had just seen Mr. Murphy two weeks ago and he'd seemed fine, so I wondered how this could possibly be happening. I went through the standard mental checklist. There had been no signs of psychiatric symptoms. He had diabetes, so maybe he hadn't checked his blood sugar. He was also a Korean War veteran. Was this a PTSD symptom I had missed?

"Okay," I said. "I'll go there today."

"Keep your head about you, love. I know how you feel about him."

I nodded, and thanked Edie for her support.

Later that morning, I arrived at Mr. Murphy's with my stomach in knots. I knocked on the door and Mr. Murphy opened it a crack.

"Oh, it's you!" he said in his normal joking tone. "Come in and join the party."

"Hey, Mr. Murphy," I said, studying his face. He opened the door all the way, and I went in.

In every respect I could think of, Mr. Murphy seemed to be perfectly fine. He was dressed normally and his full head of white hair was neatly combed. Once inside, he politely introduced me to the psychiatrist from Mt. Sinai, an older woman with a kind face, who was sitting on his mottled sofa. As I moved through the cave-like room, I looked around to see if anything was unusual. The piles of dishes, an ashtray full of cigarette butts on the kitchen table, and untidy surroundings were pretty typical.

"Mr. Murphy, thanks for letting us come over today," the psychiatrist said. "We're here to make sure you're feeling alright."

Mr. Murphy smiled and said that he was just happy for the company.

"What day is it today, Mr. Murphy?" asked the psychiatrist.

"It's Monday."

"What year is it?"

"1996."

"And who is the president?"

"Bill Clinton."

"Great," the psychiatrist said with a smile. "What did you have for dinner last night?"

"Peas and carrots and spaghetti," Mr. Murphy said proudly. I nodded at him in approval since he was adhering to a healthier diet to keep his diabetes in check.

"Is there a reason you have the windows covered?" the psychiatrist asked, looking around the room at the newspapers and cardboard taped to the windows.

"I hate the bright sun," Mr. Murphy explained, "because it shines in my eyes early in the morning and wakes me up."

That sounded reasonable to me. I looked at the psychiatrist, trying to gauge her reaction.

"Do you ever hear voices, or think someone is watching you?" she asked.

"No," Mr. Murphy said, his voice turning in annoyance. "Do you think I'm crazy or something?"

The psychiatrist and I looked at each other.

"Mr. Murphy," I interjected, "do you know why we're here?"

"Yes, you're here to make sure I'm okay. But I don't understand why the doc is asking all these questions."

I marveled at the child-like expression on his face. "Did the paramedics come here last night?" I asked.

"No."

I glanced again at the psychiatrist. "But Mr. Murphy, we got a report that your neighbor called the paramedics last night because you were in the hallway having hallucinations."

"What the *hell* are you talking about?" he asked. "I made some supper, watched the travel channel, and that's it." A smile crept across Mr. Murphy's lips. He seemed amused by all the fuss.

"Are you sure you have the right Mr. Murphy?" I asked the psychiatrist.

It took a few minutes on the phone, but we finally discovered the Mr. Murphy they *should* have been interviewing lived a block away. John Murphy, not James Murphy, was in desperate need of psychiatric evaluation.

After the psychiatrist left, I stayed to spend time with *my* Mr. Murphy, whom I was more than relieved to discover was okay. We both laughed a lot about what had happened.

"How long will you be in Florida?" he asked a little later.

"Just for a long weekend. Someone else will be on call if you need anything. I'll be back on Monday."

"And what are you going to be doing down there? I always wanted to go to Florida to enjoy the warm weather."

"I'm visiting my dad."

"That's nice. What does he do?"

I smiled. I didn't even consider explaining to Mr. Murphy that I was going see my dad's porn stores but instead spun the same old story about his being involved in real estate. I often found it helpful to share a few details about myself in order to establish rapport with clients, but I had never shared the fact that my father was in the pornography business with any of them.

I had lived this balancing act my whole life, always wondering how or if to describe the details of my father's career.

There never was, and never has been, an easy way to explain it.

⌇∾⌇

In Orlando, I was welcomed by the warm, humid air that I so desperately missed. Dad met me at the airport, wearing a Phillies' cap, sunglasses, and his typical collared polo shirt with a pen stuck in the pocket. (He would never admit it, but he now looked like a Floridian in every way.) He stood there, smiling at me and waving. A newspaper was tucked under his arm, and I knew he had already devoured every article and the crossword puzzle.

After we greeted each other, my father said quickly, "Christopher's flight arrives in just a few minutes. We should meet him at his gate. Let's hurry."

"Hang on one second," I said. I dropped my bag on the floor and started rifling through it for my sandals.

"What are you doing?" he asked.

"Dad, I *have* to change my shoes! I've been waiting to do this all winter. It's been arctic in New York since November."

He laughed. "I guess your blood permanently thinned after all those years in Florida."

On our way to Christopher's gate, we talked about New York City and about my recent plans to move to Washington, DC, with Brian, the guy I'd been dating off and on since college.

"I would have loved to live in New York City when I was young," he said. "But DC is a good choice, too. You can't go wrong there."

"I think Brian and I will like DC," I said. "He graduates in the spring, and job prospects for someone with an MBA are looking good."

"Brian is a nice guy," my father said simply.

And I knew that he meant it.

We arrived at the gate just in time to see Christopher emerge into the terminal. I gave him a hug and Christopher extended his hand to my father. They shook hands and I could tell by my father's broad smile that he was pleased we were both there with him. As we left the airport, Dad reviewed our itinerary. "We'll head south to the Fort Pierce store first, then circle back north to the Cocoa Beach and Orlando stores. Fort Pierce is only about a two-hour drive from here. Sound good?"

We agreed. I didn't mind the drive and looking out at the barren space along Interstate 95 was a welcome change after viewing countless city buildings from the bus, or the underground darkness of the subway. My father never really asked why we wanted to see the stores; instead he seemed proud that he finally had a chance to share his story.

"So, Uncle Anthony," Christopher said awkwardly. "Which store opened first?"

"The Premier in Orlando opened in 1973," my father said. "Then, in the late seventies we opened the Todd in Tampa, and later the Lakeland and Daytona stores. Uncle Coke, Cousin Danny, and I opened the Beach Video about ten years ago. And about five years ago, we opened the Fort Pierce store that Cousin Carl and Steve now manage for us."

"That's quite a lineup," Christopher said.

"Well, it keeps me traveling all over the state," my father said nonchalantly. "The hard part is that for years the conservative officials in the local governments have tried to close us down. The legal battles have lessened recently, though. It's nothing like it was back when I started out in the business."

Then he talked about *Deep Throat* and how he had first become involved in the pornography business. Christopher was finally hearing the story his parents had never told him, and I, too, was hearing some aspects of my father's life for the first time.

⚜

"I never imagined that distributing a movie would lead to the legal troubles I faced," my father told Christopher and me. This wasn't the first time I'd heard him say this, but he seemed no closer to coming to terms with it. "Not to mention that *Deep Throat* started a life-long career in pornography."

As our drive continued, my father talked about the current adult business, from the types of products he sold, to how the industry had changed over the years. As I sat in the back seat and listened, I realized just how many of my family members were involved in the business. A part of me actually felt left out. My father would never want me in the family business. Did I even want to be? I'd never considered working in pornography or working for my father, but I knew I could be good at it. I had held a few sales jobs in high school and college and did fairly well. And with my father's guidance, I could easily learn how to run a retail business.

⚜

After our two-hour drive, Dad pulled up to a small storefront in an average looking strip mall. We had arrived at Southern Exposure, the store in Fort Pierce. I climbed out of the car and stretched my legs. I was tired from the long trip but curiosity gave me extra energy.

A jingle of bells signaled our arrival as we opened the glass door to the store. My cousin Carl appeared immediately from behind the counter to greet us. Carl was the son of my father's first cousin, Danny Dicolla. I hadn't seen Carl in a long time, and I noticed that he'd gained a lot of weight. But he still had that sweet round face, which was now framed by a beard, and those crystal blue eyes that I remembered as a child. His curly black hair was pulled back into a ponytail. My father reintroduced us, then praised Carl as a good manager—he was grateful to have a reliable family member running the store.

"How's New York treating you, Kris?" said Carl.

"It's okay," I said. "But I might be moving to DC soon to be closer to Christopher."

"It's been a long time, my man," Christopher said, shaking Carl's hand. "How are you doing?"

"Been pretty good," Carl said with a casual shrug. "Business is always good."

The front section of the store looked to me like a regular video rental and magazine shop. The latest copies of *Time* and *Newsweek* stood neatly on small racks next to the cash register, and to the left side were shelves of regular mainstream rental movies.

"Where's all the adult stuff?" I asked, confused.

"Oh," my father said. "The adult products are in the back. Fort Pierce's licensing ordinance mandates that to sell adult material, at least half of the inventory must be mainstream items." My father didn't seem uncomfortable with my presence and finally acknowledged I was an adult. He motioned us in that direction, and Carl followed behind us.

As we walked toward the rear of the store, the merchandise on the shelves went from VHS cases featuring comedies, to naughty cheerleaders and women in strained bodices. Finally, at the back wall of the store, movies were piled from floor to ceiling, with a variety of titles categorized by fetishes, series, or actors and actresses. There was even a specialty section for gay pornography. And then, of course, there were adult toys—penis pumps, bachelorette kits, his-and-her bondage items, and vibrators and dildos in different shapes, sizes, and colors—all displayed neatly on wall racks. Outwardly, I looked like a customer browsing in a supermarket but inside I was blushing. I was not a sexual free spirit and everything here was so explicit. Nothing was left to the imagination on these shelves.

My father rattled off all the different brands he stocked, and he preached the importance of offering customers a wide selection. As he pontificated, I couldn't help but smile; he sounded like a walking porn encyclopedia and he clearly understood what it took to sell this merchandise. He also told us that he regularly attended conferences to check out the latest products, and I realized that any retail shop— whether in the mainstream or more on the fringe—would benefit from my father's knowledge.

"What's your hottest selling product?" I asked my father.

"That's easy," he said. "It's the Pocket Rocket."

"What's that?"

"It's a miniature vibrator. Women love it because it's small enough to fit into any handbag." My father picked up the box on the shelf and handed it to me. I took it awkwardly, unable to look him in the eyes, and I noticed a sticker on the front of the box that read "waterproof."

"Clever," I said, realizing I was having perhaps the strangest conversation that any daughter has ever had with her father.

Over the next few minutes, I took a good look around to get a feel for the place. It was clean, organized, and well-lit, and there was nothing seedy about its appearance. It seemed to me exactly like any other retail store.

"Do you mind if I take a magazine for the road?" Christopher asked.

"Go ahead," said my father with a wry smile.

I, of course, would *not* be asking my father for porn. I couldn't even imagine it. Not only was I mostly uninterested in watching pornographic movies or looking at nudie magazines, I knew that expressing anything beyond an anthropological interest in his stores would just be too strange.

❧

An hour later, we left Fort Pierce and headed to the Premier in Orlando. This was the store I most wanted to see. In its heyday, the Premier had been a popular adult theater before being converted into a retail store in the 1980s. It was the first operation that my father and Tony Arnone had launched back in 1973, for $25,000, an investment that they had recouped after only one month by showing *Deep Throat*.

There was nothing flashy about the white stucco building on the outside, but what caught my eye was a sign that read PREMIER SINCE 1973. I couldn't believe that after more than twenty years, this place still was in business. The Premier was an established landmark in Orlando and people tell me today that they still remember the Premier's radio commercial jingle from their childhood.

We walked through the Premier's glass double doors into an expansive warehouse-like room that seemed to go on for miles, lined with many shelves laden with products even more diverse than at the Fort Pierce store. It was easy to imagine this store's past life as a theater. I could visualize the rows of seats and the floors coated with sticky soda and crushed popcorn and a large screen positioned directly opposite from where I was standing at the entrance. The childlike part of me wanted to run up and down the aisles but I stood frozen as my father introduced us to his staff and to his longtime partner, Tony Panzino.

I felt like everyone was staring at me. They must have wondered why I was there, and the answer—that I just wanted to better understand what my father did for a living—seemed too weird to utter out loud.

Our stay at the Premier was short, and since we had been traveling all day, it was time to head to our hotel. My father had made plans for us to go out for the evening to a strip club called Club Juana, which was another landmark in Orlando and was owned by his good friend, Mike Pinter.

"Mike and I never worked together, but we fought many of the same legal battles," my father told us.

"So efforts to close the Premier were also used to try to close down Club Juana?" I asked.

"That's right. The only business we shared is adult star appearances," he went on. "Whenever a popular actress came to the Premier to promote a new movie, Mike would also hire her for a performance at Club Juana."

It turned out that Mike Pinter and my father were kindred spirits who, together, had helped bring "smut" (as Grandma Maria would say) to Central Florida. Mike had even famously created the "Macbeth in the Buff" show in the late nineties, which was a strategy he used to successfully circumvent an anti-nudity ordinance. In the show, actresses and strippers would recite Shakespeare on stage while naked. A local judge ruled the stage act was a form of art, thus creating a new loophole in the law and allowing the show to continue. This stunt landed Mike's performers on the *Howard Stern Show*, and the publicity generated from the act had been great for business. The law never changed on the books but this strategy permanently changed the way nudity was handled in this community.

I had never been to a strip club before, and to make things even stranger, I was going with my father. What would we talk about as naked women paraded past us?

When we arrived at the club, we were immediately ushered past the long Friday night line. Once inside, Mike Pinter greeted us with a toothy grin. I had met Mike many times before. His thick dark hair, with a slightly receding hairline, was pulled back in a tight ponytail. He wore jeans with a big belt buckle and cowboy boots. He had just opened a country western bar, which was doing quite well, and his clothing reflected it.

My father shook Mike's hand, and by the firmness of their grip, it was obvious that they had a deep respect for one another. Then Mike escorted us through the crowded club to a large reserved booth with white vinyl seating, purple lighting, and a small lamp in the center of the table.

Mike's girlfriend, Marlene, appeared from back stage and joined us at the table. She wasn't a stripper, but she had free range of the club. She was a pretty, petite blonde who dressed in the typical Florida fashion: big jewelry, a tight-fitting dress that showed just a hint of cleavage, and slip-on high-heeled sandals. She sat down next to me and we chatted like old girlfriends. I had known Marlene for a long time, too, and had met her at family parties and when my family traveled to Orlando for vacations or was passing through on our way to Philadelphia

A waitress wearing a skimpy black tank top and short-shorts—basically a dressier version of a Hooters' uniform—took our drink orders. From our table, we had a clear view of the large stage, which had four runways jutting out into the audience. The stages were just low enough so that dancers could easily bend over to collect their tips and chat up customers. And there was enough room between each stage for pole acrobatics.

I studied the dancers. They wore assorted styles of G-strings and easily removable tops that were variously styled to fit their personalities. Some donned black leather with thin chains dangling over their butt cheeks. Others wore sailor caps or cowboy hats, and one girl even managed a hippy flower-girl-ensemble—complete with a white daisy tucked behind her ear—giving her a naughty-but-innocent allure. I also noticed that all the dancers seemed to have different body types ranging from thin to full-figured, short to tall, small-breasted to large-breasted, and everything in between.

"There's something for everyone here," Marlene said, noticing that I was observing the room. "No two strippers are the same."

"I guess I always thought that all strippers had big boobs," I said with a laugh.

"This is a great place!" Christopher said to no one in particular, and I watched him lean back into his seat and laugh, taking in the view with wide eyes.

Then I glanced over at my father, hoping not to catch his eye. He barely seemed to notice the nude women all around him. Instead, he was engaged in an intense conversation with Mike, who was seated just to his right. *He's seen this stuff a million times*, I thought. *It must be boring to him.* To me, he looked like any ordinary businessman, chatting with another businessman.

The music at Club Juana was booming, making it difficult to talk too long to anyone. And at times, I just didn't know where to put my eyes—what with so many interactions occurring between the strippers and customers all around me. I was like voyeur in plain sight and in awe that someone could be so free with her body. I wished I wasn't so shy.

"Let's take a minute to welcome Brandi to the stage!" I heard the DJ announce over the crowd. "She's from Atlanta and loves hunky cowboys!"

Throughout the night, different dancers were introduced in this way, and after a short strip performance, each girl would then disappear into the crowd to talk with eagerly awaiting patrons. Marlene and I watched the performances as if everyone was fully clothed and chatted like we were in a regular dance club.

"So," Marlene said. "How's New York?"

"It's okay," I said.

"It must be exciting to live in a big city."

"Manhattan has been good, but I think I've lived there long enough."

Marlene smiled and nodded. "I know what you mean. I love it when Mike and I go to New York to shop, see a show. But it would be hard to live there I think." After a pause, she leaned over and said, "Aren't you glad you went to school so you don't have to do this kind of work?"

I looked at her in surprise. "I guess," I said. "I don't know."

"You would strip?" Marlene asked, surprised herself.

I told her that I didn't think I'd have the guts to take off my clothes in front of strangers. "But these girls seem to make a lot of money," I said.

"Oh, yeah, they make a killer living. The best girls can make a thousand dollar a night."

"A thousand dollars!"

"Uh huh. And some of them are going to school. This is how they pay for college."

As a social worker, I was only making about $800 every two weeks. I looked at one of the dancers, who was tall, thin, and flat-chested. She was standing next to a customer whose drink was tilted almost diagonally. He looked at her like she was an angel and he seemed fascinated by every word she had to say. She gave him a smile, and he handed her a couple of bills that she quickly slipped into the side of her G-string. At that moment, I had an impulse that maybe I could do a job like this. But instantly the fear of performing and the thought of being naked in public just freaked me out.

We stayed at Club Juana for about two hours. I don't even remember my head hitting the pillow that night and I didn't even know what to think yet about my porn-a-palooza day. But I was glad to have finally caught a glimpse of my father's business. Tomorrow we would head to Cocoa Beach to see the Beach Video Store, which was owned by a collection of my family members. My father had owned this store with both Cousin Danny and Uncle Coke, who was Danny's father, but Uncle Coke had passed away the previous year of lung cancer, leaving all his business interests to Danny. My father missed Uncle Coke tremendously, and Danny was still grieving over the loss of his father—in fact, he had left Uncle Coke's house, car, and personal items untouched since his passing.

Whenever he traveled to this part of Florida for business, my father stayed at Uncle Coke's house. When we arrived, we immediately opened the widows to circulate fresh air. Everything was left in its original place as if Uncle Coke might return at any moment. Uncle Coke's dentures were still in a cup the bathroom.

"Dad, can't you do anything to help Danny sell the house?" I said as I came out of the bedroom. "Or at least box up Uncle Coke's things?"

"I've tried, but he just won't do it. He hasn't paid the property tax either."

"That's crazy," Christopher said. Christopher and I gave each other a knowing look about the strangeness that seemed to exist in our family.

"You should call your mother," my father said to Christopher, changing the subject.

Christopher reluctantly agreed and he picked up the phone and dialed. "Hi, Mom. We're at Uncle's Coke's house in Cocoa Beach."

I could hear my aunt asking him, "So what have you been doing down there?"

"Nothing much," Christopher said, and he shot me a coy glance. "Went out to dinner last night, did some sightseeing."

I tried not to laugh.

When Christopher finished his call, we walked over to the next street to visit Danny and his family and were greeted at the door by Danny's wife, Martha.

"We were wondering when yous would get here," she said, her Philly accent still thick.

Martha led us into the family room where Danny was watching TV. He swiveled his recliner around to face us, then struggled to get to his feet. He weighed at least three hundred and fifty pounds.

He hadn't lost a pound since his father's funeral.

"How's your trip been Kris?" Cousin Danny asked in his soft spoken way.

"Good, so glad to be away from the cold weather up north."

"You're headed to Beach Video?"

"Yes, I have never been there."

"Well, it's doing well. We're quite happy with it."

After our family visit, we all headed to the Cocoa Beach store, which was located across the street from the wildly popular flagship Ron Jon's Surf Shop and in close proximity to the beach. It was a tiny shop—about a quarter the size of the Premier. Christopher and I browsed the narrow aisles as my father went into the back room to account for some inventory and to make note of new products he needed to order.

As I browsed, I noticed a Traci Lords video on the shelves. I had heard about this famously underage porn star who had hoodwinked the industry into believing she was eighteen years old when, in fact, she had begun performing in adult movies at age sixteen. She was later busted, and many people with whom she had worked were put under investigation for child pornography. Just before Traci Lords was discovered for this, she had started her own production company and launched her first movie starring, of course, herself. This was the only Traci Lords movie ever to sell legally, since she made it just after turning eighteen.

"Dad, is this Traci Lords title still selling well?" I asked.

"I can't keep it on the shelf."

I looked at the box, titled *Traci I Love You*, and I thought about how Lords was, at that time, beginning to have some mainstream acting success. It was interesting to me that people found her fascinating and I wasn't sure if it was her business savvy or if she really had talent. Maybe both, but she seemed to have a lot of control over her business.

"Let's walk to the pier," Dad said after he finished his work. We left the store and we walked across the street. The smell of salty air filled my nose. We watched the fisherman lazily awaiting tugs on their lines. Cocoa Beach was not nearly as busy as other Florida beaches like Fort Lauderdale or Miami. It was a quiet town on the verge of being discovered.

It was hard to believe my father's store in Cocoa Beach managed to do a healthy business but it did because there was very little competition. My father knew what he was doing. Though the exteriors of his stores didn't look like much, they'd been successful for decades.

～～～

The next day, Dad drove me and Christopher to the Orlando airport.

"If you were staying one more day, you would have seen the space shuttle taking off."

"I haven't seen one take off since I was in middle school," I said, thinking back to a seventh grade trip to Cape Canaveral. I felt sad to leave Florida but I was ready to return to my boyfriend, to my clients, and to the place that, for the moment, I considered home.

"I'll call you tonight," Christopher whispered to me as he prepared to board his plane. "We need to debrief about all this."

"Absolutely," I said with a knowing look.

Then we both broke down in laughter.

After Christopher left, I waited at the gate with my father as he read the day's paper. We made small talk about his next visit to New York, and about his schedule for the upcoming week. We didn't mention anything more about our tour of his stores, or about Club Juana, or about our family. I was reviewing Monday's client list in my mind and steeling myself for my return to New York—which seemed a world away from my past, and from my father's present.

# 17

# *Married to the Mob?*

I placed my suitcase in the trunk of the rental car that Brian, my boy-friend, had parked in front of my apartment building on Columbus Avenue and Eighty-Ninth Street. It was the summer of 1996 and Brian and I were finally moving to Washington, DC. We were at a good place in our relationship. We were in love and had a deep respect for one another, which by that point in my life I realized was hard to find.

"You almost ready to go?" Brian asked, leaning out the window.

"Almost," I said. "I have to run back upstairs one more time."

"Hurry up," Brian said, smiling anxiously. "I can't stay parked here for too much longer."

I rushed back into the building. I had to retrieve one last bag, pick up my dog, and say a last goodbye to my roommate Kara.

Brian and I had met during our sophomore year in college at Florida State, at a football keg party. I still remember how his eyes locked onto me the minute I entered the room. He was cute, with boyish features, blonde hair and blue eyes, and a dimple in his cheek when he smiled . . . but at first, I had no interest.

"Can I use your phone?" I asked him that day, a few minutes after I'd arrived. "I have to call my boyfriend."

Brian and I became friends, and later, when I was single, we started seeing each other. That lasted about a year, but like many young undergrad couples, we broke up during our senior year. I wanted to date other guys, and I was feeling confused about my future. You see, Brian was the person I'd lost my virginity to and I was in love with him—but I couldn't decide if he was my future husband without testing the waters to see what else was out there. At least, that was my rationale at the time.

After the breakup, Brian and I stayed in touch and two years later we decided to meet up while I was visiting Tallahassee to attend the Miami versus Florida State football game. (While living in New York, I always tried to come back at least once a year for a game.) Then, by coincidence—or a twist of fate—I ran into Brian's parents at the game. His mother coyly invited me to dinner at their home, since they lived in town.

At dinner, as I looked at Brian sitting across the table, I had an overwhelming realization that I missed him and that I wanted his family to be *my* family, too. Fortunately for me, Brian felt the same way. After that trip, we began dating long distance, since he was still living in Florida working as a stockbroker at Merrill Lynch and I was finishing up graduate school in New York City. Within a year, Brian moved to New York City to attend Columbia University for his MBA.

By the time we were ready to move to Washington, DC, we had been dating for three years.

That day, I said a tearful goodbye to Kara, my roommate and grad school classmate. She was a short, blond firecracker, and we had lived together for two years, sharing many memorable moments, like our summer trip to the Caribbean, escapades caring for two Maltese puppies, Roxy and Madison (Kara's idea), and supporting each other as we started our stressful social work careers.

"Well, I guess this is it," I said, misty eyed, and I leaned in to hug Kara with the dogs smushed between us.

"Oh gosh, this sucks," Kara said, wiping away her tears.

"I know," I said. "But I'll visit and you'll visit. Right?"

The two dogs would now be separated—Roxy stayed with Kara, Madison went to DC with me—which seemed to make everything more tragic. I left the apartment in tears and scurried down the stairs, dog in tow, to begin my future with Brian.

As we drove over the George Washington Bridge, the city now receding behind us, I felt relief and sadness that my time as a New Yorker had come to an end. I had lived in Manhattan for nearly four years but it surprised me that I was sad about leaving, especially since I had been desperate, for so long, to get away. New York had never been a natural fit for me—I had merely learned to cope with it, biding my time until I could leave. While some people thrive on the city's fast pace, I found that it just drained me. But for all the things that I disliked about the city, I was still grateful to have had the experience. New York City changed my life and my perspective on everything.

 ෴ 

Brian and I arrived four hours later at Aunt Rose and Uncle Gabe's house in Potomac, Maryland, for an overnight stay. We'd be moving into a brick townhouse in Arlington, Virginia, the following morning. My aunt and uncle were excited about our move to the area, and they liked Brian. Uncle Gabe had even graciously introduced Brian to his business contacts, which had led to Brian's job as a financial analyst at KPMG even before we moved. This, as much as anything, had made our move possible.

But as much as they liked Brian, they still weren't altogether comfortable with me living with my boyfriend with no ready intention of marriage.

"If you ever need someplace to live, our door is always open in Potomac," Uncle Gabe said.

I thanked him, and I appreciated his concern but his traditional thinking didn't make much sense to me. And it was especially puzzling because Aunt Rose and Uncle Gabe were about to divorce after thirty years of marriage. Uncle Gabe would later marry a soulless blonde who became a toxic element in our family, poisoning everyone's relationship with my uncle. They divorced after only five years. No one in my family, it seemed, had the perfect formula for a happy, lifelong marriage.

∽৩৶

Brain and I discovered that we loved the suburban Washington, DC lifestyle. Simple things excited us, like driving a car, shopping at a normal-sized grocery store, and having access to green grass. And as far as our careers went, DC was on the cusp of the dot-com boom; there were business opportunities all around us for Brian, as well as great non-profit and political work for me.

Through my uncle's connections, I landed a full-time job as a legislative assistant at The Dutko Group, a lobbying firm on Capitol Hill. At Dutko, I found myself in the same awkward position I'd faced many times before and I hesitated to mention anything about my father's career. So I did my best to avoid the subject entirely, partly to spare my uncle any uncomfortable moments and also to establish my own career in DC without dealing with people's negative perceptions about pornography. This seemed easy enough to do, and mostly I was just thought of as "Gabe Battista's niece."

I was enamored with Capitol Hill during my first years in DC. Sometimes at lunch I would walk up to the edge of First Street and Independence Avenue just to take a glimpse of the white gleaming Capitol Building. This work experience was, in every way, a stark contrast to my days at The Burden Center. Now, I spent my days attending hearings for the firms' oil, telecommunications, and health insurance clients. I didn't always agree with our clients' assertions about the impact of certain legislation on their businesses, but despite this, I worked hard churning out hearing reports and attending lavish fundraisers. Even though the work wasn't exactly what I wanted to do, it was an important first step in a career in public policy and advocacy. As dysfunctional and messy as it could be, there was something about DC that made it an almost magical place—a true democracy.

∽৩৶

In December 1997, Brian and I planned a trip to New York City to attend a friend's wedding. While in town we wanted to go back to one of our favorite Indian restaurants in the city, Nirvana, which overlooked Central Park West. I had a feeling we were about to get engaged.

"How do you know for sure?" Kara asked me over lunch at a bagel shop on the Upper West Side. Her eyes widened as she flipped her short, blonde hair.

"Brian's been acting suspicious," I said. "And more nervous than usual."

"Well, knowing Brian, he's probably spent forever planning this."

I laughed. Kara knew Brian very well.

"So, Brian, you got anything special planned?" Kara asked jokingly when we returned to her apartment.

"Nothing out of the ordinary," Brian responded, his voice deadpan, like he had nothing else on his mind other than hanging out on Kara's couch.

Behind Brian's back, I gave Kara a dirty look and shook my head no.

"Well," Kara said, ignoring me, "I'm sure you guys will have a nice time tonight."

We arrived at Nirvana just after sunset and the sky was orangey-red, silhouetting the dark green trees of the park.

"I know you think we're getting engaged tonight," Brian said. "I don't want you to be disappointed."

"It's okay," I said, staring down blankly at my menu. "I'm not disappointed."

"Well," he said, "then the good news is that we *are* getting engaged tonight."

"I think he's pulling out a ring," I heard someone at a nearby table whisper, even before I saw the case he was easing out of his pocket.

"Will you marry me?" Brian said. As typical with a New York City dining experience, the tables were too close together for him to get down on one knee, so he just smiled at me and held out the ring.

"Oh, my God! Yes!" I stared at the stunning two-carat, marquee-cut diamond with deep blue sapphires set on both sides.

"*Awww*," I heard from all around me and I felt the intense gaze of restaurant well-wishers.

Afterward, we walked to Rockefeller Center to see the Christmas tree. Fifth Avenue was decorated for the holiday season, my head was light with excitement, and New York City was, once again, the backdrop for another life-changing moment.

⁓ⅇ∽⅁∽

My parents were ecstatic about the engagement, especially my father, who had always liked Brian. By this time, Dad had been divorced twice, so I didn't quite understand his excitement, since marriages never seemed to go well for him. But his encouragement pleased me, nonetheless.

Brian and my father had similar interests in business and they shared a deep love of Italian culture and food. My father would reminisce with Brian about his days as a stockbroker, always sounding a little regretful at not being able to fulfill his dream of conquering Wall Street. I enjoyed the fact that I'd brought home a man to make my father proud.

That Christmas, just a few weeks after our engagement, Brian and I traveled to Florida where both of our families lived. Once there, we shuttled between Brian's sister's home in South Miami and my mother and father's places in Fort Lauderdale. My father took us to his favorite Italian restaurant, Fra Diavolo, which was next door to a Jewish deli of which he had recently become part owner.

Fra Diavolo's owners, Carol and Raul Oliveros, had also become close friends with my father and my future stepmother, Angie.

When we opened the door of Fra Diablo, the smell of garlic triggered a memory of my Aunt Mary's house packed with relatives on Christmas Eve. "We're so glad you will be celebrating your engagement here tonight," Carol said, giving me a hug. She seemed like one of my relatives, with her dark hair, glasses, and Philly accent.

We were escorted to a table in a quiet corner. Angie sat across from me, her red hair nicely coiffed in smooth round curls. I had known

Angie my entire life as she had been a family friend for years before dating my father.

"Your father couldn't be happier about this engagement," Angie said.

"Thanks," I said, smiling at my father. "That's nice to hear."

"When do you think you'll set the date?"

"This fall, we think. DC is so nice that time of year."

"Oh!" Angie chirped. "What a wonderful idea to have the wedding in DC! We weren't sure if you'd have the wedding in South Florida or not."

"Well, I think DC is our home now."

Halfway through our meal, Raul visited our table. He was a thin, short man with thick glasses, and he wore black-checkered pants, a white apron, and a beret-type hat, which hid the perspiration forming at his temples from his labors in the kitchen. "Hello, beautiful daughter of Tony and fiancé!" he bellowed in his boisterous Cuban accent. "Welcome! And congratulations on your engagement! May you have a happy life together. This is what life is all about!"

"Well, thank you," I said, looking at Brian and smirking. I smelled marijuana and liquor on Raul's breath and realized he was totally stoned.

"Your father is a good man," he said, slapping my father on the shoulder. "The best!"

"What's up with that?" I asked my father after Raul had disappeared in to the kitchen.

"Raul?" my father said. "He's amazing. I've never seen anyone drink and smoke as much as he does and still get a hundred plates out for a dinner rush."

Raul was yet another addition to my father's wide collection of eclectic pals.

Later, after having a few too many glasses of wine, my father became unusually talkative and he began to share stories with Brian about *Deep Throat*. "People were up in arms about pornography, like it was a witch hunt. I felt like I was just caught in the middle."

"It sounds like it was . . . really something," Brian said genuinely interested in the story. "Kristin's told me about your involvement in that trial."

"Yeah," my father said, taking another slug of red wine. "There were some interesting people involved. Like the Perainos. Oh God, the Perainos. They owned the distribution rights to *Deep Throat.* Most people thought they were in the mafia."

"What?" I chimed in. This was a detail I'd never heard before.

"Sure," my father said. "They even approached me and my partner, Tony Arnone, about going into business with them at the Premier in Orlando."

I shook my head in confusion.

"Tony and I didn't think it wasn't good to, you know, 'marry into the mob,'" Dad continued. "Then the old man, Anthony Peraino, came to us and said, 'We either part now while we can as friends, or work together for life.'"

I couldn't believe what I was hearing. "Have you heard this part of the story before?" I asked Angie, cocking my head to one side.

"Oh, yes," Angie said in her deep smoker's voice.

"It sounds dangerous," I said, turning to look at Dad. *Was my dad in the mob?* I thought. *Was I a mafia princess?* "So what happened?" I asked insistently.

"Well," my father said, "Tony and I decided it was best to get away from them."

"And they just let you walk away?"

"Yes."

"But doesn't the mob, like, usually get what it wants?"

My father shrugged. "Not this time, I guess."

Later, on the way home, Brian and I rehashed the dinner conversation.

"I never heard that story about the mob before," I said in a worried tone.

"It was interesting. Your family is definitely more . . . unusual than mine."

Brian was right. His parents had been married for thirty-five years. They seemed so normal. The only oddity in his family was an eccentric aunt who owned an alpaca farm.

"I guess you didn't know you'd be married to the mob yourself?" I said jokingly.

"I guess not." Then Brian laughed and glanced at me quickly. "Don't worry so much. It all happened a long time ago."

And this is what I love about Brian: all of my family's craziness has never been big deal to him.

∽∾

Shortly after we returned home from Florida, Brian asked me, "Do you think we'll be together forever?"

Our conversation leading up to it had been playful but it now took a serious turn.

"I don't know," I said. "But I'll do the best that I can to make it forever."

Brian looked at me in shock. I realized he wanted reassurances, but instead I'd given him an answer like I was an accountant calculating the odds.

"I don't want to make it sound like I don't have faith in us," I said defensively. "But let's face it. Fifty percent of marriages fail."

I hoped he would appreciate the statistics, but I also knew that his parents had been happily married for decades and that he aspired to be just like them. By the time Brian and I got engaged, my father had already divorced his second wife, and my mother had just married for the second time. Many more of my relatives, as well as the parents of most of my friends, had gone through divorces. I didn't have a lot of faith in the institution of marriage.

"Look," I said. "We've been together a long time already. We've been through a lot as a couple, and we still decided to get married. So that gives us a head start, right?"

"That's a good point," Brian said, smiling and looking relieved.

I had faith in our relationship, but I guess I was just being too much of a realist. We had taken a thoughtful approach to marriage and I knew we were very different than my parents. The stress my parents endured in their marriage surely wouldn't be repeated.

∽∾

For my wedding, my mother wanted me to wear her first wedding dress. At Grandma Maria's condo, we pulled both my mother and grandmother's wedding dresses down from the top of the hall closet.

"I just loved this dress!" my mother gushed when we opened the large dress box.

"It's very nice," I said, though I wasn't nearly as excited.

"Silk organza is the best material. You just can't find dresses like this anymore."

"I remember when we purchased this at John Wanamaker's," Grandma Maria said, smiling at my mother. "You looked so perfect in this dress."

I looked at them both oddly and thought, *Why are they so excited about a wedding dress for a marriage that went down in flames?*

"What?" my mother asked, noticing my puzzled look.

"It just seems weird how you feel about this dress," I said, shaking my head.

"It's not weird," she replied. "You're weird."

"Very funny," I said.

As we removed the dress from the box, my mother and grandmother gasped slightly.

"It's held up so well," my mother said.

"The material is only slightly discolored," Grandma Maria said. "But the cream color still looks beautiful."

It *was* a beautiful dress, but the silk lace and tiny beading all over the length of the gown was definitely not my style. The straight cut with a matching pill box hat and small veil gave the dress a 1960s look, while I was hoping for something with a full skirt.

"Go try it on," my mother urged.

I hesitated for a moment. "What if it's cursed?" I asked, shocked at my own gall in giving voice to my visceral response. I didn't even want to touch the dress, let alone put it on. It symbolized failure and dysfunction—which was nothing I wanted in my marriage.

"Listen to you!" my mother cried. "*What if it's cursed?* Kristin, that's ridiculous." A moment later, she pushed me into the bathroom with the dress.

I stood in the bathroom alone, holding the dress against my body and studying myself in the mirror. I realized that if my hair were darker and shorter, I would look almost exactly like the wedding photograph of my mother I'd seen in an old photo album. I took off my clothes, stepped my legs into dress, and tried to pull it up over my hips. But I couldn't. The dress was too small.

"Mom, how much did you weigh on your wedding day?" I yelled through the door.

"I don't remember. Maybe 118 pounds?"

"I can't even get this on," I said. Then opened the door and said through the crack, "If I pull this on, it'll tear. Come here and look."

She peered in, and I could tell she was terribly disappointed when she realized that the dress would never slide over my hips.

"Did you gain weight or something?" my mother asked.

"No," I said, annoyed. "I think you were just really skinny back then."

"Certainly not anymore," my mother said.

I hoped this would end the discussion, but when I came out of the bathroom, the conversation continued.

"We can take it to a seamstress to add material to make this bigger," my mother kept on.

"But wouldn't it be impossible to find the same material?" I argued. "And wouldn't that be expensive anyway?"

My mother persisted, but I cut her off. "Mom, I'm sorry," I said. "I just don't want to wear this dress."

She looked at me and sighed. "Okay, if you feel that strongly about it. I guess we can just save it for another family member."

"Well, that's a shame," Grandma Maria inserted delicately. "Why don't you try on my wedding dress?"

Much to my mother's consternation, I loved the idea of wearing my grandmother's dress. It was a beautiful 1920s style dress, made of pure satin, with long sleeves and buttons from the cuffs to the mid-forearm. And there was no lace, flowers, bows, or beads, which was exactly to my taste.

And on top of that, my grandmother had been married for more than sixty years. I thought this dress might bring me luck. I carefully removed it from its box. The satin looked even more fragile than my mother's dress.

I went into the bathroom to try to slip it on, and this time, I couldn't even fit one leg into the dress. Then I remembered that my grandmother had only been fifteen when she was married, and five feet tall, so I should have known that it would be too small.

"Grandma, your dress is smaller than Mom's!"

Weeks later, my mother and I went wedding dress shopping on Las Olas Boulevard, where all the fashionable boutiques in Fort Lauderdale can be found. But despite the fun we had that day, I still didn't find the perfect dress.

Back at home, I went shopping alone. It seemed easier than having people with me, all giddy with excitement and the expectation there would be this magical moment when I found the perfect dress. In Alexandria, I finally selected a dress in less than an hour.

I loved the dress, but still, I was beginning to think there was something wrong with me. No matter how hard I tried, I wasn't gushing with excitement about planning this wedding. I had no doubts about Brian, whom I knew was the love of my life—but all this hoopla just didn't seem worth it.

⌇⌇

As it turns out, I was a very laid back, complacent bride. I didn't care much about the details of the wedding party, nor things like the flowers and table settings. In my mind, as long as the party was nice and the flowers weren't dead, I'd be happy. My father was willing to pay for an expensive wedding, which was generous, of course but also a bragging right—Italian fathers love shelling out for large weddings for their daughters.

So it was left to Brian to meticulously manage our budget, and he outlined all the costs on an Excel spreadsheet, which I thought was hot (his thorough nature was one of the reason I was marrying him).

"So, when you think about being marriage, what are your expectations?" asked Reverend Alice Anderson, the minister who was going to marry us.

"I just don't want it to be like my parents' marriage," I said.

She looked at me, waiting for me to go on.

Then, in the space of about thirty seconds, I went from a calm bride-to-be to a crying, blubbery mess.

Brian just sat beside me and squeezed my hand.

"Your marriage will not be your parents' marriage," Reverend Alice reassured me.

I nodded my head in agreement and I quickly wiped away my tears.

Reverend Anderson's question had touched upon the heartbreak I had always felt about my own parents' divorce and about the tumultuous time leading up to it. To me, marriage seemed like an overwhelming burden, like you had to be a perfect person to succeed. I knew I wasn't perfect and that I wasn't ever going to be. I also feared coming to a point in my relationship with Brian when we'd end up disliking or even hating each other. I couldn't imagine a scenario where that would actually happen, but still, I couldn't silence the memories of all the arguing my parents had done when I was a child.

I was embarrassed by my sudden emotion. But after a lot of talking, both with her and with Brian, I began to alter my expectations little by little. My marriage couldn't be about "not being like my parents." Rather, my marriage had to be about what would truly make Brian and me happy.

❧

At my wedding dress fittings, the seamstress snitched the waist so tight I could barely breathe. "You'll lose weight before the wedding," the seamstress said. "All brides do. Because of nerves."

"I'm not nervous," I said. "So you can go ahead and loosen it."

"Okay, dear," she said, smiling a little condescendingly. "We'll let this out a bit."

Three weeks before the wedding, the alteration came back too tight. I just wasn't the bride everyone had expected. In other words, I wasn't a nervous wreck.

The best part about our wedding day was reconnecting with everyone we knew—both family and friends—and having them all in one place.

"Are you ready?" my father asked when the day finally came.

I smiled at him as we waited together outside the church. He looked so dapper in his tuxedo. "I'm ready, Dad." I saw a lifetime of faces as I made my way toward Brian waiting at the altar. My father lifted my veil, a little teary eyed, and he gently kissed my cheek. Then he gave my hand to Brian.

⌒⌒⌒

The reception was well underway, and as the Italian men of my family stuffed envelopes brimming with cash into Brian's jacket pocket, my father-in-law, George Frazee, said to him, "Everyone on Kristin's side of the family looks like they should be in the mafia!"

When Brian told me, I knew George was joking and I couldn't stop laughing. Even though my family had brushed company with the Perainos, I wasn't a mob princess, nor was my father a gangster. Brian's parents had learned long ago about what my father did for a living and they'd accepted it. I was now, like I'd wanted to be, a part of their family.

# 18

# *Like Mother, Like Daughter?*

"Brian, I know I'm pregnant," I said after three years of marriage. "But you haven't even taken the pregnancy test yet," he said. "How do you know?"

"I just know."

We'd only been trying to conceive for about two months, but we'd taken a very methodical approach to getting pregnant, charting my temperature to pinpoint exactly when I'd be ovulating. I was thirty-one years old and Brian and I had decided it was time to have children. Why leave anything to chance when we knew what we wanted?

Brian insisted on buying two pregnancy test kits because he doubted my intuition.

"Wow," Brian said, his face bewildered as he looked down at the stick with "+" mark on it. Then a huge smile bloomed on his face. "I'm going to be a dad!"

Of course, I was happy, too. But the prospect of having children was daunting. I'd never loved all-things baby, and at that point in my life, I felt very connected to my career. I knew "doing it all" (meaning both family and work) would be very, very difficult. I'd watched many female friends struggle to raise a family while continuing to work full time. They were often exhausted, having to endure endless sleepless nights, and were often sick because of germs brought home from school or daycare. The only thing that made having children possible for me was knowing that Brian would be a great partner and father.

"That's so wonderful!" my mother said over the phone that night. "I'm finally going to be a grandmother!"

Over the next nine months, whenever I was on the phone with my mother, I would always pick her brain about being pregnant. Since we carried the same genes, I reasoned that she could give me clues about the trajectory of my pregnancy.

"Do you remember when your morning sickness stopped?" I asked. "I'm not throwing up, but I feel nauseated *all the time*."

"I didn't throw up much either. I think I felt better after three months."

"Well, that's not too bad."

"I craved Italian bread and water ice constantly."

"Really? I don't have any cravings."

"Not yet," she said, laughing.

"But how much weight did you gain?" I asked, cringing.

"About twenty-two pounds," she said. "Pregnant girls today, they gain like fifty pounds. In my day, doctors wouldn't let women get that heavy."

My father was also thrilled about becoming a grandparent, but, of course, he and I didn't talk about the same things. Rather, ours were general discussions about how I was feeling as well as the shared excitement as my due date drew closer.

Brian and I found out we were having a daughter during my fifth month. I was relieved because I'd wanted a little girl most of all. And both of my parents were elated about the arrival of a granddaughter, since they knew what it was like to have a daughter.

We prepared, as most new parents do, by reading lots of books. The amount of "stuff" that seemed necessary to care for an infant was overwhelming—the bobby nursing pillow, two types of strollers, high chair, crib, the breast pump, the bouncy chair, and a million other things. . . . I had my share of minor panic attacks thinking about how to use all them.

Even Brian, who normally enjoys making a heavy analysis of any purchase, said to me with a furrowed brow, shopping for a stroller, "I can't even tell the difference between them anymore!"

Fortunately, my pregnancy was an easy one. But during a routine sonogram three weeks before my due date, I was admitted to the hospital for monitoring when a test came back with some concerns.

After a full day of more tests, my doctor strongly advised that we induce birth.

"I thought we were just doing some testing," I said to the doctor, my voice quavering with worry. Brian sat next to me and squeezed my hand. "I'm not due for another three weeks."

"The tests from this morning showed a stop in the heartbeat for an unexplained reason, and although we didn't see this again, I still don't think you should go home," the doctor said.

My jaw clenched. "Well, what if I decide I don't want to have the baby now?"

"Then you take the risk of your baby dying," my doctor said plainly.

All we had to hear was "your baby dying" and Brian and I decided to proceed with inducing labor. Brian called our families, a few friends, and my office to keep them informed. After thirty-six hours of steadily increasing the Pitocin dose and the doctor breaking my water, the delivery progressed very slowly, then after twelve hours of active labor, my doctor was now considering a C-section.

"Okay, let's check to see if you're dilated," my doctor said. "If there's no progress, we'll do the C-section."

I'm not even sure how I responded, only that I spoke groggily, and at that point, I hadn't slept in over two days.

"Well, it looks like we're ready to have a baby," the doctor said, her head popping up over the top of my knees. "You're dilated at ten centimeters."

"It's time," I said weakly to Brian, who had been crumpled in the chair next to me asleep.

"What!" Brian said, startled awake. "It's time?"

Our daughter, Grace Kelley, was born on June 29, 2002 around 2:30 a.m., more than two weeks before my due date. She was the perfect little peanut, less than seven pounds, with her nose slightly smashed as a result of being pushed through the birth canal. It was quiet in the room and Brian and I took turns holding her.

"She scored perfectly on her APGAR test," Brian whispered to me proudly. I sighed in relief—this meant that the stress of the birth had hopefully not caused any serious complications. Brian looked exhausted, but he was also glowing with some sort of inner light as he looked down at his daughter.

When I held Grace on that first day, I realized that my turn at being a mother would be nothing like my mother's experience. I would keep chaos out of our lives, I would be a calm, steadying influence, and I'd already chosen a spouse who didn't have a risk-taking bone in his body. I would always strive for my daughter to have the perfect childhood, learning from the many mistakes—as well as the many good things—that both my parents had done.

For Grace, Brian, and me, things would be different.

⁓∾∾⁓

Brian and I arrived home a few days later and we had a week alone before our families started to arrive for visits. In those weeks (and the weeks and weeks after that), I barely slept and I cried frequently as I adjusted to taking care of a newborn. Grace developed jaundice and wasn't feeding well. Our pediatrician was concerned about her getting enough nutrition and she ordered a bilirubin blanket to manage the jaundice. The blue glow of the blanket helped Grace's yellowish features subside within a few days.

"I don't know how you did this," I said to my mother on the phone.

"Well, it's tough being a new mom," my mother empathized. "I'll be there soon."

"The breast feeding isn't going well because of the jaundice. So I'm supplementing with formula."

"I had so much milk with you. I had to wake you up to relieve the pressure."

"I don't have that problem," I said, feeling very much like a failure.

"You're going to be fine, Kristin," she said soothingly.

"Did Dad help you a lot when I was an infant?"

"Oh, no. Men back then didn't take care of children at all."

"Brian is doing a lot," I said.

"That's because Brian's a great husband."

"Mom?"

"Yes."

"I just feel so tired. When did you start getting sleep?"

"After about three months. You were a good sleeper."

More and more, I came to rely on my mother for advice, and during that time I developed a new, mature empathy for her. Now I realized—truly realized—how easy it was to feel isolated when you have small children. The responsibility is constant; it's not like you can pick up and go whenever you want. The whole post-partum experience was taxing on me, both physically and emotionally. The thought of my mother raising a small child without hands-on assistance from my father—either due to his work or the cultural mores of the time—was striking to me, especially since Brian was so actively involved.

≈≈≈

My father and my stepmother, Angie, arrived first for a five-day stay. During that trip, they transformed into Pepop and Nana, and they helped Brian and me out as much as they could. My father's main mode of "help" was walking around the house videotaping every moment and cooking meals, while Angie watched Grace as I tried to sleep. "No offense, Kris," Angie said, "but you look like shit. Go take a nap." It was nice to have them there, and ever since Grace's birth, they've visited almost every few months, just to help out.

My mother arrived next—after my father left, of course—and a few days after that, Grandma Maria would be arriving to meet her great-granddaughter.

"Let me see my granddaughter!" my mother said excitedly as soon as she crossed our front door.

Grace was in a bouncy chair in the center of the living room and my mother leaned over and scooped her up.

"Aren't you so beautiful," my mother cooed. "Kristin, she's just perfect. I know I'm biased, but she's such a good looking baby."

"Thanks, Mom," I said wearily. It was three weeks after the delivery and I was still feeling like I'd been hit by a truck.

My mother went to work right away, doing laundry, cooking meals, and cleaning. During the afternoons, we would watch cooking shows and *Oprah*. It was nice to have company during the day and to have my mother right there to answer any questions, instead of having to call her all the time.

My mother and I both went to pick Grandma Maria up at Union Station and we easily spotted her in an orange top and denim skirt as she made her way toward us through the crowd. Even at seventy-nine years old, she still had swiftness in her step

"There's my mommy," Grandma Maria said, hugging me.

The highlight of all the family visitors was seeing Grandma Maria meet Grace for the first time. Like a pro, Grandma Maria scooped her up and rocked her like it was the most natural thing in the world.

"You're no longer the baby in the family," Grandma Maria whispered to me, now cradling Grace on her lap.

"Well, I'm okay with giving up that title," I joked.

"I *have* to get a picture," my mother said. "This is four generations here." Then she called in Brian from the other room and asked him to snap a photo.

*Mothers and daughters have such a complicated relationship*, I thought. As I looked at my grandmother and my mother, I realized that their relationship was completely different than the relationship between me and my mother. It was difficult to imagine, at that moment, how my relationship with Grace might evolve. I was sure there would be times when Grace wouldn't understand me at all, just as I often hadn't understood my mother. And of course I knew that Grace would be a mystery to me in many ways. But I hoped that the vital family currency—of time and attention—that I banked with Grace in her younger years would later be the foundation of our future relationship.

I was lucky that Grandma Maria had the chance to meet her youngest great-grandchild, because I knew she would miss many things in Grace's life—graduations, wedding, and the birth of Grace's children. And there would be so much that Grace wouldn't learn from Grandma Maria. But my mother and I would always tell the stories—like the hilarious time when Grandma Maria saw *Deep Throat*—and we would detail how fiercely protective she had been of her babies and, of course, of Kitty.

We all carry our family's history with us. The relationships that are forged between mothers and daughters, as well as between fathers and daughters, influence our beliefs and ideas. Exploring my parents' experience through the *Deep Throat* days, and beyond, is something I will never forget. My daughter now inherits our family's past, and how she chooses to use it to address the decisions in her own life will be up to her.

❦

In June of 2008, I traveled to Fort Lauderdale for my twenty-year high school reunion. I couldn't believe that much time had passed since I had graduated from high school. So much had changed in my life and, luckily, I wouldn't be sharing sob stories of divorce or hard times with my classmates. Everything was going well. Brian and I had been married for ten years and Grace was already six years old. Kelley accompanied me to the reunion since Brian and Grace did not make the trip to Florida.

"Let's drive by our old neighborhoods," Kelley said as we were leaving a St. Thomas Aquinas charity golf tournament in Plantation.

We turned off Broward Boulevard and headed down Seventieth Avenue. We arrived at Kelley's old street and drove slowly passed the house where she had lived. It was at the end of a cul-de-sac among other houses with nice, manicured lawns.

"Still looks the same, except the color is different," I said staring up the driveway. "I remember when you were fifteen years old, you couldn't wait to get your driver's license and we would drive up and down your street in your mom's car."

"Yeah, that was fun. I was a better driver back then than you are now," Kelley said jokingly and I laughed, not disagreeing. She then paused in a reflective way, "A lot of bad stuff happened here but we had some happy times, too."

We took some back roads and arrived at West Planation Circle and drove the twisty road around until we reached my old ranch style house. It looked smaller than I remembered and the landscaping was more mature and overgrown.

"I always loved this house," said Kelley.

"I did too," I said with a weak smile, wishing we hadn't moved years ago. "It's surprising how much our lives have changed since we lived in Florida."

"It was a lifetime ago," said Kelley.

"I think we did okay, don't you?"

"We did more than okay; we hit the jackpot."

We both had wonderful families. We earned our graduate degrees and had successful careers in the non-profit world. The big plans we made as teenagers, even though our direction wasn't always clear, came to fruition. Our lives were everything we had hoped for.

As I sat in the passenger seat, it saddened me to imagine what my life would have been like if my family hadn't move to Florida and my father remained a stockbroker. I would not have met Kelley or many other great friends in my life. I might not have attended Florida State University and married Brian either. Despite the heartache of the *Deep Throat* days, I didn't wish my father never distributed *Deep Throat*.

Being a pornographer's daughter, I felt, brought me wisdom I might not have otherwise gained. And I learned that a seemingly small decision could change the direction of my life, so all my small decisions were important. I never wasted time on a friend or a boyfriend who didn't deserve it, I chose trustworthy people to have in my life, and I developed a strong empathy for others.

It was clear that what my father did for a living didn't shape who I was. It was how my parents handled being in the pornography business and raising a daughter that did influence me. My father overcame many challenges and succeeded in business despite a very bad situation. I also learned from his many mistakes and the missteps my parents had made in their marriage. Their dysfunction was certainly magnified with the fall out from *Deep Throat*. I wished that they had stayed together, but I had to respect their choices as they had respected mine.

"Come on. We should get going," I said snapping back to present day.

"Okay, I'm glad we took this trip down memory lane," Kelley said.

"Me too," I said, grateful for the perspective it had given me.

We drove off giggling about our younger years and excited about who we might catch up with that evening.

# Epilogue
## *Daddy's Little Girl*

My very first memories are of the time just after my father's first arrest in 1974, when I was four years old. Mostly I recall my parents' heated arguments and my father's limited time at home. He would appear at most family meals but then quickly head off to work again at the Golden 33. I would often pull on his hand and beg for one more minute but he always had a clever way of making me giggle as he slipped away. My sadness about him leaving would pass quickly because, despite his busy schedule, I never felt like he was gone for good.

Some people, when they learn that my father works in the pornography industry, have a perception that our relationship must be perverted or that I must have low self-esteem because his work is thought to be demeaning to women. But the truth is quite the opposite: our relationship has always been positive. There are a few reasons why this has been possible. The first is that my mother never believed that what my father did for a living was wrong, and she felt that he had been unjustly accused of crimes. She never maligned my father in front of me, even though she was, quite often, very angry at him.

Also, my father was always very present in our moments together. He was not a harsh disciplinarian nor a setter of arbitrary rules, like so many men of his generation. He was often able to say yes to me and I don't ever remember him having a harsh word with me.

Although my father didn't share the day-to-day responsibilities of raising me, he did attend all the piano and dance recitals, the Indian Princess father/daughter meetings, the school plays, and the graduations—and he was always a proud, beaming presence in my life. I remember once, when I played soccer in a community league in the eighth grade, how he would run up and down the sidelines like a maniac, pointing at the direction I should be running. "Go after the ball!" he would yell, a happy smile on his face. "That way! That way!" I was a terrible athlete and I was embarrassed by his sideline antics. But I also knew that he just wanted me to be good at the game.

He's been like that about the rest of my life, too—and wanted me to be a successful and independent woman. And he's been my biggest fan, running down the sidelines of my life with that smile on his face, and not at all the detested pornographer that the courts and the press made him out to be.

# *About the Author*

Kristin Battista-Frazee, in addition to her roles as an author and writer for *The Daily Beast*, is a marketing professional and social worker who has spent more than sixteen years working for non-profit organizations raising awareness about mental health issues and online learning start-up companies.

Kristin was born in Philadelphia but hails from Florida and currently lives with her family in McLean, Virginia. She graduated from Florida State University with a bachelor's degree in psychology and Columbia University with a master's of science in social work.

Follow the author on Twitter @porndaughter and visit her website at www.kristinbattistafrazee.com. Request an in-person or virtual visit for your book club.